To De Witt,

Happy Birthday Feb. 1985.

from Peter

Frederick III
III
German Emperor 1888

Ex Libris

De Witt Bailey II

German Emperor 1888

John Van der Kiste

Alan Sutton
1981.

Alan Sutton Publishing Limited
17a Brunswick Road
Gloucester

First published 1981

British Library Cataloguing in Publication Data

Van der Kiste, John
  Frederick III.
  I. Title
  943.08'4   DD224

  ISBN 0-904387-77-1

Typesetting and origination by
Alan Sutton Publishing Limited.
Photoset Stempel Garamond 10/11
Printed in Great Britain
by Redwood Burn Limited
Trowbridge & Esher.

Contents.

Illustrations.

Foreword.

Frederick III, German Emperor and King of Prussia for the last three pain-racked months of his life, has received meagre attention from biographers; his self-effacing personality has always been obscured by those of his vivacious wife Victoria, the eldest child of Queen Victoria, and his larger-than-life son William II, the controversial 'Kaiser Bill' of the Great War. One-volume histories of modern Germany mention in passing the Crown Prince who fought in the Franco-Prussian war, and who later reigned briefly after his father William I and before his son, but very little more. For almost a century he has remained a shadowy figure, one of history's 'might-have-beens'; an enigmatic 'not wholly Prussian Prussian'; a war hero who came to detest the battlefield; a patron of the arts and a champion of parliamentary government; a ruler who might have changed the destiny of Europe's most aggressive military power. This so far has been the picture, and a faithful if superficial one at that, but not for a long time has anyone revealed the man beneath it all.

Precisely four biographies have appeared in English since his death; that they were all published within the ensuing thirteen years, while his unfilial son was at the height of his glory, and the last of these during the same year that his widow died, gives some indication of how much had to be left unsaid. The first, **Frederick, Crown Prince and Emperor** by Rennell Rodd, his friend at the Berlin Embassy, was little more than an extended obituary in book form. Written at the request of the widowed Empress, who contributed an introduction, and sold to help raise funds for a throat hospital which he had visited as Crown Prince while undergoing medical treatment in London, it was published before the end of 1888, the year he died. Two years later Gustav Freytag's **The Crown Prince and the German Imperial Crown,** originally issued in German, was translated for the English reader. Far from being a reliable history, however, it consisted largely of a series of allegations that Frederick and his English relations had assisted in betraying secrets to the French commanders during the Franco-Prussian war. Freytag had been a close friend of the Crown Prince at that time, but he later suffered financial difficulties and was rescued by Frederick's lifelong political enemy Bismarck, on condition that he played his part in furthering a ruthless propaganda campaign against the late Emperor and his widow, then at its height.

Fortunately, two more faithful biographies were not long in appearing. The first was Lucy Taylor's **'Fritz' of Prussia** (1891), a pleasantly-written but chiefly domestic portrait. The second, Margaretha von Poschinger's **Life of the Emperor Frederick** (1901), was an abridged translation of the three-volume account originally published in Berlin between 1898 and 1900. It dealt more fully with his military career and politics, but like Taylor's book it could only touch on the latter with the utmost indiscretion.

A few biographies of varying merit in Germany and France followed, but in the light of the royal correspondence which has been published since the fall of imperial Germany, none of them do Frederick justice. There are two reasons for this. One, of course, is that the letters of his relatives remained hidden in the archives of both Britain and Germany for several decades, and so much had to remain private — partly because of the longevity of his mother-in-law Queen Victoria, and of the Emperor William II. (The latter survived his father by over half a century). The other is that he was so out of tune with the arch-conservative circles in Berlin, and the Empress so hated and feared, that volume after volume of statesmens' memoirs published in the early years of the present century — not least the reminiscences of Bismarck himself — portrayed him as a characterless nonentity totally dominated by his wife. The legend was fostered particularly after 1918, when nationalist writers attempted to put the blame for William II's instability and the empire's subsequent collapse onto his parents, culminating in Emil Ludwig's notoriously distorted **Kaiser Wilhelm II** (1926). As Ludwig was soon to admit, his portrait had of necessity been based on very one-sided contemporary state papers and memoirs, and it provoked the Empress's godson Sir Frederick Ponsonby into producing the extremely valuable **Letters of the Empress Frederick** in 1928[*]. This and several similar volumes, notably those containing passages from Frederick's private diaries, and Roger Fulford's more recent selections from letters between Queen Victoria and her daughter, have helped to present a far truer portrait of his personality; at the same time, they have emphasised the lack of an up-to-date biography. Hence the present volume.

John Van der Kiste

---

[*] A full account of Ponsonby's acquisition of the correspondence, his decision to publish it, and the ensuing controversy, is related in his letter to **The Times**, 23 February 1929, and his **Recollections of Three Reigns,** pp. 110-15. After threatening to sue for theft, the embarrassed ex-Emperor William wrote a foreword to the German edition; an extract is quoted in context in the present work, p. 186.

CHAPTER 1

Childhood and Youth, 1831 — 51.

On 11 June 1829 Prince William of Prussia, the second son of King Frederick William III, and heir to the throne which had belonged to the Hohenzollern dynasty since 1701, married Princess Augusta of Saxe-Weimar-Eisenach at Berlin. It was a typical royal marriage of convenience.

In the words of a Prussian courtier writing a century later William's mother, Queen Louise, was a cheerful girl when she came to the rigid Prussian court, 'where her spirit sank under the crushing load of cold, unbending etiquette then prevailing.'[1] It seemed to be a common fate for Prussian Queens, certainly for two of Louise's successors. Her delicate health was unable to meet the sacrifice of comfort she had to make as a result of Prussia's misfortunes in the Napoleonic wars, and she died in 1810, aged thirty-three. Her widower remarried fourteen years later, but the vacuum in the boyhood of Prince William, who was fourteen at his mother's death, was never filled. A lonely adolescence was followed by the one love affair of his life, with the pretty Elise Radziwill. It lasted passionately for a few years, but unfortunately the Radziwills, a Polish nobility, were considered unequal in rank to Hohenzollerns. Had they been permitted to marry they might have been an unusually happy royal pair, but the 'monarchistic code' in Prussia was severe, and even if they could have married, their children would have been barred from the succession. At the age of twenty-three, he wrote in his diary that he had at last come to the decision to give up all thoughts of Elise, although he still hoped against hope. Several schemes were considered to try and make the match possible. It was proposed that the girl might be adopted by the Tsar, and after his refusal, by one of the Hohenzollern princes, in order to give her royal rank. Not until he was twenty-nine did a specially-convened royal commission issue the final decree forbidding the *mésalliance.*From this, the King sympathetically but firmly assured his son, there was no appeal. William tried to bury his sorrows in hard work in the traditional family manner, at soldiering, and was soon appointed a general in the Prussian Garde-de-Corps. His character changed almost imperceptibly, but those who knew him well commented that the conclusion of his infatuation with Elise had left him more taciturn and serious. On her death in 1834 he attended her funeral, and was described by another mourner as looking 'shattered'.

Three years after the final decree he married Princess Augusta, a great-granddaughter on her mother's side of Catherine the Great of Russia. She had been brought up in a very different atmosphere from her husband; Weimar was the first state in Germany to grant its subjects a free constitution. Her grandfather had had the poet Goethe as his childhood tutor, and it was the latter's influence that had helped to make the Weimar court the most progressive not only in the German Confederation of thirty-nine states, created by the Congress of Vienna in 1815, but in the whole of Europe. Prussia at this time was no more than an average military state, recovering from the aftermath of the wars earlier in the century; not until the 1840s did it display the signs of nationalism which were built on by Bismarck to assume the leadership of an united Germany. For Berlin, the years between 1815 and 1848 marked a period of tranquility and incipient industrialisation, with a rapidly-expanding population which almost doubled to a figure of 400,000. In some aspects Prussia was surprisingly modern; it was the first state in Europe to pass factory legislation forbidding the employment of children under nine, and limiting the working day to sixteen hours. On the other hand, the conditions of the working-class were no better than anywhere else, and many of the lowborn, who were responsible for the increase in Berlin's population, lived just outside the city in makeshift huts, where those who could not find employment, or who had large families to support, lived by thieving. Moreover, while schools of liberal thought were stirring in states other than Weimar, Prussia continued to ignore or suppress them.

At the time of her marriage Augusta was a tall, vivacious girl of seventeen, with classical features which made her handsome if not beautiful. Even allowing for the flattery of Winterhalter and other court painters, her portraits show that she kept her striking looks well into middle age. Had she found a husband who was her equal in her literary tastes, her generally free-thinking outlook, and her pro-Catholicism — or at least able to complement them — she could have developed into a remarkable personality. William was a good-looking, dignified man with a deep sonorous voice, a fine head of hair, a moustache and magnificent side-whiskers — the kind of prince many a girl would have loved to marry. They could have made an idyllic couple, but this was sadly not to be the case. Like the mother-in-law she never knew, and in time her daughter-in-law, Augusta was completely taken aback by the bigotry of her new home. Unlike them she made the best of a bad job in her ability to adapt to the petty, tittle-tattling ways of the court, but the cheerful and cultured young woman became in time sour and embittered.

William was undoubtedly prepared to try and grow fond of her; he was a man with profound sense of duty, having obediently renounced his heart's desire in the interests of his dynasty, and then having become a model soldier. Yet she made his task very difficult. She was niggling, intolerant, and jealous of the memory of Elise, about whom she had been fully told. Paradoxically she made friends with the girl's family, thus making it all the harder for him to banish the memories of his blighted youth. With true magnaminity he struggled, and to some degree succeeded, to respect her talents and artistic qualities, which reminded him of his mother. Yet her intelligence and subsequent desire to 'have a finger in every pie' must have been hard to live with in a time when men were brought up to believe that women, particularly princesses, should have no genuine interests outside the three K's: *Kirche, Küche, Kinder* (Church, Kitchen, Children). Catherine the Great would have had a battle against anti-feminine prejudice in Prussia. Augusta's liberal views were no secret on the continent, and a French minister told his colleagues that as soon as her husband came to power, she would ensure that Prussia would follow Weimar's example and grant a constitution.

It was not only over politics that the couple argued; even the most trivial domestic matters caused friction, and some contemporary courtiers said that they quarrelled daily. One of the sources of trouble led to an incident little short of farce. William had been left a tea service by his mother, with a hideous pattern of intertwined bright blue and grass-green ribbons. Augusta loathed it, and frequently requested that they might be allowed to use something a little quieter, but he would not hear of it; what was good enough for his mother was good enough for his wife. Eventually her favourite maid, Fraulein von Neuendorff, came up with a solution to her problem. Knowing that Augusta was afflicted with trembling hands, she suggested that she could 'accidentally on purpose' drop a few of the cups and saucers whilst entertaining her guests, whom she always served personally. Soon a fair amount of china was broken, and she thought the wretched service had gone for good. Imagine her horror when on her next birthday her husband, doubtless struggling to keep a straight face, presented her with a new one. With no expense spared he had had the identical design, so beloved by his mother, reproduced by the Royal Berlin Porcelain Company.

It was to this ill-matched couple that Prince Frederick William, destined to be the second German Emperor, was born on 18 October 1831, in the Neue Palais at Potsdam, where his parents had temporarily gone to avoid an outbreak of cholera in Berlin. The date, an auspicious one, must have pleased his father and grandfather; it was the anniversary of Napoleon's crushing defeat at the battle of Leipzig in 1813. Bawling so loudly at the font that one of the guests likened him to a little general giving orders, he was christened on 13 November, with the names Frederick William Nicholas Charles; throughout his life he was Fritz to his family, and in more formal terms he was known as Prince Frederick William.

At his birth, he was third in succession to the throne. His uncle Frederick William, then Crown Prince, had been married to Princess Elizabeth of Bavaria for several years, and they were still childless, although Tsar Nicholas had given them a bronze statuette of a baby boy for encouragement. That children might be born to them was still possible, as the Prince was only thirty-six and his wife ten years younger, but while their nursery remained empty Prince William remained heir presumptive.

The Hohenzollern family were, almost without exception, a typical product of their military environment — an unprepossessing group of philistines. The princesses had all Augusta's instinct for quarrelling among themselves, without her intelligence; their main interests in life were gossip and parties. The princes were summed up neatly in Crown Prince Frederick William's remark: 'If we had been born as sons of a petty official I should have become an architect. William a sergeant-major, Charles would have gone to prison, and Albrecht would have been a ne'er-do-well.'[2] After William's accession to the throne his permission was asked for the erection of a statue in Berlin to the Humboldt brothers. He agreed, adding: 'Though not as big as those of my generals.'[3]

The Neue Palais was Fritz's favourite home, both as a small boy and as a married man. Built by Frederick the Great between 1763 and 1769 in the rococo style, it had about two hundred rooms. The King had filled it with magnificent silver furniture and priceless tapestries, but none of his immediate successors shared his appreciation of the arts, and by the time William had lived there for a few years nearly everything had either tarnished or faded, and was infested with moths, lice and dead bats. The palace boasted no bathrooms or lavatories, which were considered needless extravagances. On the rare occasions when somebody wanted a bath one was borrowed from a nearby hotel. The only source of water was a pump in the courtyard. Eggcups were unheard of, and liqueur glasses served the purpose instead. But such were the conditions in which the family grew up that Fritz found nothing strange about them; eating cold food and washing in dirty water was all part of life — even for royalty. Not until he was married did he find anything remotely squalid about his home, and even then he found it hard to comprehend his young wife's disgust.

Although he had no brothers, and only one sister Louise, born in December 1838, he shared his toys and games with several childhood companions. Princess Charlotte of Prussia, later Hereditary Princess of Meiningen and mother of his future son-in-law, was an early friend, as were his cousin Prince Frederick Charles, three years his senior, and cousin's sisters. His adult memories were always of a lonely childhood, for fond as he was of these contemporaries they could not compensate fully for the unhappy home life dominated by his parents. William, whose early days had been motherless and lonely, should have understood, but as a father he was unimaginative to the point of cruelty. All that mattered to him was that the lad should be a good soldier. Sources agree that Fritz was more devoted to his mother than to his father; he inherited more from her than from him. The gradual understanding of her unpopularity as he grew up made his formative years sadder still.

His childhood education followed the usual pattern for Hohenzollern princes. He was looked after by nurses and governesses till he was seven, when Colonel von Unruh, his father's aide-de-camp, was appointed his military governor and Herr Godet, the son of his governess, became his tutor. The military element predominated in the life of all the dynasty's sons at this time. His tiny fingers had felt their way over dozens of toy soldiers by the time he was able to walk. To Prussia belonged the distinction of having pioneered soldiers in tin and lead, both painted and plain, first made in a burst of patriotic fervour to commemorate the victorious campaigns of Frederick the Great. While still small he became accustomed to the routine of being punctually and smartly turned out on parade no matter what the weather. One wet day a servant, who had been watching him exercise while soaked to the skin, dashed out to the parade ground with an umbrella. Much as he appreciated the thought Fritz declined it; who had ever seen a Prussian helmet under an umbrella before? His military education was a thorough one, being not only confined to drill and the study of artillery, but also embracing the more practical aspects such as shoeing, harnessing and grooming the cavalry horses, as well as cleaning their tack. On the cultural side he was taught languages, music, dancing, gymnastics, book-binding and carpentry; he was always proud of the chair he made his father. He learnt the rudiments of typesetting, and when he was twelve the proprietor of a Berlin printing firm presented him with a small hand-printing press.

Yet little of the more intellectual aspects of his learning appear to have taken root at first. He loved reading, and spent a good deal of spare time in the royal library. He had inherited his mother's enjoyment of poetry, but neither liked nor understood mathematics and science. The library contained no novels, and he rarely attended the theatre or concert hall as a boy. Such outings were rare for the family who, apart from Augusta and the future Frederick William IV, completely ignored the Romantic trends in philosophy, music and literature sweeping Germany at the time. Prussia could boast no Goethes or Schillers, and it is revealing that Beethoven, who was born and raised in Bonn, had to settle in Vienna to find fame and fortune. In spite of her love for literature and arts Augusta detested music, saying it set nerves on edge.[4] As for William, he declared it gave him a headache, and he once walked out of a Wagner opera to go on manoeuvres. It was not surprising, therefore, that their son was nearly thirty before he could recognise any music other than the Prussian national anthem. His favourite subject fittingly was history, which stemmed from the days when William in his rare demonstrations of fatherly affection had lifted him on his knee and told him about his homeland's past, as soon as he was old enough to understand. His eyes had often opened wide at the tales of Frederick the Great's victories, or brimmed with tears as he listened to the family's temporary decline in fortunes at the hands of the conquering Napoleon. And it was with fascination that he had wandered through the rose-scented apartments at Charlottenburg Palace, his small hand in that of his father, examining with awe his grandmother's finely-wrought embroideries and treasured Indian muslins, before looking at her marble effigy in the palace mausoleum. Perhaps his happiest moments, however, were those which he spent with his grandfather the King, who like many monarchs of the time was stern with his own children but in turn devoted to the second generation.

In June 1840 King Frederick William III died after a reign of forty-three years, and his eldest son ascended the throne as Frederick William IV. The new King, a bald, ugly man with very small features and a high-pitched voice, was a contradictory character. Basically kind-hearted, he wanted to leave his mark on Prussian history as a progressive monarch, but his horror of the French revolution and subsequent upheavals culminating in the Napoleonic wars had fostered in him an almost medieval view of his exalted position. The idea of becoming a constitutional monarch in the British sense was equally unpalatable to him. Unlike his brothers he was no philistine, and his military interests went little further than designing a new style of helmet. He had a passion for planning and building castles in a mock-Renaissance style, and he was one of the few members of the family who really enjoyed the fine arts; his purchase of works by the Romantic landscape painter Friedrich showed a sense of appreciation well ahead of his time. But in other ways he was just as reactionary as his contemporaries, agreeing that only soldiers were any help against democrats.

As he was still childless, the title Crown Prince went into abeyance; William as heir apparent assumed the title Prince of Prussia and Fritz at the age of eight became heir presumptive. The following year on his tenth birthday, in accordance with family tradition, he received his commission as Second Lieutenant in the First Infantry Regiment of Guards, and was invested with the Order of the Black Eagle.

Remarkably few childhood impressions of the handsome red-haired boy have survived. Those that have indicate that he was generous, unselfish, and very rarely lost his temper; he was also quiet and serious-minded like his father. A few incidents from his early days were recorded by his tutor Unruh. One evening after the boy's guests had gone home from his eighth birthday party he found his pupil, still dressed in his best velvet jacket with high-waisted trousers, close-buttoned jacket, and silk waistcoat, apparently engaged in calculating something at his desk, and left him to his work. A while later, he returned to discover him asleep with his head on his hands. After a servant had carried the boy to bed, he had a look at what lay on the desk; it was a list of presents that Fritz was going to buy for other people, using the money given him by his uncle, 'with reference to the estimated merits of each case, as well as their separate circumstances and conditions.'[5] Even though he knew Fritz so well he was most impressed by the earnestness of the work, and touched by the charitable motivation behind it.

On another occasion Fritz had a trivial argument with his father, and wanted an impartial opinion as to who was wrong. Unruh was asked to arbitrate, and after listening to both sides of the dispute said he believed Fritz to be right. He cautioned him not to boast about it, but need not have bothered; the boy immediately threw himself on the floor, sobbing, 'Now all is lost!'[6] He had desperately hoped that his father would have been judged right, and was not comforted until William took him in his arms and told him that he was in the wrong, but right at the same time. This has an affinity with the incident in which he reprimanded one of his teachers for bringing up a subject connected with his father's death, whenever it should occur. Both illustrate the tremendous obedience, almost to the point of anti-rebelliousness, to his father with which he was imbued, and perhaps to a degree his lack of self-confidence. The consequences of this were to prove crucial in the future; one might say that it eventually proved to be his undoing.

Meanwhile thoughts regarding his consort-to-be were gently stirring. In the royal palaces of England lived the reigning and predominantly German dynasty of Saxe-Coburg-Gotha. There was very little English blood in Queen Victoria and none in Prince Albert, and they would undoubtedly continue the British royal trend, introduced by their Hanoverian forebears, of looking to Germany for eligible sons- and daughters-in-law. On 21 November 1840, nine months after their wedding, the Queen gave birth to the first of their nine children, Victoria, Princess Royal, otherwise known as Vicky. Similar ideas were slowly but surely forming in the court at Windsor, and as an overture King Frederick William IV was invited in January 1842 to stand as one of the godfathers to Albert Edward, the baby Prince of Wales. Vicky was fascinated by the King; after the christening, he dandled her on his knee while she played with his gold watch chain. She failed to repeat the performance a couple of years later, when her second brother Alfred was christened and William came to be one of his godfathers. Frightened by his gruff voice, which for her failed to compensate for his friendly manner, she refused to meet him but fled without a word of greeting for the protection of her embarrassed father.

Nobody welcomed the prospect of closer connections with Britain more than Augusta. Her husband was indifferent, while the more conservative

Prussian elements — including at times the equivocal King — were not impressed; to them, the country was tainted by a constitutional monarchy. All the same, Frederick William played his part in the new phase of Anglo-Prussian relations, toasting Queen Victoria and Prince Albert at a gala banquet when they visited him at Aachen in August 1845.* Thirteen months later Augusta repaid the visit, spending a week at Windsor. Away from the oppressive atmosphere of the Berlin court, and in a country she liked and respected, she was a very different woman. The Queen and her husband were very pleased with their guest, who was eight years their senior; for the former it marked the beginning of a long friendship. Victoria's enthusiasm poured forth in a letter to her uncle Leopold, King of the Belgians: 'I do believe that I have a friend in her, who may be most useful to us.'[7] Not for many years was she to see in her the domineering small-minded princess who was so unpopular at home. Augusta had at least one very strong reason for wishing to have an English princess as her daughter-in-law, for William had suggested marrying Fritz to a Russian Grand Duchess. Despite her Romanov ancestry she hated everything Russian, particularly as she suspected her sister-in-law Charlotte, consort of Tsar Nicholas I, of maintaining a reactionary influence over William.

The following Christmas presents arrived at Windsor from Berlin, including toy shops with fruit and vegetables for Vicky, and five boxes of wooden and lead soldiers for the Prince of Wales. One hopes they were much better received than Queen Victoria's present to Fritz on his twelfth birthday — a complete Highland outfit, which to his intense embarrassment his mother made him wear when he was brought in to meet her guests after a state dinner. Arrayed in this 'fancy dress', he was shown into the dining room, and for half an hour had to endure the 'impudent exclamations, horrid caresses, and familiarities' of the assembled company.[8] As soon as he could make his escape he rushed back to his tutor who, expecting him to have been flattered by the admiration of the court, was surprised to find him almost in tears. Looking back on it, when he later came to wear the kilt regularly at Balmoral, it was an amusing enough incident — but, at the time, he had wished that the floor could have opened and swallowed him up.

Prince Albert noticed the progress of the prospective alliance with quiet satisfaction. He was idealistically treasuring the dreams of King Leopold and Baron Christian von Stockmar, the Coburg physician who had come to personify all the liberal hopes of their generation: visions of a Prussia which was not only a British ally, but also the leader of an united and more constitutional Germany. In 1835, as a tentative step towards German unity, the state had established a *Zollverein,* or Customs Union, by which it

---

* However, the King refused to give Albert precedence over an Austrian Archduke who was present. The Prince apparently accepted the slight without undue complaint, but Queen Victoria was furious and it permanently coloured her opinion of the Prussian court.

virtually controlled the Confederation's trading activities; only Austria, Hanover and Mecklenburg were not members. It was also the leading Protestant state in Germany, had some claims to being a centre of learning and science, and possessed an assembly. The power of this body was negligible; it was summoned (usually to ratify royal taxes) and dissolved by the King at will, but Frederick William IV was a romantic at heart — albeit a mentally unstable one, as later became apparent, and sometimes open to persuasion. From time to time he professed to hold certain liberal principles, in theory if not in practice. Further concessions to liberalism might therefore be expected.

Meanwhile Fritz continued with his studies and army training, as yet presumably unaware of the tentative matrimonial scheme being planned for him. Nevertheless his mother's political views left their mark; he showed signs of becoming just as steadfast a liberal thinker as she was. At the age of seventeen he attended a banquet at Potsdam and was seated next to the conservative Leopold von Gerlach, the King's Adjutant-General. The latter remarked how he envied the prince his youth, as he would doubtless 'survive the end of the absurd constitutionalism.' Fritz shocked him by replying that he believed some form of representation of the people would become a necessity.[9]

Therein lay a simple statement of the political beliefs from which he was never to waver. Whatever his detractors would eventually write or say of him, he did not take his creed from his father-in-law or his wife; it came to him from his mother.

It was partly brought home to him by the events of the previous year, 1848, when Germany was only one area of Europe to be shaken by the spirit of revolution. In March street fighting broke out in Berlin, and the temporarily unnerved King promised reforms, including summoning of the *Landtag* (the Prussian Parliament). Fritz and Louise could see shots being fired between guards and revolutionaries from the palace. After a few days Augusta decided that the capital was no place for her children and she took them to Babelsberg, the summer retreat three miles from Potsdam built by William in 1835. Here they were approached by Otto von Bismarck, one of the most reactionary members of the United Diet in Germany. Having considered and discarded several schemes to nip the revolt in the bud, he came to Augusta with the idea of persuading the King to abdicate, getting William to renounce his right to the succession, and placing Fritz — young, innocent, untarnished by any connection with the past, and therefore more acceptable to the rebels than any other Hohenzollern — on the throne. The plot was not his; it had been suggested by Prince Charles, the King's arch-conservative younger brother, who intended that he himself should be the power behind the throne. By coincidence exactly the same manoeuvring brought the young Habsburg Prince Francis Joseph to the imperial Austrian throne in succession to his uncle, the epileptic Emperor Ferdinand, later that year. Taken by surprise, however, Augusta's loyalty to her husband and brother-in-law — or more possibly the desire to see herself on the throne in time, rather than surrender the privilege to her son — overruled her. She indignantly refused to contemplate the idea, and never forgave Bismarck for it.

Whether Fritz knew of it at the time or found out later is uncertain; yet it was not the last time that he was to be offered the throne to which he succeeded so tragically late. Had be accepted it on either occasion his life, and almost certainly German (if not European) history, would have taken a very different course.

While his wife and children were sheltering away from Berlin, William fled to Britain. He had been regarded by the Prussian Conservatives as their champion at court, and it was due to him that troops were called into the streets to put down the rioting. For this he became known as the Grapeshot Prince, and mobs in Berlin demanded his blood. Trimming his very conspicuous whiskers with a pair of scissors in the hope that he would not be recognised, a gesture his son considered most undignified and never forgot, he made for the safety of the Prussian Embassy at Carlton House Terrace in London. Prince Albert lost no time in calling on him and inviting him to Windsor, where he poured out his schemes for a united liberal Germany, and explained how England had adapted herself to Parliamentary government without any diminution in the nation's loyalty to the crown. William listened silently, more out of good manners than agreement. If he had ever entertained such ideas favourably, which was unlikely, Augusta had doubtless unwittingly put him off them. Interpreting his silence as both depression at events and tacit agreement with everything he had heard, Albert wrote of him in glowing terms to King Leopold: 'Germany can ill spare people like him.'[10]

William returned to Prussia during the summer, by which time the revolution was dying a natural death. As hopes of further democracy wilted, the Frankfurt assembly decided to go ahead and create an united German Empire from the Confederation. After the Imperial crown was refused by Francis Joseph it was offered to King Frederick William in April 1849, who was dissuaded from accepting it by his ministers, warning him that by 'picking it up from the gutter' he would be surrendering himself to democracy. The assembly therefore shelved the idea for the time being, and few people were more disappointed than Prince Albert.

Fritz's minority was coming to a close. With his family he spent the summer of 1848 at Babelsberg, where he was prepared for confirmation; the ceremony took place on 29 September in the Charlottenburg chapel, where he read out an essay of his own composition on his belief in Christianity. In the following summer, after Unruh's retirement, he began full-time military service with his regiment, and was promoted to the rank of First Lieutenant; that autumn he commanded the regiment for the first time during seasonal routine manoeuvres, and in October he came of age. The eighteenth birthdays of Hohenzollern princes were celebrated in a spectacular fashion; a levée was attended by the family and countless officials, including the Prussian state ministers, military commanders, and deputations from town magistrates, all in full dress. He received their congratulations, and the Mayor of Berlin, Herr Naumyn, read out addresses from the town officials; he then made several short speeches of thanks in return.

Three weeks after his eighteenth birthday came his first break with Hohenzollern tradition, namely an university education. Until then military training was considered adequate for the heirs to the Prussian throne and their kin, but Augusta had used her influence to have her nephew Frederick Charles (son of the Prince Charles who had schemed with Bismarck) enrolled at the University of Bonn, where Prince Albert had studied before his marriage. In doing so she set a precedent for sending her son there; in November 1849 he settled in Bonn, on the first floor of the university building, the former Elector's castle, to study literature, history and law. This system of education was not just a course of study for its own sake, but also something of a democratic experiment. In Fritz's view it was a complete success, as the long essay he wrote on its value in his third term shows. In it he recognised that 'no true picture of the life and doings of man' could be gleaned at court, but one had to meet and exchange views regularly with people from all social classes.[11] Under his mother's upbringing he found the court nearly as stifling as she did, and he never forgot the atmosphere on frequent occasions when royal fellow-students and others gathered in his rooms at Bonn for a 'social round table'. That he worked hard there is no doubt; he preferred studying into the small hours to the all-night drinking and singing parties enjoyed by other students, and recalling descriptions of him handed down by his childhood tutors there are grounds for supposing that, like Prince Albert, he may have seemed to some a little too angelic to be human. But he was never priggish; there is ample evidence that he mixed freely with his contemporaries and the citizens of Bonn, being fully accepted by all as 'one of the crowd'. He tactfully avoided becoming involved in political discussions, preserving total impartiality, but he was not without a sense of humour, being as ready to joke as anyone. Only those who forgot to treat him with the respect due to a prince of the blood royal had anything to fear; like his future brother-in-law, later Edward VII, he had the 'common touch', but insisted on the appropriate deference to his rank. Not surprisingly he preferred living in Bonn to Berlin, and generally only visited the capital when court festivities or functions demanded. Such an occasion was the confirmation by oath of the new constitution by the King in February 1850; another was the celebration of the creation of Prussia in January 1851.

When not at Bonn he was happiest visiting his mother and sister at Coblenz, their rural retreat in West Prussia. Despite the seven years in age between them, the childhood lack of intimacy between Fritz and Louise had lessened by the time of his early manhood, and they were often to be seen together strolling along the banks of the Elbe, shopping in the nearby towns, or exploring the fairs, a small pug dog scampering at their heels.

The train journey which returned him to Bonn in January 1851 from Berlin almost cost him his life. The express train ran off the rails at one point, probably through part of the engine near the left wheel breaking while crossing a bridge. Five carriages fell after each other down the embankment, the sixth rolled over, and the rest eventually came to a standstill; the driver and two passengers were killed. Fritz in the fifth carriage received a slight blow on the back of the head, but nonetheless got out to help the injured. A stone monument was later erected to mark the site of the accident at which Providence had intervened on his behalf.

During vacations he was allowed to indulge his fast-forming taste for travel. To his father journeys abroad were a needless luxury, and no experience nor landscape could compare with the barracks, though he sometimes yielded in the face of opposition from the rest of the family. Before his student days Fritz's longest journeys from Berlin and Potsdam had been to Switzerland for a walking tour at the age of ten, and four years later to the island of Rügen, off the north German coast in the Baltic Sea. Between his university terms, he saw something of Southern Europe. The first of his expeditions, as a guest of his cousin Charlotte, who on her marriage had become Grand Duchess of Meiningen, took him to Lake Como in Italy. After a few weeks on the sunny shores and in the neighbouring villages he visited Switzerland, the Tyrol, and the south of France, happy days of sightseeing in foreign lands enhanced by perfect weather. Before returning home in the autumn, impatient to tell his friends and lecturers of all he had seen, he vowed to visit some if not all of these places again. He was allowed to fulfil his promise, albeit during some of the less cheerful times of his life.

The following year, however, the memories of his southern European travels were temporarily eclipsed by a journey to England, which as his biographer Margaretha von Poschinger writes was undoubtedly 'the greatest influence upon his whole life.'[12]

CHAPTER 2

Engagement, 1851 — 55.

While Fritz was beginning his second year of study at Bonn, one of the university's most illustrious former students was equally hard at work in London. Prince Albert was planning the Great Exhibition at Crystal Palace, a monumental tribute to the industrial and artistic skills of peacetime Britain and her empire. Having fought all opposition to the scheme, he and Queen Victoria decided to try and bring another idea to fruition. They had met the Prince and Princess of Prussia; when were they going to meet their son and heir, of whom his parents had spoken so enthusiastically? The whole family should be invited to the opening ceremony of the exhibition, and in order to disguise the implications other European royalties should come as well.

William accordingly accepted. He had reckoned without his elder brother, who was persuaded by the Anglophobe clique that such a gathering of princes in that constitution-ridden country would be an easy target for anarchist attacks, and at first refused to let him go. A persuasively-worded letter from a desperate Albert changed the King's mind, and on 29 April 1851 William brought his wife and children to Buckingham Palace; the exhibition was opened two days later.

Amid all the excitement, Victoria and Albert soon found that all they had been told about Fritz was true; he was 'so good and amiable'. For his part he was equally captivated by everything: the respectability and technological superiority of Victorian England, the liberal and tolerant outlook of Prince Albert, so different from the narrow-minded conservatism prevalent at home, and the warm happy royal family life, where the seven children behaved so naturally and benefited from having such loving parents. To the lonely nineteen-year-old youth accustomed to a very different home atmosphere and the most spartan of surroundings, this visit was nothing short of a revelation.

But the greatest impression made on him, as hoped, was by the eldest of these merry children. At ten Vicky was something of a child prodigy. She was her father's delight, already sharing with him the intellectual, artistic and political interests which evoked so little response in the Queen, She had spoken English, German and French fluently from a very early age, the German with an English accent and vice versa, which later proved to be a rather appropriate analogy. One day at the age of three, riding in Windsor Park, she exclaimed to her governess with a theatrical flourish of her hand at the view: *'Voilá le tableau qui se déroule á mes pieds,'*[1] a line from a poem she had just learnt. She was also endearingly proud. If anyone called her Missy she retorted indignantly that she was not Missy, she was the Princess Royal. If she wanted to chat with her when the latter was receiving ministers at court, and they refused to go away, she tearfully asked the Queen to make them obey her.[2]

How aware was Fritz of the elder generation's match-making? The German biographer Martin Philippson believes that he knew of it; if he had not actually been told, then he must have guessed. His excitement with England was therefore tempered a little at knowing what was expected of him, but like his parents he would in due course do his duty; love was not the motivation for Hohenzollern marriages, but an unexpected bonus which occasionally followed. In this respect he was to be most fortunate.

It would certainly have been a little premature for him to fall in love with a girl of ten. But he could not have failed to be impressed by her; even allowing for hindsight, he can have exaggerated only a little if at all when years later, as a grandfather, he told one of her first biographers, Catherine Radziwill (Elise's niece), that even at such a tender age, she was so perfect he often caught himself wondering whether she really was a human being.[3]

At their first meeting, in Buckingham Palace, he spoke to her in halting English, and she replied in perfect German. Having visited the exhibition before it opened to the public, she knew so much about the items on display that she astounded him with her knowledge when she took him on a conducted tour around the Crystal Palace, and continued full of energy despite the heat and dust which gave him a headache. At the same time, with tact well in advance of her years, she neatly took him by the arm to show him something different every time his parents began to argue. She had sensed that the connubial harmony of Windsor was not to be found in Prussia.

An all-too-short stay with the family at Osborne, and a visit to Liverpool, followed for Fritz before his return home. He went back with his liberal convictions considerably strengthened. For he had grown up inclined more towards his mother's political ideas, particularly after the horrors which the revolutions of 1848 had threatened,* than to the views of his father, who was prepared to make half-hearted concessions to liberalism provided they did not conflict with his military principles, but was still scarcely more flexible than his reactionary brothers. But how was he to be sure? His parents were on such bad terms with each other, owing largely to their differences of opinion; who was right, who was wrong? In May 1851, it

---

* A mob in Paris had forced King Louis Philippe of France to abdicate that year. He fled to England as an exile and died in 1850.

seemed he had the answer. Prince Albert's advice to him was much the same as that given to his father during his temporary exile; in brief, that constitutionalism and monarchy were not only compatible, but also potentially far safer than absolute monarchy. All that he had seen in England confirmed Fritz in this belief. While Berlin had experienced street fighting in 1848, the nearest that England had come to internal revolt that year were a few lukewarm Chartist riots and the smashing of windows at Buckingham Palace; the contrasts were obvious. In the light of this, Augusta's visions of liberalism and German unification did not look nearly so remote now that Prince Albert had expounded on the same theme, albeit in his rather theoretical, unworldly way.

This was not to say that Prussia did not have a constitution of sorts, but as Gerhard Masur wrote, the state was a constitutional monarchy with the accent on monarchy.[4] What constitution there was provided for a division of power between the heads of the great aristocratic families and persons nominated by the monarch. The consent of the King and the two chambers, the *Herrenhaus* (or Upper House) and an elected assembly were necessary to pass new legislation. Yet the elected representatives could not propose legislative measures on their own initiative and the electoral system, devised after the revolution and remaining in force till the collapse of the monarchy seventy years later, strongly favoured the property-owning classes. It can thus be said that Prussia under Frederick William IV was a constitutional power, but without democracy in the modern sense of the word. It was certainly absolutist in comparison with the governments of Britain and Weimar, both possessing systems with which Fritz, his mother, and others of liberal opinion identified themselves.

None of the parties concerned was slow to exploit the advances made after the visit was over. Fritz and Vicky began to correspond regularly, while the Queen had for the first time gained some insight into the unhappiness of her guests' family life. She was in a good position to sympathise. After the marriage of her half-sister Feodore her own childhood had been bleak, surrounded by her ambitious widowed mother and a grasping comptroller with only a middle-aged governess for a friend. The letter she wrote Augusta in June after their departure was perceptive: 'I beg of you to show confidence in your dear son, so that he may likewise show confidence in himself. I am always afraid in his case of the consequences of a moral clash, should his father strongly recommend something and his mother warn him against it. He will wish to please both, and the fear of not succeeding will make him uncertain and hesitating.'[5] Uncertainty and hesitation were to dog Fritz in the years ahead, as the Queen had so prophetically foreseen.

Not surprisingly, on his return to university his increased love of England was reflected in his studies. His English tutor Dr Copland Perry gave him three lessons in English language and literature a week, and was struck by his sincere affection for the country, not just for the Queen and her family, but also for her political and social way of life. At the end of each formal study session, they would amuse themselves 'by writing imaginary letters to ministers and leaders of society'.[6] At a party he told another student how much he had enjoyed staying there, and when asked why, he suddenly looked very serious. Asking him to keep his secret, he pulled out a large gold locket which hung around his neck, and pressed the spring to reveal a miniature of Vicky. He kissed it lovingly before replacing it — a gesture that the girl who so relished attention would have greatly appreciated.

His university studies were interrupted for a while by further military training. Within a week of returning from England, he was in command of the castle guard at the public unveiling of a statue to Frederick the Great in Berlin. Later he accompanied his father to observe Russian manoeuvres at Warsaw, where he was appointed commander of a Russian regiment, doubtless giving rise to further friction between his parents. The autumn was spent on duty with the First Regiment of Infantry Guards, after which he was promoted to the rank of Captain. Not until October did he return to Bonn for the final session of his studies. A testimonial, various gifts, and a torchlight procession by the other students were among the celebrations when he left the university in March 1852.

The next three years of his life began with another session of soldiering. At camp near Potsdam he celebrated his twenty-first birthday with a supper and dance for the officers of his regiment. Manoeuvres and the study of theory occupied the next few months until he contracted an inflammation, the result of a chill, in May 1853. On medical advice he went to recuperate at Ems, a holiday and health resort in Hanover, lying in an attractive valley among wooded hills. From there he left for Switzerland, making his home for a few months on the shores of Lake Geneva, with views of the vineyards and the perpetual mantle of snow on the Alpine slopes. Sailing, climbing the lower mountain reaches, and visiting the picturesque castle of Chillon, which stirred his historical enthusiasm, greatly deepened his love for foreign travel.

Yet at the same time his absence and ill-health had unpleasant consequences at home. The trouble began with Prince Charles, to whose intrigues there was no end. On this occasion he took it upon himself to exaggerate his nephew's illness, making it appear that he was a delicate youth. Would it not be more practical to have an heir apparent who was 'healthy and capable of work' — namely his own son Frederick Charles?[7] William and Augusta were angry, and insisted very properly that the succession could not be tampered with in this way. But this defence of their son could not prevent the gathering of supporters in both camps among the army officers, one party upholding Fritz's rights, the other those of his cousin.

The affair never went any further, but Fritz never really trusted either of them again. From his father he had inherited an inviolable respect for the laws of royal succession; within a few years it was to be cruelly tested.

In August he resumed his duties for a while, and took part in an inspection of the Austrian contingent in the German Federal Army at Olmutz with the Tsar and Francis Joseph, the latter awarding him a Colonelcy-in-Chief of an Austrian regiment.

How much did his military activities really mean to him in the aftermath of May 1851? Before that golden month he had accepted it unquestioningly as part of his life, but now it must have seemed a contradiction to his liberal inclinations and conception of a peacefully united democratic Germany. War went hand-in-hand with absolutism and revolt, he recognised, not with liberalism. The days when he would denounce war as butchery were a long way ahead, but for the present he enjoyed army life; he had his share of the Hohenzollern character, and it brought him into contact with people of his own age, as his university days had done. Moreover camp life was preferable to the hidebound court life at Berlin, now all the less pleasant in comparison with his spell in England. All the same, the parade ground did not suit him as fully as it did the typical Prussian prince; already he knew that life and an apprenticeship to a throne should have more to offer.

By December 1853 he was on his travels again, this time in classical Italy. Just before Christmas he met Pope Pius IX for the first time, in circumstances which neither forgot. The Pope held out his hand for the ring to be kissed but Fritz, either not realising the significance of the gesture or else deciding that Protestants such as himself should do otherwise, grasped it and shook it heartily. On subsequent occasions the Pope kept both hands carefully behind his back. It was in the ensuing months that Fritz's interest in art and archaeology, already fostered by his classics tutor Professor Ernest Curtius, came to life. He was enthralled by the Roman ruins, churches, palaces and art treasures, which till then had been little more than names in a book to him. He stayed in Rome until March, visiting Naples, Vesuvius, Pompeii and Sicily among other places, returning to the papal capital for Easter, and attending the Good Friday service in the Sistine Chapel. After leaving Rome for a second time, he travelled home via Florence and Venice, taking with him various treasures, including an exact model of the triumphal arch of Titus made from marble, two vases, and several copperplate engravings of paintings hanging in the Vatican. His later patronage of museums during his long years as Crown Prince, greatly eclipsing that of any other Hohenzollern before him, never failed to remind him of those happy days in Italy.

To the background of more military training and the inevitable honours which followed, there was a sinister note which threatened to sour if not

William I

Prince Frederick William, c.1849

undo the Anglo-Prussian unity, which had anyway taken something of a back seat since 1851. Relations between Britain and Russia had deteriorated while Fritz was in Italy, and now both nations were at war with each other in the Crimea. The Prussian court came close to splitting, while the state remained neutral as far as fighting was concerned; the King sided with his brother-in-law the Tsar, and when William suspected him of victimising pro-British ministers and ambassadors, his protests led to his temporary banishment from Berlin. Britain became furiously anti-German, destroying for a while the good impression created by the visit of the royal family to the exhibition. Was Vicky, now thirteen, still writing enthusiastically to the prince she had not seen for three years? It was more than likely that she was too thrilled by the course of the war to keep up her correspondence without a considerable break. Yet the Queen continued writing to Augusta. Could Fritz come to stay again soon, she asked in January 1855; the political situation between the two countries was difficult, but surely better times would come?

Come they did. At the beginning of September the Queen and Albert took the family to Balmoral, their new home in the Scottish Highlands; Fritz arrived there a few days later. Understandably he was apprehensive, for he knew he was not coming just for a cosy fortnight's holiday, in spite of Prince Albert's remarkable understatement to the Duchess of Kent, his mother-in-law: 'he wishes to see Scotland'.[8] Had it not been for his mother's encouragement, he would probably have refused the invitation; four years was a long time in the life of an adolescent girl, and once his father's temporary anti-Russian phase had passed, he would most likely be looking for a suitable daughter-in-law among the Romanovs as an alternative.

Nevertheless he had parental permission to propose — he hardly dared consider returning without having done so — and his reception at Balmoral soon put him at ease. The family were the same happy unit as before, and as for Vicky, whom he only remembered as a pretty little girl, she was maturing into a beautiful woman. Contemporary photographs of her show that she had none of her mother's plain looks at the same age; the combination of her childish roundness, awakening beauty, and unforced charm was irresistible. They sat next to each other at dinner that first evening, chatting gaily in French and German. She could not keep her eyes off this handsome young suitor, still the same gentle unaffected friend she had known before, but twice as manly with his tawny moustache, which seemed to make him look taller and more magnificent than ever;* her father was watching them. Had she but known it, Albert was trying not to blush himself. Both he and the Queen did their best to look unconcerned, but they were secretly overjoyed that all appeared to be turning out as planned. They had decided

* His height was about six feet two inches.

firmly beforehand that, had no signs of love between the two appeared, they would not attempt to force the issue.

The next day Albert took Fritz out deer-stalking, but his mind was on game of a different sort. Getting soaked to the skin proved too much for the elder man, who then took to his bed with an attack of rheumatism. Both this and the Queen's exaggerated coyness towards the young couple were most disconcerting to Fritz, who once again became as nervous as he had been on the journey to Britain. Fortunately Vicky could read his thoughts, and as soon as they were alone for a minute she took his hand and squeezed it. He was so elated and relieved that he had his first good night's sleep since his arrival. The next day after breakfast, he plucked up courage to ask the Queen and Albert for a quiet word; in the Queen's words, his wish was 'to belong to our family'.[9] He had permission from the King as well as from his parents, he told them, and 'proposal had long been his wish'. But, she insisted, Vicky was to know nothing until after her confirmation at Easter the next year; he ought to attend the ceremony if possible and propose immediately afterwards. In strict confidence Albert notified the Prime Minister, Lord Palmerston, and his Foreign Secretary, Lord Clarendon.

Yet Fritz could not wait. Vicky would not have been a normal girl if she had not guessed what was afoot. On 25 September he asked for permission to give her a bracelet. The Queen granted it, adding that 'something had to be told her and he had better tell her himself'.[10]

On 29 September came the climax of the happy drama. That afternoon the family went out riding up the heather-covered slopes of Craig-na-Ban, pausing to admire the view from the summit before riding down. Fritz and Vicky lagged behind, and he picked her a sprig of white heather, an emblem of good luck, telling her that he hoped she would come to stay with him in Prussia, always — a roundabout way of asking her, but she understood. When they reached the carriage where everyone else was waiting, he winked at the Queen to imply that his mission was accomplished. Back at the castle, an agitated and half-remorseful Vicky threw herself into her parents' arms and told them everything.

Two days later, amid tears and embraces from all, Fritz returned to Prussia, having already extended his visit beyond its planned duration, and with a considerable weight off his mind. Vicky confessed to her parents that she had never been so happy as at the moment when he had kissed her. As recognition of her new status, from that time onwards mother, father and daughter dined together *á trois* in the evenings.

'The description of the rapid development of my dear Vicky's character,' Fritz wrote in October to Prince Albert, 'in consequence of our mutual declaration, is an extremely joyful piece of news for me . . . I can vividly imagine how the dear child has suddenly moved closer to her parents, and on both sides this development is a very beneficial, amazing one; but it would not be easy for me to say any more, for because I just feel so drawn towards her and discovered so much depth of mind and feeling in her, I really cannot put into words what it was that so specially attracted me.'[11]

Several writers have criticised the parents for allowing their daughter to be swept off her feet and accept a proposal at the age of fourteen, thereby robbing her of the chance to exercise her own judgment. Was she really just a pawn in the hands of the elder generation? Was she being sacrificed on the altar of the visions of a liberal Europe led jointly by Britain and a constitutional Prussia? Should Fritz have been more patient? It is difficult to answer yes to these questions. Under normal circumstances it would have been unfair to let a girl get engaged so young — although everyone agreed that the wedding should wait till she was seventeen — but Vicky was remarkably mature for her age. She was oustandingly intelligent, even if her intellect was often at the mercy of her emotions, and also allowing for the fact that she knew she was as good as expected to accept Fritz at Balmoral. It was an early age to fall in love, but their affections never wavered. Throughout the tragedies of the future, this was the one constant factor of their life together. While there is some justification for the view that Albert sacrificed his favourite daughter to his visionary ideals, it is interesting to note that two of Vicky's sisters made unhappy marriages. He could have made a far worse choice; as regards his first son-in-law, he could hardly have made a better one.

If the select group of a dozen or less who knew at once of the engagement believed that the secret could be kept for long, they were optimistic. On 3 October the first leader of *The Times* drew the attention of its readers to Fritz's arrival at Balmoral, for the sole purpose of 'improving his acquaintance with the Princess Royal'. Emphasising King Frederick William's tacit pro-Russian attitude during the Crimean war, which was not yet over, it believed that an alliance with Prussia would be tantamount to one with Russia. If Fritz was called up to join the Russian army, it continued, then Vicky would be placed in a situation where loyalty to her husband would be treason to her country; and if Prussia lapsed into the status of a petty power, she would be sent back to England as an exile. 'For our part, we wish for the daughter of our Royal House some better fate.'[12]The criticisms wounded Albert. He had unbounded faith in Fritz, but he knew that there was some truth in this view, despite his snort of derision that the newspaper, 'our sulky grandmother (was) deeply offended that its permission was not first asked'.[13] Would the King and his brother become dependable British allies? The future, he believed, undoubtedly belonged to Fritz, who was surely destined for a long reign, although as yet only second in line to the throne.

On his way back Fritz visited King Leopold in Brussels, who was delighted that his plans were materialising. Proceeding to Bonn he called upon Dr Perry, his former tutor, to whom he had already confided his hopes. 'It was not politics, it was not ambition,' he told him, 'it was my heart.'[14] It was to a double family celebration that he returned; by coincidence his sister Louise, now seventeen, had become engaged the same week to Frederick, Prince Regent of Baden. As adults, brother and sister were never very close. Louise had inherited nothing of her mother's progressive qualities, and was much more attached to her father; like her aunts, she was 'ignorant and proud of it', and doubtless eager to avoid Augusta's unpopularity. Her husband-to-be, however, came from one of the more democratic German states, and had much in common with Fritz.

Whatever may have been his initial doubts about an Anglo-Prussian marriage alliance, the King defended it cheerfully. When Gerlach waved a copy of the right-wing *Kölnische Zeitung* at him and complained of the absurd reports that his nephew had gone to England merely to propose, the monarch laughingly told him they were true.

But in general the other princes and princesses were far from pleased, as he noted ruefully. 'Most of (the family) do not really know what to make of me, and one can feel their curiosity, uncertainty, etc.; only they are always letting off random shots in the form of sarcastic, barbed references with pretty unkind content! The unhappy party is seething with anger at not having been informed and consulted in advance, and is now trying to get revenge by incredibly petty cackling that sheds a most revealing light.' Fortunately his friends were more gracious in their comments 'expressing joy about the probable purpose of my journey to England [*sic*]. This warms my heart, and without more or much enquiry such indications suffice to give me real happiness.'[15]

CHAPTER 3

Marriage, 1855 — 58.

That winter, Fritz's military duties were interspersed with obtaining some insight into contemporary Prussian government, which pleased both Prince Albert and Princess Augusta; it was largely due to their combined pressure that he was given any such 'training' at all. He was most unfavourably impressed with what he saw of Otto von Manteuffel's reactionary ministry, particularly the corruption in the elections for the House of Deputies, which took place as he was returning from Scotland. No efforts were spared, he told his future father-in-law, to get elected as deputies the provincial councillors who were completely subservient to the government and would only vote as the ministers wished. 'In Berlin it is incredible what shameless devices the all-powerful police used in order to deliver to people's homes the names of those who were to be elected. And now it has been achieved that completely spineless persons are appearing as deputies, to whom the household gods of popular representation are being offered, and we are probably achieving everything that has long since been intended. Many people are saying that motions will probably be brought forward for abolishing the constitution, and that this is what the party manoeuvring is aiming at . . . May God protect us, and enlighten our poor most gracious King, who is no longer allowed to see things as they really are.'[1] Prince Albert could not agree more, replying in words which were to prove prophetic: 'designs such as those contemplated by the reactionaries . . . may result in extreme danger to the monarchy'.[2]

Announcement of the betrothal to the European courts was made in April 1856, a month after Vicky's confirmation, which Fritz could not attend because of his army commitments; it was now discussed openly for the first time. The comments of Bismarck, then Prussian Ambassador in Paris (where he had been presented to the Queen and Prince Albert the previous summer) have passed into immortality. What did he think of the English marriage, Gerlach asked him. He did not like the English part of it, replied Bismarck, but the bride-to-be was said to be a lady of intelligence and feeling. As long as she could leave the Englishwoman at home and become a Prussian, she would be a blessing to the state, just as long as she did not bring any reprehensible influence from her parents' court with her. He had his own good reasons for being apprehensive; he was no political ally of

Prince Albert, and he had heard how much her intellect resembled his.

Privately, Augusta's views were not so very different. Much as she disliked Bismarck and all he stood for she envied the love, denied her in marriage, that her son and his betrothed shared, to say nothing of the influence at court she would undoubtedly have over her fond husband when they ascended the throne. The laudatory letters about Vicky she continually received from Queen Victoria did nothing to reassure her. Nearly thirty years of loveless married life had left her with little human warmth, and she was pleased that her wishes were going to come true solely for the prestige that a British princess would bring Prussia. She found Vicky too clever by half, and secretly thought her much too full of her own importance to be a suitable daughter-in-law, but nonetheless the Princess Royal of the powerful nation the whole continent respected was not a prize to be scoffed at.

Fritz paid his third visit to Britain in the early summer of 1856, to coincide with the Queen's birthday. The engagement had not yet been formally announced to Parliament, and the visit was again private. It did not pass altogether smoothly; the Queen insisted on the Victorian, un-Continental custom of chaperonage, although she found it as tiresome as the young couple themselves. Yet here they had an ally in the Prince of Wales. When ordered by his mother to keep them company he made a point of playing with the younger children in an adjoining room, though for caution's sake leaving the door ajar in case she should suddenly return. In the course of his visit, a few weeks after his arrival, a rather alarming incident occurred. While melting sealing-wax over a candle, Vicky set fire to the sleeve of her dress. Although the flames were quickly smothered with a hearthrug, her arm was badly burned from wrist to shoulder. Fritz was distraught and sat beside her holding her hand for hours. Later he was full admiration for her fortitude; she could even jest at her own clumsiness, although obviously in intense pain.

With increasing duties as a Prussian ambassador abroad, and as a fond fiancé, he was for a while giving less time to his army career. In August 1856 he went to Moscow to represent his uncle at the coronation of the new Tsar, Alexander II. The Dowager Tsarina, his aunt, had come to stay at Potsdam soon after her husband's death, and it was with her that Fritz and his aide-de-camp Helmuth von Moltke set out on the long journey. From Prussia they travelled to Warsaw by coach, arriving there at three in the morning to a reception by ambassadors in full state dress. After a mere two hours' sleep they went by rail for the remaining one hundred and twenty miles, a distance which took them a whole day and night to accomplish. By the time they reached Moscow, they had not undressed for six nights, apart from their meagre rest at Warsaw.

Fortunately the magnificence of the ceremony made up for the uncomfortable journey they had just endured, although the celebrations were not without mishap. The day's festivities opened at seven in the morning with gun salutes, a signal for the guests and guards to fall into their places in the procession to the cathedral. Fritz was spellbound by the costumes of the Tsar and Tsarina, the former clad in green tunic, red trousers, a brilliant plume of feathers in his helmet, and the latter in a white silk robe studded lavishly with jewels. The uniforms of the generals and the other foreign representatives were equally colourful, their scarlet and gold trousers, plumed helmets and dazzling displays of jewellery eclipsing the resplendent flags and drapes adorning the cathedral walls. Not so marvellous, however, were the fire precautions, a pitifully small number of water carts wheeled along at the end of the procession, lest the firework displays got out of hand. The wonder with which Fritz watched the illumination of the St Basil Cathedral, 'outlined in fire' the evening after the ceremony, would have turned to a feeling akin to dread had he known of the ridiculously inadequate supplies of water in the barrels which were to be emptied in case of accident. He was also quietly scornful of the preparations for the ceremony in which medals struck to commemorate Alexander's accession were distributed; the official in charge was mobbed and his carriage destroyed by the impatient crowd. The medals were given out in the end, but it was the strongest who secured the lion's share. As a military man Fritz was not impressed by such poor organisation, much as he had been fascinated by the coronation. It was a memory which remained with him all his life; to his distrust of Russian reaction was added another black mark for inefficient security, and he vowed to himself that any similar ceremonies in which he was to be involved in future years would be better managed.

After attending his sister's wedding in Berlin that September, he returned to England for a month to celebrate Vicky's sixteenth birthday. It was marred by court mourning for Prince Charles of Leiningen, the Queen's half-brother, who had just died. He had been a wastrel with few redeeming qualities, but the formalities of Victorian mourning demanded that the departed should receive the same attention whether worthy of it or not. Fritz was not so much touched as piqued when Vicky took to her bed for two days with a 'sick headache' in mourning for a reprobate uncle she did not even know.

Luckily for him, he did not know that the Queen was beginning to be tortured by misgivings at having let her eldest child commit herself so young. Only four months after the engagement, she had confided to her journal that she did not fancy the idea of her daughter 'going to Berlin, more or less the enemy's den!'[3] Fritz later came in for indirect attack behind his back. Only days before his visit Albert had written a critical note to his wife (as he was frequently obliged to do when her Hanoverian wrath drove her beyond her capacity to reason verbally with him), taking her to task for being angry with their future son-in-law for preparing to devote his life to their child, of whom she was only too pleased to be rid.[4] How much of this strained atmosphere communicated itself to Fritz is a matter for conjecture, but at least his parents-in-law to be, unlike his own mother and father, had the grace not to quarrel in front of others. For this, he would gladly put up with his betrothed's emotional ups and downs. He would even bear with her tearful sister Alice, who was so overcome at the thought of the coming separation that she started to cry every time she saw him.

At home he was already making preparations for his married life. On his return from Moscow in September he had begun to arrange the palace at Babelsberg, which had been chosen as one of their first residences, doing his utmost to model it on the lines of Balmoral and Osborne. From England he went to Paris in December to reassure the French Emperor. Napoleon had obtained the imperial throne by an extraordinary combination of good fortune and social climbing, and was regarded as a *parvenu* by most of his fellow-monarchs. The one firm bond of friendship he had made was with Queen Victoria, the least snobbish of European sovereigns, and he felt it to be threatened by the impending Prussian match. Fritz did his best to overcome his apprehensions, and the Empress Eugenie was conquered. She could not help comparing her tall handsome guest, 'with a touch of Hamlet about him',[5] with her short, undignified husband, whom contemporaries likened not unfairly to a circus ringmaster. She was much kinder than Mary Bulteel, Queen Victoria's Maid-in-Honour, whose first impression of Fritz had been 'that of a good-humoured lieutenant, with large hands and feet, but not in the least clever.'[6] Mary, like Vicky, was exceptionally well-educated and intelligent, and her judgments were often rather blunt; one dreads to think what her opinion might have been of Fritz's uncles had she ever met them. Napoleon, for his part, wrote sardonically that he tried to make the visit pass as well as possible, but found that his guest's thoughts 'were always either at Osborne or Windsor'[7] — a rather unnecessary observation.

On 16 May 1857 the Prussian Official Gazette issued the public announcement of the engagement. Three days later Queen Victoria opened Parliament, choosing the occasion for notifying the Commons and requesting financial provision for the marriage. The ministry's apprehension that the match would find little sympathy was unfounded; by a majority of 328 votes to 14, a dowry of £40,000 and annuity of £4,000 were granted.

A month later, Fritz and Moltke paid another visit to Britain. Now that the news was public, it was permitted for he and Vicky to be seen together. Their first such appearance was at the History of the Art Treasures Exhibition at Manchester on 30 June. The royal party — which also included the Queen, the Prince Consort,* the Prince of Wales and Princess Alice —

---

* Thus created by letters patent five days previously.

viewed the display together. On the following day the Queen paid a second and strictly private visit, while the princes attended a reception at the town hall. An address was read to Fritz congratulating him on his engagement, to which he replied gracefully: 'I hope that God's blessing may rest upon this union, in which to secure the happiness of the Princess Royal will be the dearest duty of my life.'[8]

Later they went to Madame Tussaud's premises in London, where they inspected their newly-made wax likenesses; Fritz's was dressed in the Fusilier uniform of the Prussian Guards, while Vicky's was in a light blue silk dress decorated with lace and pearls. They posed for a full-length portrait side by side at a photographic studio in Regent Street, and when the Queen visited the races at Ascot they accompanied her. *The Times* may have scorned the engagement, but the public were thrilled by these subsequent festivities, and in any case they welcomed the match with far more enthusiasm than they had the Queen's marriage in 1840. Music lovers were pleased when the family attended a performance of an oratorio by Handel at the Crystal Palace and, led by Albert and Vicky, continually beat time with their scores. Theatre managers in the city did big business when every play which received royal patronage immediately afterwards drew vast audiences. The day before he left, Fritz was given the Freedom of the City. Before resuming his military command at Breslau, he visited Berlin and noticed with mixed feelings that all the souvenir shop windows were sporting cheap badly-executed busts of Vicky and himself.

The closing months of the engagement were not without their difficulties. The first was an argument over the composition of their future household, which had been planned to consist solely of middle-aged Germans chosen by Queen Elizabeth and Princess Augusta. For Vicky it was a daunting prospect, and the Prince Consort asked them to include with some reluctance a few British girls of her age. Queen Victoria told the Prussian court that some of the German ladies might like to accept invitations to Windsor so that they and their future mistress might meet each other beforehand, a suggestion which was received rather haughtily. Even Dr Wegner, who been appointed their physician, was brought over to attend the Queen's last confinement,* 'to see how these things are managed here'. Their secretary-to-be, Mary Seymour, was a daughter of Prince Albert's equerry, and Count Ernest von Stockmar, the Baron's son, had been chosen as their treasurer, despite Fritz's protests. Like his father, the Count was to wield more influence than his position demanded; it would have been as well for the sake of their future popularity in Prussia if the Prince Consort had listened to his future son-in-law's views.

---

* Her youngest child Beatrice was born on 14 April 1857. Fritz and Vicky were among the godparents.

But such troubles paled into insignificance beside the Queen's wrath when she heard that Prussia expected the wedding to be in Berlin. She firmly disagreed with the court's not unreasonable desire for their future King to be married 'at home', as she made plain to Lord Clarendon: 'Whatever may be the usual practice of Prussian princes, it is not every day that one marries the eldest daughter of the Queen of England. The question therefore must be considered as closed.'[9] It was.

Her Majesty might have had considerable opposition if only the Prussians had not had other worries on their minds at the time. The King's health had been giving cause for concern over the last few months, and while the remainder of the family were preparing for his nephew's marriage, the doctors were diagnosing his symptoms as softening of the brain. Before long he was certified as incurably insane. In October William was declared Regent for three months, an appointment which was later extended to last until his accession to the throne. It proved a mixed blessing for Fritz, as he soon discovered when Augusta tried once again to use her influence over her husband. 'Sometimes when opinions differ it is wiser to pretend to agree so as not to irritate her still further,' he wrote to Vicky. 'Papa tries to do everything to please her but Mama does not think so.'[10] Now they were closer to the throne, they argued more heatedly than ever before, making their son doubly glad that setting up his own establishment as a married man would allow him to withdraw more from such an unpleasant atmosphere.

After an engagement of over two years, both he and Vicky were only too eager to settle down as husband and wife, and they corresponded on a considerable scale when apart. In August Moltke allegedly found him reading a forty-page letter from her; how the news must have accumulated, he sardonically told his wife.[11] 'In you God has allowed me to find what I had hoped for, my one and all, what more can I want?'[12] Fritz wrote affectionately in November. From the middle of December, there was ceaseless activity on all sides. In London a banquet, ball and concert were being arranged to coincide with the wedding, while in Berlin preparations were being made for the state entry. Fritz inspected the coach, the 'gilded monkey-cage' to be used for the purpose; it shook and swayed like a ship at sea, he told Vicky.[13]

Rather nervously he arrived at Dover on 23 January 1858, two days before the wedding, and made for Buckingham Palace, where the court had moved from Windsor a week earlier to receive the first of the ninety-odd guests. That evening he joined the family at a state performance of Shakespeare's *Macbeth* at Her Majesty's Theatre. After the final curtain the National Anthem was the signal for a massive cheer, followed by repeated calls for 'the Princess'; the Queen led Vicky and Fritz to the front of the box and the cheering increased. The representative of the 'paltry German dynasty', to quote *The Times* of 1855, was already regarded as one of the family.

Such a welcome, following that given him by the family on his arrival, calmed him, particularly as he had sensed how much their emotions were in turmoil. As the previous year had worn on, Vicky's fond letters had dwelt increasingly on how much she would miss her father once they were married. The Prince Consort was more restrained, but he had found her such an apt pupil and valuable political confidante that he would himself miss her deeply. As for the Queen, she was in two minds. At times she was jealous of her daughter's intellect and the way in which she commanded her father's attention, which had led to stormy scenes in private between husband and wife; on the other hand, she would often reproach herself for having encouraged the girl to marry so early and commit herself to the distant court of Berlin. Fritz knew his betrothed well enough to understand that, much as she loved him, for all her intellectual qualities she was still a very young seventeen, and not looking forward at all to leaving her beloved family. As he knew only too well, family and court life in Prussia were not to be compared with the happiness found in England. He was aware of the bad impression made on their hosts by the other German princes with their bad manners and crude conversation; they would have gladly told Victoria and Albert that the match was by no means as popular in Berlin as the romantic bridegroom had given them to understand. Even Prince William had provided them with an unpleasant moment before Christmas by writing off-handedly that he was too busy as Regent to spare any time to attend the wedding; only a desperate letter from Albert had persuaded him to come.

The day before the wedding, the Queen led the couple into the large palace drawing-room, where they were dazzled by the array of wedding presents. Three candelabra, the gift to Fritz from her and the Prince Consort, filled up three tables and dwarfed all the jewellery. Even Vicky's pearls, which her mother declared were the largest she had ever seen, paled into insignificance beside them.

At last the long-awaited and long-dreaded day, Monday 25 January, arrived. St. James's Palace, where the Queen had been married, was chosen again for her daughter. To mark the occasion, Fritz was promoted that morning to Major-General of the Prussian First Infantry Regiment of Guards, and arrived at the chapel in his new uniform. He was accompanied by his father on his right and his uncle Prince Albrecht on his left. Approaching the altar, he stopped near the Queen's seat and bowed to her and his mother, then knelt to pray at the altar steps. At that point Vicky, in a dress of white silk trimmed with Honiton lace, trembling and very pale, entered on her father's arm, both being escorted by King Leopold. She curtsied to her mother and William, then Fritz came forward, dropped on one knee before her, and affectionately pressed her hand to his heart. Both spoke the responses firmly, which reassured the nervous Queen. Even the officiating Archbishop of Canterbury was 'agitated'; he faltered and omitted several passages of the service, as he had done at the bride's confirmation. The ceremony was concluded with the *Hallelujah Chorus*, after which bride and bridegroom led the procession out of the chapel to the strains of Mendelssohn's *Wedding March* — the first time it was so used — and in the throne room there were embraces and kisses all round as the family signed the register.

They all returned to Buckingham Palace where Fritz and Vicky appeared on the balcony, both with and without their parents, to the delight of the loudly cheering crowds. After the wedding breakfast, dominated by an enormous cake, the young couple left by train for their two-day honeymoon at Windsor. At the station the boys of Eton College, shouting merrily, unhitched the horses and dragged the carriage to the castle gates, to the delight of the cheering crowds.

Inside the castle, they found themselves in a strange position; for the first time in their lives, they were alone together. After the excitements of the previous few hours, surrounded by enthusiastic admirers and a phalanx of relations, it was oddly quiet. As Vicky recalled years later, they were 'two young, innocent things — almost too shy to talk to one another.'[14] But they were glad of a brief respite from being the centre of attention. Their parents were attending a state banquet at the palace, followed by a concert where the Queen and the Prince Consort were unable to appreciate the music as everyone within earshot was still talking about the wedding. Not until the small hours of the following morning did the exhausted parents get to bed; the young couple had hopefully retired much sooner.

On 27 January, having seen most of the guests depart, the rest of the family joined them at Windsor, and on the next day Fritz was invested with the Order of the Garter. On 29 January they all returned to London, and in the evening the Queen, the Prince Consort, and the newly-weds again attended the theatre, the audience demonstrating their approval of the match once more by cheering the couple as they stood at the front of the royal box during the Anthem. On the following day a small drawing-room ceremony, with 'no presentations, only congratulations'[15] was held, and in the evening there was a private party for the bridesmaids and their families. Meanwhile Fritz was taken out to see the sights of London by night.

But by now the glitter of the festivities was wearing thin. Fritz knew that behind the gaily smiling face Vicky presented in public she was filled with increasing anguish as the time approached to leave her home. A less perceptive bridegroom than he would have sensed that she would not find Berlin a suitable home after having experienced only London, Osborne and Balmoral; on the contrary, it would seem more like living in a barracks. It was hardly a place for a girl in her teens, let alone one who was known over Europe to be schooled in advanced political theory directly opposed to the views held by most of her in-laws, but at the same time had had such a sheltered upbringing that she had only 'dined out' once before her marriage, and even then with her cousins. He could tell that the immediate few months would be a testing time for both of them, over and above the normal adjustment of adapting to married life.

On 1 February, he spent most of the day talking — or more probably listening — to his father-in-law, while Vicky spent the last precious day at home with her mother. For each, it was a sad day which everyone wished would last forever. But the departure could not be postponed, and so the next morning there were not a few tearful farewells on the stairs. The weeping Queen stayed at home, so it was left to the Prince Consort and the two elder boys to see Fritz and Vicky on their way. He wrapped a blanket tenderly around her shoulders to protect her from the wind and snow as they waved goodbye from their open carriage — a supreme sacrifice of comfort on such a bitter day — to the crowds of well-wishers lining the city street. 'Be kind to her, or we'll have her back,' shouted a group of cockney draymen. At Gravesend they boarded the royal yacht, the *Victoria and Albert;* Fritz led Vicky to the cabin, where she clung to her father in a last embrace, loth for the final farewell. As Albert sadly stepped ashore he waited in vain a few moments to see if they would reappear on deck. The only one in the small family group not to break down at the parting, he was too overcome to speak. Only when he wrote to his daughter the next day could he express himself: 'My heart was very full yesterday . . . I am not of a demonstrative nature, and therefore you can hardly know how dear you have always been to me.'[16]

For 'England's flower', it was only her second journey abroad. For her husband, it was the sixth return from Britain to Prussia; but his first as a husband. It was also a dynastic alliance of considerable importance, made more significant by it being that rare event in the house of Hohenzollern, or indeed in any royal family — a genuine love match. Vicky was certainly no ordinary princess. Once the heart-rending scene at Gravesend was over, one of the foremost thoughts in Fritz's mind was — what would his family make of his wife?

CHAPTER 4

Husband and Wife, 1858.

It was a stormy crossing that carried the royal yacht across the North Sea that February night, but its passengers had more on their minds than the weather. It was not just the howling winds, the incessant hail, or the waves beating against the hull, that kept them awake; a new way of life was ahead of them.

They anchored at Antwerp on the following morning, ready for the first of a series of celebrations and receptions planned for them on their way. Dutifully they accepted these as inevitable, though privately all they wanted to do was to get to Prussia as soon as possible, in order to settle down to the life they had awaited for nearly three years. Being the more seasoned traveller of the two, Fritz found nothing new in the cheering crowds everywhere, and he was relieved when his bride put on a smiling face as she waved to the multitudes at Antwerp as he led her off the yacht. During a brief visit to Brussels, they danced together at a ball given in their honour. Reaching Cologne by rail, they were welcomed by the Mayor and town council, but they found more pleasure in walking around the specially-illuminated cathedral. Fritz had been there before, and he guided her round in the same way as she had pointed out the exhibits at Crystal Palace in 1851; they later paid a similar visit to the cathedral at Magdeburg, closer to Berlin.

One incident did nothing to enhance their German welcome. They stopped at Hanover to call on King George, son of Ernest Augustus, the last surviving son of George III, who had been heir to the British throne until Vicky was born. He had always been on bad terms with his niece, and a gold dinner-service which had belonged to his father had been the subject of disputed possession until a British commission had decided in favour of Hanover. Vicky was naturally rather piqued at the dinner given in their honour when this same service graced the table.

But there were lighter moments too. At Wittenberg Field-Marshal von Wrangel, a veteran of the Napoleonic wars, welcomed them on behalf of the army. As he stepped into the carriage the train started with a jolt, and he found himself suddenly sitting rather untidily in a large apple tart they had just been given. All three of them were helpless with laughter as Vicky called for the attendants to clear up the remains.

After breaking their journey at Potsdam to stay with William and

Augusta, they entered Berlin on 8 February, another bitterly cold day, in the state coach Fritz had tested a month earlier. At the Bellevue Palace, the royal family were waiting to greet them. For Vicky it was her first sight of the King and Queen. The story goes that the latter was so taken aback at the sight of the young girl running up the steps to greet them, apparently oblivious of the cold — she was wearing a low-cut dress without any wrap or coat — that she temporarily forgot her hatred of England, and asked if she was not frozen. Back came the smiling answer: 'Completely, except my heart, which is warm.'[1]

The Neue Palais was far from ready for them to settle into, and for the time being they were given apartments in the Berlin Schloss, the traditional home of the Prussian monarchy. Built mostly by Andreas Schluter at the end of the seventeenth century, it was a maze of endless dark corridors which connected the vast rooms, and in the winter the wind whistled mercilessly down the chimneys. It was believed to be haunted by *die weisse Frau*, the ghost of a long-dead family member.[2] Not lived in since the death of Frederick William III, the state apartments however were the setting for most of the court's social gatherings, receptions and dinners.

To Fritz, one palace or castle was no better and no worse than another. In spite of having seen the glories of Italian architecture, and having stayed at Windsor and cosy Osborne, the lack of comfort in which he had habitually lived meant nothing to him. He found it hard to understand the bitter complaints of his wife, who had only been in Berlin for a few days before her eyes were bright red and her nose was streaming with a cold, about everything she saw — or did not see. Where were cupboards for her clothes, the bath, the lavatories? Why were all the carpets so threadbare? Why had the family portraits, some darkened beyond recognition by the smoke from the old stoves, never been kept clean? Where was the lighting — surely she was not expected to read by the light of a flickering candle, which struggled to stay alight under the force of the Arctic winds which penetrated the north-facing windows? Why was there no modern attempt at heating?

What nobody had ever thought of explaining to her was that Hohenzollern reverence for the dead being what it was, the building was kept almost as a shrine to the late King. The room in which he had breathed his last had been left undisturbed, except thankfully for the removal of his body; this death chamber was between Fritz's and Vicky's bedroom on one side and their sitting room on the other. The kitchen and servants' quarters were right at the other end of the Schloss, so that the domestic staff likewise had plenty of cause for complaint at the distances they were expected to walk.

Loving his wife as he did, Fritz was sympathetic to her desire for improvements, and it was not long before he braved the derision of their

Master of the Household to ask that a bath, with hot and cold running water, be installed for her benefit. But he should have gone further; at first he showed little more imagination than his father. He was used to these medieval conditions, but he should have realised that she was not. Windsor had its faults, notably its deplorable drainage, but like Osborne and Balmoral, at least it had its share of modern conveniences. Even if he did not sufficiently notice the difference in physical conditions between his country's palaces and those in Britain, he should have foreseen that she would. If he had reasoned gently with her as soon as she started belittling the Schloss, and advised her that it was in her best interests in the long run to tolerate more and complain less, then he would have spared her much of the opprobrium that his intolerant relatives brought upon her. Perhaps he had become too accustomed to his mother's perpetual nagging to find anything out of the ordinary in her behaviour.

As he knew, his family had been eagerly waiting to see what kind of princess he had brought back with him. Her reputation for being a girl of character had reached Prussia ahead of her, and in a pro-Russian court where Britain had not yet been forgiven for victory in the Crimean war, it was inevitable that she would be watched with suspicion. Within a few days of arriving at the Schloss, he naively sent a telegram to his parents-in-law worded: 'The whole Royal Family is enchanted with my wife. F.W.' As the Prince Consort dryly remarked, the Berlin telegraph office must have been amazed.[3] Queen Victoria's half-sister, Princess Feodore of Hohenlohe-Langenburg, who praised Fritz when she visited Berlin for his 'expression of goodness and candour in his countenance', commented on the 'enthusiasm and interest' the family showed in Vicky.[4] They were certainly fascinated by her, for she had so little in common with them. Not only was she much shorter than they were; none of the princesses was less than five foot ten in height, while at her marriage she was a mere five foot two, and her small features made her look even younger than her age. She was, as Augusta had been, astonished by their lack of interests, and could not even share her mother-in-law's appetite for tittle-tattle and endless parties. The princes she found equally difficult to relax with. Her father might have warned her beforehand what a pompous, reactionary set they made, though they also had their coarser side. Fritz's uncles so delighted in 'improper jokes' at family dinner that even the hardened Prussian princesses sometimes found it hard not to blush delicately. By comparison Prince William seemed a kindly, dignified old soul, but Vicky was ashamed when he admitted proudly that his only interests in life were military; to her this was a dreadful confession from a man so close to the throne. Then she found endless fault with court etiquette. She did not take kindly to the Sunday dinners between two and five in the afternoon on the ground floor of the Schloss, attended by the whole family in full evening dress and decorations. Everyone present was shocked when she accidentally sneezed while standing behind the King's chair on one occasion, and Queen Elizabeth reprimanded her, only to be told rather scornfully that such attitudes were not to be found 'at home' in England.

As to her complaints about the shortcomings of their living quarters, Fritz was partly to blame. He should have cautioned her to be more circumspect in the presence of her in-laws. Her parents wrote her voluminous letters in which there was no shortage of often conflicting advice — 'your place is that of the husband's wife, and of your mother's daughter'[5] — 'be very civil but keep your position'[6] — but they were too far away to understand much about the surroundings in which she was living, particularly as the frequent tampering with letters (even in royal post) made it inadvisable for her to write too frankly. Fritz ought to have explained that the character of the average Hohenzollern was nothing like the typical member of Queen Victoria's family, as he had seen himself on his first visit to Britain. It was obvious to him, if not to her, that the anti-English element at court was only too ready for an excuse to criticise, and her youthful impetuosity and almost exaggerated honesty would hardly be taken into account. Above all, he should have asked her at once to suppress her natural homesickness, by not referring to England as 'home'. The sooner she tried to break this habit, the sooner she would stop missing her childhood home so badly, and giving such offence at court.

The young couple had had little opportunity to get to know each other well, yet there is no doubt that he was genuinely in love with her. It was a relief to spend what time he could with a loving wife instead of with his quarrelsome parents and uncles. When they did not have to endure the company of their hordes of relations, it was a pleasure for him to read to her in German from his favourite histories, and listen to her reading aloud — usually in English — from her newspapers, sent to her regularly from London, or from her treasured set of Shakespeare bought with her pocket money as a girl. Such precious evenings were sadly rare. It was as unwelcome to him as to her when his father thoughtlessly ordered him to take part in yet another course of military training only a few days after their arrival, for this meant that the only part of the day they spent alone together was breakfast. Unless they were visiting the theatre or seeing relations, he insisted at first on his nightly walk alone in the streets of Berlin, a habit from his bachelor days. In vain, partly out of fear for his safety and partly from possessiveness, did she beg him to give it up or make it less frequent.

If he had hoped that his married status would have made any difference to his relationship with his parents, he was in for disappointment. The Prince Consort was right when he complained that his son-in-law was a victim of Prussian 'army-mania', but he was living in a dream world if he seriously expected his letters to both him and Vicky to ask for more training as heir-presumptive — attending council meetings, studying state papers, and so on — to have the intended effect. The King was so ill that he was under constant medical attention, and it was no use approaching him, so spurred on by her father, Vicky held her breath and asked Prince William. As she had half-expected, he told her in no uncertain terms to mind her own business. Very set in his ways, the Prince refused to accept that statecraft, even for a future sovereign, was more important than ritualistic drilling or marching. It was of apparently no consequence that he was over sixty and his son was in all probability not so far away from the throne; it may have been because of this that he was so obstinate. In his occasional moods of depression, William feared that his brother's illness might be hereditary, and being only one year younger himself, he felt he could go the same way at any time. Much as he would have loved to, Fritz was too shy 'for fear of appearing ambitious or pushing'[7] to ask for further responsibility himself. He pessimistically saw the certain futility of it.

As for Augusta, she treated him just as she had always done, continuing to scold and bully him, venting on him all the irritation her husband caused her. At first she was civil and occasionally kind to Vicky, but jealousy of her soon overcame all other considerations, and it was not long before she treated her as unpleasantly as she did her son. They stayed with her for a few days in April, in her native Weimar, and although they had been looking forward to the visit for weeks, they were only too pleased when the time came for them to take the train back to Berlin. The atmosphere was just as frigid and uncomfortable as it was in the Schloss; Fritz caught a heavy cold, and they were even given separate rooms on different floors. Augusta was bored, and rude to family guests and servants alike.

So depressed were they with everything that they employed the only safety valve possible; Vicky poured out her heart in a long albeit careful letter to her parents. On reading it, the Prince Consort took the most reckless course imaginable; in turn he wrote bitterly of Fritz's anomalous position to his mischievous brother Ernest, Duke of Saxe-Coburg-Gotha. The latter was the last person in the family to be trusted with anything even remotely confidential, and soon rumour was rearing its ugly head throughout Europe. A frustrated Fritz was ill-treating his poor defenceless wife, it was said, and had thrown her down a staircase (she had in fact fallen headlong down a flight of stairs in the Schloss, and sprained an ankle), and Queen Victoria made a lightning visit incognito to reconcile the pair; or according to another version, the Prince Consort had marched over to rescue his daughter from 'those horrid Prussians' and take her home.

In all this there was not the slightest element of truth, and there is no evidence that Fritz ever ill-treated her; indeed, there is abundant proof to the contrary. But gossip-happy tongues and ears loved nothing better than royal scandal, in this case reinforced by the high incidence of unhappy Hohenzollern marriages. At least William was never physically violent to Augusta, and even if he had been so inclined she was tough enough to give as good as she got, and they never officially separated. Princess Marianne of Anhalt, the wife of Prince Frederick Charles, was less fortunate. She had to put up meekly with a brutal husband who was so angered by the birth of their third daughter that he allegedly boxed her ears, leaving her deaf, while still suffering from the effects of childbirth. In his later years, it was said, he would drunkenly force himself upon her and drag her through the palace by her hair. Such stories may be exaggerations, if not idle rumours, but such barbarity was not unknown in royal households during the nineteenth century. At any rate, one night Marianne felt she could endure his treatment of her no longer and fled intending to seek a divorce. She was dissuaded by the pleas of her uncle William, by now German Emperor, who detested nothing more than family scandal, and for his sake she tolerated her partner until his death released her in 1885.[8]

Rumour or no rumour, it was an inauspicious start to the married life for which they had waited so long. They had each other's love, but Fritz to his dismay was soon to discover that he did not possess his wife's confidence as fully as he had believed. The trouble arose in the early summer, just after — much to her mother's horror — she became pregnant. It had done her no good to be told by Dr Wegner that should rest indoors all day with the windows closed, and nobody was spared her subsequent bouts of temper. Her gloom was dispelled in a flash when the Prince Consort wrote to say that he was about to visit Coburg; would she go and meet him there? She was overjoyed, and for days could think or talk of nothing else.

The chickens were coming home to roost. She had brought up to love and respect her father as a paragon of virtue, a fount of wisdom, to whom she could turn with all her problems. The Prince had unwittingly done nothing to dispel this impression after her engagement. Although he had told her that her place was that of 'her husband's wife', he never seems to have hinted that she might place a little more confidence in Fritz and correspondingly less in himself. It would have been a hard thing for a father to tell his favourite daughter, but necessary if she was to learn how to stand on her own two feet. Lord Clarendon pointedly considered Queen Victoria to be 'really insane about the maintenance of her maternal authority', and not recognising that marriage justified the smallest transfer of allegiance from herself to her son-in-law. He could equally have been referring to Albert. As a result he became a barrier between husband and wife, and the only one to realise it was the unfortunate husband himself. He had taken it for granted that she would turn to him after marriage for everything, and it was something of a blow when she did not. 'Dearest papa' remained the open sesame for all her difficulties.

It was brought home to him bluntly when she merrily talked about her father's imminent visit to Coburg. Dr Wegner told her that she could not go because of her pregnancy, to which she answered regally that she could not and would not put her father off. The doctor knew it was useless to argue with her, and instead he asked Fritz to try and make her see reason. Confident of his ability to talk her round where the doctor had failed, he begged her to do as she had been advised — it was most important, for every reason possible, for her to have a healthy child, be it a son and heir or a daughter.

Overestimating her feelings for him, he was unprepared for the shock he got in return. Her incredulity changed to fury as she sobbed that, if her body belonged to the state, then she did not want their child.[9] Refusing to let him answer, she screamed that she would never speak to him again, and she wished they had never married. In the heat of the moment, he did the only thing possible; by now equally furious, he turned on his heel and, slamming the door on her, went for a stroll in the garden to cool off. It seemed like a nightmare. How could his wife ever place her father above their unborn child?

At the end of May they moved to Babelsberg, where the change of scenery did them both good and enabled them to forget their recent quarrel. Yet the castle had its drawbacks, notably that it smacked too much of William and Augusta with its heavy tasteless furniture and ungainly hothouse plants, for either of them to feel completely at home there. They were not allowed to make any major alterations, though hanging their own photogaphs and a selection of Vicky's paintings was permitted. But it was still comforting to escape from the Schloss, which had been like a prison to her, and for ever afterwards reminded both of the worst days in their early married life.

It was here that the Prince Consort came to visit them at the beginning of June. For the sake of harmony Fritz agreed to look after his father-in-law's travelling arrangements, so that Vicky need not go to Coburg, her ankle injury being given as the official excuse for her staying at home. Suppressing his jealousy, he allowed her to spend as much of the first day as she wanted with her father, delightedly showing him round the palace and garden, with its attractive woodland setting and view of the countryside overlooking the river Havel. He took comfort from knowing how happy she was at seeing Albert again, and also from the hope that his forebearance would bring its just reward; she would surely be grateful to him for keeping himself in the background. He was similarly thankful the next day when the King, Queen, Prince and Princess drove over from Charlottenburg to see his father-in-law, treating him as an old friend despite their fundamental political differences. Only the alarming deterioration in the King's condition marred the gathering for Albert, but it was compensated for by his seeing that rel-

Neue Palais, Potsdam

Babelsberg

ations between his daughter and son-in-law were 'all that can be desired'.[10]

Fritz was right. Even if Vicky had heeded her mother's advice not to overburden papa with her worries, and not told him half she would have liked, she recognised her devoted husband's self-sacrifice for her sake, and he immediately noticed how much more frank she suddenly was with him. The message came across clearly a couple of weeks after the Prince Consort's departure, when he had to spend a few days at military camp. Missing him deeply, she wrote: 'What shall I feel like this evening when I have to go to bed without my angel; you my all, my darling husband, I can see only too well that I cannot live without you.'[11] Had her conscience told her that she had wronged him by thinking less of him than of her father? Even if this was not the case, it was the best expression of her ripening love that Fritz could have had.

He was almost as happy as she was when both parents-in-law came to Babelsberg in August, which went a long way towards recreating the happy family evenings at Windsor in which he had revelled as a guest. Remembering those not-so-distant days, he leant over the piano as he turned the pages of the music while Vicky and father played and sang duets. He took great pleasure in introducing them to various Prussian notables, such as the scientist Alexander von Humboldt, and 'old Wrangel', who could still talk of nothing but how glad he was that Fritz had chosen Vicky; she was indeed a 'blessing to the country'. The only character to whom the Queen and Prince Albert found it difficult to be civil was Manteuffel, whom they privately blamed for Fritz's enforced political ignorance; they considered him 'most unpleasant, cross, and disagreeable'.[12]

Little did the Minister know that his period of office was coming to an end. Even the omnipotence of a Hohenzollern King had its limits, for Frederick William was by now little more than a human vegetable. By October William had been his representative for a year, and he insisted that he could only continue to act as such if he was granted the full powers of Regent. A royal decree accordingly conferred the position upon him, and Fritz proudly attended the ceremony in the Berlin Schloss at the end of the month, in which his father took the oath 'to exercise the royal authority to the best of his ability as Regent with sole responsibility towards God,' and observe the constitution of 1850.[13] Intent on creating a new era, he asked Manteuffel to resign, creating him Count and a life member of the *Herrenhaus*, and called upon Prince Hohenzollern to form a government. Prince Anton Hohenzollern-Sigmaringen was an unusual choice for William; he was selected partly to please Queen Victoria and Prince Albert, whose close friend and confidant he was. The next general election produced a large liberal majority in the house of representatives, the *Landtag*, and on the new Minister's advice Fritz was allowed to attend the meetings of the house. In addition Privy Councillor Brunnemann was appointed his political secretary in all but name, with responsibility for keeping him informed on state affairs.

It was not everything, but Fritz was encouraged. A passive role it might be, but it was a step towards the further state involvement to which he felt he was entitled, and for which Prince Albert had pressed so hard. All things considered, his future appeared to be taking the right course. His father did not share Prince Hohenzollern's pacific outlook any more than he did the liberal rejoicing at the election results, but he had sworn to uphold the constitution. As the young couple moved into the Palace Unter den Linden in Berlin, their official winter residence, on the eve of Vicky's eighteenth birthday, there was every reason to be optimistic; the frustrations Fritz had known earlier in the year had now largely disappeared, and they felt the imminent joy of parenthood.

CHAPTER 5

Parenthood, 1859-61.

Fritz bore patiently with Vicky's pre-natal miseries over the new year of 1859. Like any young father-to-be he gladly made the effort, putting up with her fretfulness and her petty outbursts of temper. Not for some time did he know how extremely fortunate both wife and child were to survive.

Dr Wegner found nothing unusual in her lethargy, pooh-poohing her protests that she felt worse than she believed she ought to. Queen Victoria sent her favourite physician, Dr Clark, who according to Lord Clarendon was 'not fit to attend a sick cat',[1] to examine Vicky, and take home a first-hand report; neither would he believe that anything was wrong. Only Mrs Innocent, the Queen's experienced midwife, who arrived at the palace after Christmas, recognised that her youthful patient was not crying wolf. She was certainly not coping with pregnancy as well as her mother used to. The first year of adjusting to her new home had left its mark, as had her fall downstairs; not the most favourable circumstances for a pregnant girl of barely eighteen. By chance the Queen, distrusting German doctors, had sent her own Dr Martin to attend the confinement. The consequences fully justified his presence. Yet for some reason best known to the household at the time — probably contempt for 'British interference' — Martin was put in lodgings some distance away from the Unter den Linden.

Sources vary widely as to exactly what went on between the doctors and the servants immediately before the birth, as they naturally had no desire to record for posterity what must have been at best a piece of clumsy mismanagement, at worse a petty chauvinistic conspiracy on their part, which all but resulted in double tragedy. What apparently happened was that Vicky's labour began in the small hours of the morning on 26 January. Wegner then scribbled a noted to Martin asking him to come at once, and gave it to a servant who posted it instead of taking it by hand. Whether he did so out of thoughtlessness, or contempt for everything and everyone British, is a matter for speculation. It was quite possible that the other servants or Wegner's assistants, out of spite or professional jealousy, bribed him to delay the note. Whatever the reason, Martin received the message by post some thirty-six hours after it was written. Seizing his instruments and hurrying by coach to the place, he was spurred to desperate action by the horrifying scene he found there. Fritz, struggling to retain his self-control, was kneeling at the bed holding Vicky in his arms; deprived of the chloroform which had eased her mother's last two confinements, she was weak and exhausted, but just conscious enough to realise vaguely what was going on around her. Incredibly, Wegner and his assistants had given up hope, and were sitting in a forlorn group several feet away from the bed, presumably waiting for the end. The Scottish doctor was greeted with the encouraging words — in English — from one of them that the Princess and her unborn child were beyond salvation, a remark which the patient seemed to understand, judging by the resigned look in her eyes. Luckily he was not one to take no for an answer; while there was life there was hope. Producing both anaesthetic and instruments he brought Vicky through, perilously weak but alive, able to appreciate that she had given birth to a living son.

Fritz too was quite exhausted. Not only had he physically supported her since her confinement began, but the anguish of the last few hours when he was certain that she was going to die had also taken its toll. His relief was restrained when he was told that she would live after all, but he was too weary at first to understand that their child had been saved as well. Meanwhile the news of the near-catastrophe had reached the press before the rest of the family. He would have been most upset had he known that, during the afternoon and evening, newspaper assistants throughout the city were hurriedly composing his wife's obituary.

None of this was known to the crowds who stood waiting patiently outside the Schloss, braving falling snow to await the salutes that would be fired to announce the birth. At three in the afternoon the cannon began to roar one hundred and one times to denote a new prince. In his boyish excitement Wrangel put his fist through the window to tell the gathering that the infant, third in succession to the throne, was as fine and sturdy a new recruit as they could wish for.

All Fritz wanted now was a good night's sleep. But first he had to go to a reception, 'a grand family festival' given by the proud grandfather, the Regent. Tired and dazed at the end of the worst day he had yet spent in his life, his expression was taken as being 'radiant with happiness' by Gustav zu Putlitz, a member of the *Landtag*.[2]

He could never have attended the reception without breaking down if he had known at the time of his baby son's condition, which ill-suited Wrangel's hearty description. The doctors devoted all their attention to saving Vicky after the birth, and Mrs Innocent was the only one to think about the baby. She picked him up firmly and slapped him for nearly half an hour before he moved or cried; at first she had feared him to be dead. The next day she showed him to Wegner, drawing attention to his left arm, which was blue and hanging lifeless from the shoulder socket, the elbow joint dislocated as well. Fritz was told at once, but he agreed that Vicky should not know until she was better, as in her still precarious state the news

might cause a relapse. He had just received Queen Victoria's ironic telegram:
'Is it a fine boy?' How bad was the injury, he asked Wegner. Was it
permanent? The doctor valued his exculpation more highly than the father's
feelings, and was irritatingly vague. The 'paralysis', as he called it, could be
treated at once with a little careful massage, and when the baby was older he
could have special exercises. Yes, of course the arm would respond, given
time. If the doctor was ignorant and not prepared to admit it, Fritz knew
even less, and all he could do was believe in the limp reassurances he was
given.

Frederick William Victor Albert was christened on 5 March, the
ceremony being postponed in order to give Vicky time to recover sufficiently. Queen Victoria was annoyed that a new sitting of Parliament
prevented her from attending, and she felt it degrading for her and Albert to
be just two of the child's forty-two godparents, but she was consoled by
her daughter's narrow escape; Dr Clark had given her a full account of the
dangerous confinement. Fritz was as proud as he could be of William, later
Willy (there were enough Fritzes in the family already without adding to the
confusion, as he noted). He spent much of his spare time carrying the baby
dressed in an enormous frilled bonnet and little white robe around the
castle, beaming at everyone who would stop and admire him, or dandling
him on his uniformed knee while both posed in an armchair for the court
photographer. 'In his clear blue eyes we can already see signs of sparkling
intelligence,'[3] he wrote fondly. His baby-worship — Vicky's too, once she
was strong enough — far excelled that of his parents and parents-in-law. The
Prince Consort could not 'quite enter into Fritz's ecstasy about (Willy)',
while the Queen wrote that she found even the prettiest of small babies quite
ugly until they were about four months old.[4] Augusta agreed. She was
inclined to blame Vicky for her grandson's deformity — her attitude to her
daughter-in-law made it abundantly clear in later years — and insisted that
she hand him over to a wet-nurse instead of breast-feeding him herself.

As winter turned into spring, the Neue Palais at Potsdam was at last ready
for them. It was here, as he watched his wife's girlish enthusiasm trans-
forming the musty old rooms into a comfortable home, and restoring the
overgrown garden, that Fritz heard of the worsening European situation. A
congress of European ministers of state to discuss the future of Italy, slowly
reaching unification under the tenacious Count Cavour, was blocked by
Austria. The latter owned the state of Lombardy, and demanded the
disarmament of Piedmont-Sardinia as the price of her attendance. Backed by
the Emperor Napoleon, who had Italian interests, the state refused to do so.
Confident of his military superiority, Francis Joseph sent an ultimatum —
disarmament or war. By the end of April, Austria was mobilising against the
combined Franco-Italian forces, and the proposed congress was cancelled.

Like Queen Victoria, most of Europe remained hesitantly neutral; Napoleon's intrusion was hard to justify, but Francis Joseph was undeniably the aggressor. In Germany, however, opinion was naturally on the side of its fellow-member of the Confederation, especially as the other states were always ready to see evil in any action taken by France. The only dissentient group was made up of a few liberals and radicals who regarded the Habsburgs as absolutist oppressors, and saw in the Italian steps towards unification a pattern to be followed.

Prussia took a neutral stand, but as a token gesture of support for the Austrian Emperor the Regent ordered partial mobilisation. It was the moment for which Fritz, bored by his enforced inactivity, had been waiting. He refused to listen to Vicky's heartrending appeals to him to stay at home, instead muttering darkly about the reputation of Prussia as a faithful ally to be defended, to say nothing of his own honour as a prince and officer. His pride did not gladly suffer endless teasing from the rest of the family about his easy life any more than it relished his father-in-law's taunts about his 'playing at soldiers'.[5] Domesticity with a wife and young son, and attending council meetings, were all very well in peacetime, but he had been raised as a soldier and here at last was the chance to prove himself, not least to his wife. While she paid her first visit to England as a married woman, reluctantly leaving Willy with his nurse, he was given command of the First Infantry Division of Guards. When fighting broke out he led them eagerly towards the battleground at Italy. They were still on their way when he heard of the crippling Austrian defeat at Solferino on 24 June, and the subsequent peace treaty at Villfranca a couple of weeks later; Francis Joseph had had no alternative.

Without having so much as seen a shot fired, Fritz returned home seething with fury. The Hohenzollern in him came to the fore as his father appointed a commission to overhaul the army. Not only did he attend each meeting of the new military council, but he also pledged himself determinedly to making the Prussian forces invincible; if Austria, confident of victory, could be defeated so heavily, then so could the Prussians if they suddenly found themselves at war. For several days, from dawn to dusk, he drilled and marched his troops with a severity they had never before known of him, until he was as tired as they were. To him this was not merely the routine training over which he had intermittently spent much of his life, it was by way of an insurance policy to make sure that Prussia would never suffer her own Solferino, which had claimed nearly forty thousand Italian casualties. Nothing else mattered for the time being.

Vicky did not take her new role as a parade-ground-happy-soldier's wife without putting up a fight herself. Two other beloved male members of her family had made her summer of 1859 an anxious one to start with. Willy's arm was not improving, despite the doctors' reassurances that the exercises would help, and the Prince Consort was perpetually tired from overwork; she had been alarmed in May to see him looking so aged. It was the last straw when Fritz returned home from his campaign that never was, angry at what he called Germany's humiliation, and thinking of nothing but the army. Finding him deaf to her entreaties to spend a little time at home, she impulsively dashed off a desperate letter to her father — what was she to do? She soon regretted it. Back came the reply: she must remind Fritz that Prussia was less important than Germany; it was childish of him to behave as if the state was on the verge of war, and such action could bring the whole of Europe into armed conflict.[6] But in his present frame of mind, war was all Fritz wanted — it would make up for the lightning Austrian campaign which had thwarted his military ambitions. He was in no mood to appreciate Vicky's anxiety over her father, which she tried to persuade him to share. He answered back that it was his own fault he was overworked and worried if he was ruling England through the Queen, and trying to rule Prussia through the Regent[7] — an acid remark which stung her bitterly as it was not far from the truth.

It seemed as if he could nothing right. In devoting so much attention to the army, he was only doing what he had been brought up to regard as his duty, and because of it he was suddenly in painful opposition to two of the people he most loved and respected. He refused to give way, and so did Vicky. Was their marriage, like that of his parents, to become the story of row after row?

Thankfully the autumn brought a truce between husband and wife. Fritz went down with influenza, only to be roused from his bed before he was better. The Regent had just published his plans for army reform, demanding among other things an increase in conscription from two to three years, with extra taxation to finance it, and the abolition of the *Landwehr*, a kind of territorial army drawn mostly from the middle classes. Fritz was furious; why had he not been consulted? Without waiting till he was well again he confronted his father. The latter, knowing that his reforms would not meet with the Liberals' approval and that he would have a struggle to see them through, took all his anxiety out on his son. Both lost their tempers; William called Fritz a meddlesome amateur, while Fritz accused his father of keeping him out on a limb. He regretted ever having been so impatient with the Prince Consort, who was so right to criticise. Anyway, who had been in active command of the troops during the summer? It was hardly his fault that he had not been in time to take part in the war. The clash solved nothing. It only held back his recovery, and he now suffered badly from insomnia. He would get up at night when he could not sleep, and sit in a chair with a book until he dropped off; in the morning he would wake up in this position stiff, still tired and depressed, in no frame of mind to face what he called 'another hopeless day'.[8] It took all Vicky's powers of persuasion to induce him to visit England for a sorely-needed change of air.

Leaving Willy again in the hands of his nurse, November saw them back at Windsor, celebrating the Prince of Wales's eighteenth birthday and spending family evenings cosily in the rooms where they had enjoyed their honeymoon. Fritz recovered at once. He had boarded the train from Berlin full of misgivings, but like his wife he was soon at his most relaxed — a welcome contrast to the tense year he had just lived through. He was in such good humour that he did not feel inclined to argue with his weary-looking father-in-law. At the same time, the royal household were getting to know and like him even better. After a conversation one evening Prince Arthur's governor, Major-General Elphinstone, wrote that 'there was none of the hauteur I had previously ascribed to him.'[9] Fritz was never haughty, but shyness on previous visits to his wife's family had made him appear aloof to those who did not know him intimately.

Even the happy atmosphere of Windsor, however, could not relieve him of the worry over his inflexible father. He and Vicky returned to Berlin for a Christmas made quite intolerable by William and Augusta's endless squabbles. The anxiety over the army bill, the leak to the press of the condition of Willy's arm, and the bitter winter gave Fritz a feverish cold which he could not shake off. The reform proposals had become common knowledge, and to quote Ernest Stockmar, everyone involved was 'living in the midst of a very serious crisis.' Writing to the Queen and the Prince Consort in March 1860, he explained the situation and public feeling over it. He saw the Regent's programme, supported firmly by all but the most moderate Conservatives, as the military caste's attempt to eliminate the 'middle-class element' from the officers and thus achieve complete control of the army. The reactionaries would not stop at overthrowing the Liberal ministry or even the constitution if necessary.[10] William made no secret of his threat to abdicate if he did not get his own way.

What was Fritz's view on the army bill? He was certainly in favour of reform, in the light of what he had seen during the previous summer's mobilisation. That the number of recruits had not risen since 1815, despite the considerable increase in the Prussian population since that date, was an obvious anomaly. If the state was to pursue what might be loosely called a 'progressive' policy, it had to have a strong army; this he understood and supported, but he did not favour the reorganisation of the reserve which would in effect abolish the *Landwehr*. Above all, he had been deeply hurt by the way in which his father had not consulted him on the proposals, and he was angered by his unconstitutional obstinacy which was leading to a private war between the army officers and the Liberals. Yet it did not stop him from being dragged into the fray in the ugliest way possible.

For if William shrank back from overriding the constitution the Junkers, the reactionary landowning aristocracy, would quite happily spare him the trouble. Fritz was summoned one morning in secret to an anteroom in the council chamber, where a number of the bolder Conservatives and Liberals were waiting for him. Tired of the Regent's intractability, they intended to overthrow him and put his son in his place at the head of an army dictatorship. But they had sorely misjudged Fritz's character; he had never been so shocked in his life. Too angry to stop and think about it, or discuss it with Vicky, he went at once to his father and told him everything. Unfortunately the memories of last year's quarrels had made William suspicious of his son. He believed Fritz to be the traitor who had instigated the plot, and on being faced with failure, had lost his nerve and decided to confess in order to save his skin. This unleashed another violent quarrel, but Fritz was too confused and unhappy to shout back, and so the miserable situation dragged on. William refused to give an inch on his reforms, while the Ministry and the Liberals refused to accept them. Nothing had changed over the previous few months except that Fritz had forgotten his imagined humiliation at the hands of the Austrians in the summer, and his military ardour had cooled. Bored and depressed, he returned half-heartedly to his barracks. Having to rise at seven every morning, and spend most of the day outside in the arctic March winds, improved neither his health nor his temper. Once again he came to treasure the evenings that he could spend with Vicky, reading and being read to.

In June father and son attended the opening of the new Königsberg-Eydtkuhnen railway together, and a few days later Fritz was promoted to the rank of Lieutenant-General; but the relationship between them had only partly healed. Vicky had been seven months pregnant in May when the family had decided to turn her out of her room in the Neue Palais so they could celebrate the death of Frederick William III. It had been their custom for the past twenty years to convert her sitting-room into a mausoleum on the anniversary and there hold a 'religious ceremony', followed by a procession to the vaults where they laid wreaths on the late King's coffin. They were not going to be swayed from their purpose by Fritz, who moved Vicky away under strong protest. To her credit she pretended to accept the situation philosophically, telling him not to take such matters to heart, although deep inside she was angry too. But for her sake he complained to his mother, who brushed his objections aside and would not listen.

The recent ill-feeling between father son brought home the realisation that his family were jealous of him and Vicky, simply because their marriage was obviously so happy. Having seen little if anything of the scenes between them during the previous two years — which were thankfully water under the bridge by now — they smirked as they watched husband and wife driving, walking, going out in the evening together, a habit which was as un-Prussian as taking baths with hot and cold water. None of the other princes or princesses even went to church or the railway station together, and Fritz's departure from the rules earned him even more scorn than his wearing a cloak or driving in a closed carriage during cold weather.[11]

The somewhat macabre mausoleum arrangement notwithstanding, Vicky had an easy pregnancy, and on 24 July she gave birth to a daughter, christened Victoria Elizabeth Augusta Charlotte the following month. At first she was known in the family as Charlotte, after her father's favourite cousin and boyhood companion — whose son by coincidence his new baby daughter was destined to marry — and in honour of the Regent's favourite sister the Dowager Tsarina of Russia, who died four months later. Soon, however, the nickname of 'Ditta' was adopted, as a result of Willy's first attempts to call her 'sister'. Queen Victoria disliked the name Charlotte; she though it only fit for a housemaid, despite her cousin Charlotte of Belgium, but she overlooked it with good grace, and drank her first granddaughter's health at supper on receiving the news. She was more tolerant over the choice than Queen Elizabeth, who was 'so much displeased' that she found fault with everything possible at the christening. Fritz only put up with her moods without complaining because he felt so sorry for her.

Charlotte was normal in every way, unlike her brother. Although he was lively and cheerful, his arm still had little life in it; it remained stunted, and only with difficulty could he hold a stick when it was pressed into his tiny fist.[12] So far Fritz and Vicky had kept him away from his maternal grandparents, hoping that it would soon be all right (though Vicky had told them of the natal injury). But by the autumn of 1860 they were increasingly impatient to see the child, and with heavy hearts the parents realised it was hopeless to keep the family apart any longer. It was the Prince Consort who made the plans for their meeting; he, the Queen and Princess Alice were about to visit Germany to see old Baron Stockmar, now living in hypochondriacal retirement at Coburg. Would they meet the party there?

The reunion was to take place in the second half of September. Fritz was looking forward to it as much as anyone, but in retrospect it went down in everyone's memory as a near-disaster. A shadow was cast a few days earlier by a storm in a teacup which soon threatened to lead to the severing of diplomatic relations between Britain and Prussia. A Captain Macdonald, on holiday in Germany, refused to give up a seat in his railway carriage which had been previously reserved by another passenger. He was forcibly ejected, imprisoned and later tried; the subsequent fine would have been the end of the matter, had the public prosecutor not chosen to denounce English travellers abroad in general as 'notorious for the rudeness, impudence, and boorish arrogance of their conduct.'[13] Lord Palmerston demanded compensation for the Captain, and at least a humble apology from the prosecutor. *The Times* had never really wavered from its anti-Prussian attitude of 1855, and for the second time in five years led a storm of vituperation against the state. The Prussian press retaliated, and feeling between the two took a decided turn for the worse.

It was an unhappy overture to what was meant to be a joyful family reunion, and the shadows did not stop there. As the Queen and her entourage were travelling through Belgium on their way to Coburg, looking forward to seeing the Dowager Duchess, Albert's stepmother, they received a message telling them she had just died. Fortunately there were no further troubles before 25 September when Fritz and Vicky, dressed in mourning, met Duke Ernest at Coburg station to await the royal party. At the palace the Queen had her first sight of her grandson, dressed for the occasion in his little white tunic with black bows; as she noted in her journal, he had his father's eyes and his mother's mouth.[14] For their sake she did not look at his arm. Seeing Willy, 'such a little love', was the highlight of this German excursion for the Queen and the Prince Consort. A few days later, Albert had an accident in his horse-drawn carriage from which he emerged less physically bruised than mentally shaken. His spirits were only partly restored by a boar-hunt in the park near Coburg at the weekend, where he killed three boars; his son-in-law tactfully shot only one.

Like his wife, Fritz returned to Berlin very concerned over the Prince Consort. Stockmar and Duke Ernest had warned them that he was in a fragile state, convinced that he would never see his birthplace again — which indeed proved to be the case. The anxiety was soon overtaken by further family bereavements. In November, the Regent was shattered by the death of the Dowager Tsarina; Fritz had never seen him look so aged before. All her brothers and sisters mourned her except for Prince Charles, whose 'laughing and joking' when he heard of her death earned him general condemnation.

In Queen Victoria's words, it was the first link in the chain to be broken.[15] The second was about to follow. Fritz and Vicky had gone to see the King in June, to be horrified by the 'human ruin' they found. He was lying in a bath chair, his left hand, arm, and both legs tied up, unable to speak or direct his eyes to look at anyone, showing no signs of consciousness except for looking up feebly to his right.[16] By Christmas it was obvious that he was dying.

Vicky's second brother Alfred, now sixteen, was spending a few days with them at the time. On the evening of 31 December, after seeing him off at the station, they went to Charlottenburg for tea with the Regent; he seemed unusually low-spirited, while Augusta was 'rather low and unwell'.[17] Afterwards they returned to the Unter den Linden, only to be summoned by telegram just after one the next morning to Sans Souci. Half-awake, they hurried on their clothes, and without waiting for a cab made their way on foot through the cold deserted poorly-lit streets of the city to meet William and Augusta. Together they took a train to the palace, where by the light of a fire and a dim lamp which cast heavy shadows on the furniture and walls, the Queen sat in an armchair at the bedside, her arm supporting the King's head, and her other hand regularly wiping the perspiration from his brow. The room was silent except for the crackling of the fire and the death rattle, which lasted for an hour after their arrival.* As the clock struck the hours, still the princes and princesses came and went or stood around, only muffled sobs breaking the stillness. Augusta fell asleep in her chair, and overcome by exhaustion Vicky nodded off on a sofa, while Fritz and the others, already clad in black, paced up and down. The dramatic spectacle was not fated to come to a sudden end, and by five in the afternoon Vicky was feeling so sick and faint that Fritz sent her off to bed. He remained at the vigil with the others and was still there when, shortly after one in the morning of 2 January 1861, the 'living corpse' ceased to live.

At the age of twenty-nine, Fritz had become Crown Prince.

---

*Although this appears medically impracticable, it is stated in Princess Victoria's description of the deathbed scene,[17] on which this account is based.

CHAPTER 6

Crown Prince Frederick William, 1861-62.

The accession of the Prince Regent as William I did not usher in the new era for which Fritz and the Liberals had hoped. The new King delighted in his position, grandly signing state documents and receiving congratulatory messages from the other European courts, but those who expected him to make immediate concessions to liberalism were disappointed. The radicals wanted the dismissal of the reactionary Chief Police Commissioner von Zedlitz, who was unpopular with the moderate Conservatives as well; when William turned their demand down, the ministry refused at first to sanction the public celebration of his accession which he demanded, and only his War Minister Albrecht von Roon came to the sovereign's defence. Eventually, to prevent any ill-feeling on either side a compromise was reached, and William decided on the 'supreme act', a coronation later in the year.

Within the family, also, strife was rampant. Only moments after the late King's death Alexandrine, the widowed Grand Duchess of Mecklenburg-Strelitz, a vindictive woman who had told everyone that she would never set foot in the Neue Palais while Vicky lived there, threw herself into William's arms begging him not trust his intriguer of a wife. As it was, he had no intention of trusting her anyway. It therefore came as no surprise to anyone when a few days later Queen Augusta tried to assert her influence. She advised Baron von Schleinitz, the pro-French Minister for Foreign Affairs, to persuade the King to communicate personally with the Emperor Napoleon before he received the formal announcement of the accession, in order to establish closer Franco-Prussian relations. She also enclosed a draft of the letter, composed by herself, which she thought should be sent. Schleinitz replied to both King and Queen in favour of the scheme, but the messenger muddled the letters, handing the King that intended for his wife and vice versa. William was furious at her meddling in what did not concern her; she refused to accept a reprimand without fighting back, and soon the atmosphere at court became so strained that, for the first time in their lives, they came close to official separation — Augusta threatened to retire permanently to her summer residence at Coblenz. At this point Fritz intervened, persuading them that in the interests of the monarchy they ought to forget their differences.[1] He knew this was asking the impossible, but at least they did their duty and stayed together, still quarrelling bitterly and doubtless not without a certain malicious satisfaction.

Fritz's relationship with his father suffered at the same time, through no fault of his own. The culprit was his father-in-law, who like Augusta felt that William's accession should be the time for a renewed attempt at influencing his constitutional beliefs; both had been further encouraged by the sudden death of the feared Gerlach, who had caught a severe chill at the King's funeral in January. Long, very earnest and very frequent letters of advice went from Windsor to Berlin; most of those to the King went into the fire without a second thought. To Fritz, the Prince Consort suggested that his father ought to be crowned in Berlin to mark the beginning of the 'new era', instead of at the old capital Königsberg, the setting for all coronations since the Elector of Brandenburg had been crowned King Frederick I of Prussia in 1701. Fritz told the King, who promptly exploded and swore that everyone was plotting his downfall.[2] Albert was clutching at straws, and ten years earlier he would have known it, but in his premature old age and with increasing ill-health his judgment was losing its old power. He could no longer appreciate that William was simply an obstinate old soldier who was not likely to change his views at the age of sixty-four, and finding himself King of Prussia could be as obstinate as he pleased — he was now answerable to nobody. He would no more take advice from his son and young daughter-in-law than from the liberal Coburg prince so despised and feared by his reactionary ministers. Their potential influence was undermined by his belief that the ministry wanted him to abdicate, on account of his age and his inflexibility over the army reforms, and that Fritz could not wait for him to step down and take the throne in his place. Nothing was further from his son's wishes, as became evident the following year, but the King simply did not want to know. The arguments of the previous two years had broken down much of the father-and-son intimacy of the past, and it would have been difficult to restore it at this stage. The natural jealousy of a reigning monarch towards his or her heir, particularly when the latter held crucially different views supported by a section of the government, would have prevented this. There were several examples in both Hohenzollern and Hanoverian dynasties. From the moment he came to the throne, William's reign was in part the story of a King and heir in opposition, albeit usually of a tacit nature — with subsequently calamitous effects on the unlucky heir, whose filial integrity made it difficult for him to speak his mind as much as he would have liked.

If the political background to the beginning of the reign was an unfortunate one for Fritz, his domestic life suffered further setbacks and had to take second place to his new duties as Crown Prince. Gone for a while were the walks and drives with Vicky, which they enjoyed so much; even having breakfast together became rare. Military duties occupied the mornings, after which he had council meetings to attend, deputations and audiences to see, and his father's papers to arrange. As Crown Princess, Vicky had her audiences to receive, and the Queen came to regard her as a kind of reserve lady-in-waiting, even calling her out of bed at all hours when she felt so inclined. Guided by Fritz, she was gradually learning and accepting her duties; the days were over when she had tearfully begged him not to join war against the Italians, simply because she could not bear it if he never came back — duty had to take precedence over family life. He had always had a strong sense of royal priorities, and he adapted to his new schedule uncomplainingly, much as he missed his wife's company. Resignedly if wearily, Vicky wrote to her mother that she saw little of him from one day to another, and often she did not know whether he was in the palace or not; they might as well not be married.[3]

The evenings were often given over to long tedious court receptions and balls attended by the whole royal family, many of whom found their patience sorely taxed. The story goes that a tailor invited to one of these functions found himself next to Prince Frederick Charles and commented that he found the company very mixed that evening, to which the Prince snorted: 'Hang it! it isn't everyone that can be a tailor.' According to another version the tailor made this remark to Fritz, who answered good-naturedly: 'You are right, my good man, there are both ladies and gentle-men.'[4] Perhaps not the most memorable of royal sayings, but at least he made the effort to be pleasant where other members of the family thought nothing of rudeness.

All work and no play for a time made their stay in England during July all the more welcome. Vicky had paid a quick visit there in March, after the death of her maternal grandmother the Duchess of Kent, to find her mother temporarily bowed down by grief and her father almost worn out by the extra work the bereavement had added to his already seemingly endless chores. By June the general atmosphere was happier, particularly as Vicky and Fritz were in the process of finding a wife for the Prince of Wales. Although only nineteen he already had an eye for a pretty girl, and photographs of several eligible European princesses shown to him had filled him with dismay, for he judged them as being either plain or downright ugly. However his sister had heard of the beauty and charm of the young Princess Alexandra of Denmark, and in spite of the political differences* that led Fritz to declare gloomily that such a match would be so contrary to Prussian interests as to be 'the very worst that could happen to us'[5] it seemed that she

---

* Over Schleswig-Holstein. See p. 73.

might be a promising candidate. They were discussing the possibility of such a match when Fritz was called home by the news that a student had attempted to assassinate the King. However the bullet had only wounded him lightly in the neck, and he was delighted by the increased popularity his escape afforded him.

In September the Prince of Wales came to stay, ostensibly to attend the autumn manoeuvres at Coblenz with Fritz, but in reality to pay Speyer Cathedral a visit with his sister and brother-in-law, where he was to meet Princess Alexandra 'accidentally', and where they could talk to her parents, Crown Prince and Princess Christian of Denmark. The expedition was carefully stage-managed down to the last little detail, with Fritz and Vicky travelling under the name of Berg, although they did not remain incognito for long. While in the cathedral they allowed the bishop to guide them around and show them the frescoes, but they were secretly watching the young couple they had brought together so cunningly. Happy that Bertie was apparently pleased with his princess, and satisfied that they had contributed towards relieving Queen Victoria of the worry of finding a suitable wife for her son and heir, they returned to Berlin to prepare for the approaching coronation.

In vain did Fritz continue to suggest to his father that he should be crowned in Berlin, the capital of 'modern' Prussia, instead of at Königsberg. So as not to waste any preparations already made by the town officials at the latter, why not arrange a reception or something similar there? But the King would not be swayed over where to hold the ceremony, any more than he would over a letter left him by his brother asking him not to take the oath to uphold the constitution. It suited him to invoke the Divine Right of Kings, and he was deaf to his son's warnings about Charles I of England, whose similar stubbornness had done him little good. William gravely replied that out of respect for the dead he had no option but to follow his brother's wishes[6] — as long as they suited him. He took no more notice of the request from his ministers, who asked him not to demand the oath of allegiance from the estates of the realm, and not to crown himself — two gestures which smacked too much of absolutism.

In an attempt to mollify Fritz his thirtieth birthday — 18 October 1861 — was chosen as the date for the coronation. Vicky, dressed in white with a gold-embroidered train, was utterly dazzled by the vivid colours of the scene; the chapel was hung with red velvet trimmed with gold, to complement the bright robes of the family and the ladies-in-waiting, and sun poured in at the windows, giving 'quite magic tinges'.[7] Fritz, who always had a weakness for splendour and pageantry, looked resplendent in his Silesian Grenadier uniform and mantle of the Black Eagle, which reached from his shoulders to the ground. He forgot his differences with the King as he helped to place the coronation mantle over father's uniformed shoulders, prior to the placing of the crown on his head. The following day it was his turn to be the centre of attention when in a ceremony at Königsberg he accepted the Rectorship of the Royal Albertus University, an office previously held by the late King, and his investiture with the academic purple was a pleasing reminder of his student days at Bonn.

In the two-day whirlwind of festivity, he was temporarily too starstruck to appreciate the unconstitutional implications of his father's coronation speech — 'mindful of the fact that the crown comes from God alone . . .'[8] It was a defiant assertion of the Divine Right, and a snub for liberals everywhere. For once the Prince Consort had to agree with *The Times's* condemnation, much as he and Queen Victoria resented its practice of attacking everything Prussian at the merest opportunity. At last the Prince saw that his faith in William was sorely misplaced. Fritz agreed that his father's views were foolhardy, but he had learnt from past experience that arguing with him on the subject, no matter how good his intentions, was a waste of time; it only reinforced the old man's stubborn convictions. A little patience and hope on his and ministry's part might succeed where blunt suggestion had failed. He often wondered whether the Prince Consort would ever learn to understand his father's character. How little he realised that time was running out.

The winter following the coronation was one of perpetual ill-health for both Fritz and Vicky, she suffering from a severe bout of bronchitis, so serious in fact that at one stage Dr Wegner wrote to warn Queen Victoria that her daughter's life was in danger. In spite of being confined to bed for over three weeks, Vicky was not blind to the nervous strain which was leaving its mark on her husband. When he left Berlin in November for military service in Breslau he was obviously far from well, his complexion yellow and fatigued, and his eyes dark ringed. Queen Augusta and her hunger for society life were largely to blame. Her nerves were in a 'perpetual state of excitement', and with her 'immensely strong constitution' everybody — family and servants alike (sometimes the line of demarcation between the two became uncomfortably blurred, especially for Vicky) — had an exhausting existence. Fritz suffered his mother's domineering manner in silence, feeling it his duty to let her have her way, as it kept her happy, and this was in everybody's interest.[9]

It was in the gloomy atmosphere at Berlin that he received a telegram on 13 December from the Prince Consort's private secretary, Sir Charles Phipps, asking him to prepare Vicky for the shock of her father's almost certain death. Overwhelmed by work and anxiety, his constitution undermined by perpetual ailments, Albert caught typhoid fever, the same disease which to his distress had just carried off the King of Portugal and his brother. Queen Victoria, trying to fight her alarm for the sake of appearances, wrote optimistically to Vicky that he was ill but would soon be better: 'pray don't fred and worry — there is no reason for it.'[10] It only made her grief all the deeper when the final news came that he had died on the evening of 14 December; she was stunned by it. As Fritz had discovered during the summer before Willy's birth, marriage had not weakened the bond between father and daughter, and it was dispiriting for him now when she told him that she felt as if her life was over and she could never be happy again.[11] For several days she fell into a lethargy, punctuated only by outbursts of tears which distressed her ladies-in-waiting.

But Fritz was deeply affected as well. Forgotten was the father-in-law who had once been a barrier between husband and wife, forgotten was the prince in faraway England who had poured scorn on his 'playing at soldiers'. He only remembered the man who had introduced him to his wife, the father-in-law 'whom we thought would help to guide us through many many years.'[12]

A more detached observer would have realised that the Prince Consort had done them both — Vicky especially — a disservice by his support. It had been unwise of him to interfere so much in Prussian affairs. Nobody could deny how high-principled his ideas were, but he had never belonged to Prussia; in practice he had by marriage become an Englishman, no matter how much he claimed that he had left his heart behind in Coburg. It was therefore not his business to try and steer Prussia towards the goal of the liberal united Germany which he, Baron Stockmar and King Leopold all longed to see — or, as Fritz had pointedly said in a heated moment, to try and rule the land through the King. At the same time, it was extremely shortsighted of him to make himself the pillar of support on which they leaned and to whom they looked for advice. He should have seen that, sooner or later, the day would come when he was no longer there to help them; and he was a sick man for the last few months of his life, with little if any hope of attaining old age. His plan had been for Ernest Stockmar to assume this role gradually, but this revealed as much as anything else his lack of understanding of both situation and character. The Stockmars, father and son, were viewed with just as much suspicion by the Berlin reactionaries as the Prince Consort himself, and by his mere presence, their secretary Ernest in turn made Fritz and Vicky distrusted by the 'clique'. Moreover, the younger Stockmar did not have the drive or the visionary outlook of his father. The Prince misjudged his character in the same way as he had that of King William, both as prince and sovereign; he tended to see what he wanted to see until it was too late. Lastly, Albert was the wrong person to be in a position to offer them suitable advice. To a degree, yes; few statesmen of the day had a more astute grasp of constitutional politics than he did, but his

Albert, Prince Consort, 1861

Queen Victoria and Queen Augusta, 1867

textbook knowledge of Prussian court life was based on hearsay and not experience. Not having lived in Berlin, he was simply incapable of understanding the conditions Vicky found at court after her marriage; the stiff etiquette, the narrow-minded elderly princes, the deep-rooted distrust of any connection with parliamentary government. That she had inherited much of his analytical mind and way of thinking was her great misfortune; according to Mary Bulteel, she 'divided everything into three heads, turning them about so much that she often came to a wrong conclusion.'[13] There were men such as the liberal-minded Max Duncker, appointed political adviser to Fritz earlier in 1861, who did not have Albert's brains but were much better-equipped to offer counsel, merely because they knew Prussia from first-hand experience.*

Dr Wegner forbade Vicky to visit England and comfort her mother, as she was not only pregnant but still convalescing after bronchitis at the time of her father's death. Fritz went instead, and it was to him in those hushed joyless rooms at Osborne that the Queen unburdened her grief by describing every detail of her husband's last hours. Brokenly she told how his illness had started and progressed; how he had been reconciled with the wayward Prince of Wales, whose liaison with an actress, she asserted, had broken his heart; how she had held his hand to the end, only realising that he had passed away by the spiritual look on his face. Then, taking his hand and leading him into the bedroom she showed him the corpse dressed in a blue overcoat, the lifeless hands holding a photograph of the Queen as a young woman with her hair flowing over her shoulders.[14]

For a moment Fritz was too moved to speak. He realised that he owed it to the dead man's inspiration, his firm and honourable if sometimes misguided beliefs, to do what he could to secure a peaceful future for Europe through a firm alliance between Britain and Germany. If he had been impatient at times with the Prince's philosophy in those heated arguments with Vicky, it was something he now regretted. The long-winded theorising to which he had been verbally treated as a bachelor on his visits to England had been sincere, and to one of Fritz's liberal convictions, there was much to commend them and little if anything to condemn. The constitution, he had learnt, was not a tiresome book of rules to be sheltered behind or dis-

---

* Prince Albert's concern with Prussia (and Queen Victoria's too) at the expense of other German states may have had other unfortunate consequences apart from the personal problems which surrounded Fritz and Vicky after his death. Their unwillingness (if not refusal) to establish good relations with their uncle Ernest Augustus, King of Hanover, and the Queen's apparent silence over Bismarck's annexation of the Kingdom in 1866, indirectly contributed to Prussian supremacy in Europe and Anglo-German rivalry which came to a head after the accession of Edward VII to the British throne, culminating in the 1914–18 war. See Bird, *The damnable Duke of Cumberland*, p. 294.

regarded at will, but a vital guarantee against extremist shades of conservative opinion which could endanger personal freedom at large. Like the Liberal ministry, he never forgot the lessons of 1848; like the Prince Consort, he realised that the reactionary politics of one era could unwittingly further the revolutions of the next.

He stayed for the funeral at St. George's Chapel, Windsor, on 23 December. As the Queen was in no state to attend, he and the Prince of Wales were the chief mourners. A close relationship was forming between the brothers-in-law; Fritz could appreciate the qualities in Bertie which his mother was determined not recognise, and he worked as hard as anybody to prevent them from drawing further apart. He returned to Berlin three days later, bringing Vicky 'precious relics and hair'[15] of her father, as well as her mother's touching description of his last illnesss.

During the next few months, he visited his wife's country several times and found himself welcomed as an unofficial substitute for the Prince Consort; the Queen found him infinitely preferable to her next nearest male relations, her eldest son, and Duke Ernest, her dissolute brother-in-law. The King grumbled — why did his son have to be in England so often? Albert's funeral was only the beginning of it; Fritz was invited to open the second Great Exhibition in May, a sequel to the 1851 display, and then to act as best man for the wedding of Princess Alice and Prince Louis of Hesse at Osborne in July. At first William refused to let him go to the exhibition, but under pressure he grudgingly gave in — very well, but the young man could pay his expenses himself. When asked by the family why he made objections, he could offer no real explanation. There was nothing to keep Fritz in Prussia as far as government was concerned, for apart from attending council meetings and continuing his military training, he had very little to do in an official capacity. The reason was that the King was jealous of his son's popularity in Britain; *The Times* confirmed his nagging fears too regularly for comfort.

Nor was his popularity confined to Britain. The elections held in Prussia during December 1861 had produced a greatly increased liberal majority, and William was uneasy. He had always been restrained to a certain degree by the Prince Consort, although he chose to disregard his letters with contempt, but once the younger man was dead, he gleefully resolved that he was going to keep his family in check without interference from anyone. There was another scene between father and son in March. Fritz declared himself in complete agreement with the 'essential liberal policy for internal and foreign affairs' — basically, no unnecessary reform of the army and taxation at home, and closer links with the rest of Europe — in which Vicky supported him, and the King reproached him for being hand in glove with the Liberals. Furthermore, William went on, he was placing himself in a 'peculiar position' through his liberal views, especially as the democratic press was (rather tactlessly) describing his attitude as being in opposition to his father. At this point Augusta intervened, snapping at her husband for being so much under the influence of the *Keuzzeitung* (extreme right) party that he could say such things to his son.

Fritz was bewildered. Surely there was all the difference in the world, he wrote to Vicky then staying with her mother, between the freely-expressed opinions of an unbiased person, such as himself, and an opponent who was deliberately setting himself up against the King.[16] During sleepless nights, denied his wife's company for a while, his sense of family loyalty made him long to be on better terms with his father. But how could he do so without falling out with mother, betraying the views of his wife and her father, above all abandoning his own convictions — selling his soul? Were his beliefs worth the high price he was paying for them? The unfortunate results of a lonely childhood, overshadowed by quarrelsome parents, were beginning to show.

It was in these dark months that Vicky's influence, shortly to be seized on so vigorously by their political enemies, began to make its mark. The wildly exaggerated reports that he was completely under the thumb of 'the English-woman' were generally accepted for over half a century, and have persisted to this day; only in the light of recent research and long-unpublished material can the matter be viewed more objectively. Fritz was a mild, good-natured character who throughout his life was plagued by indecision; upset by family quarrels and torn between both sides of an argument, he could never really decide whose ideas were at fault — his or those of the people who disagreed with him. Vicky simply reinforced his belief in his own opinions, and gave him the confidence in himself that prevented him from being swayed too much from one view to the other: 'let me beg you never to miss an opportunity of showing the world by your firmness and decision who you are.'[17]

It was just the advice he needed during these difficult times. Yet it was unfortunate that she had at this crucial time been temporarily thrown off balance by her father's premature death; a few more years without his support, and she would probably have been able to see situations with a more elastic judgment, of which Albert was usually capable until the last few months of his life. But she clung so tenaciously to his example that she was for a time unable to recognise that Prussia's future developments would have eventually resulted in him revising his opinions.

With so much unpleasantness at home, Fritz was glad to go over to England often, although he doubted the wisdom of Queen Victoria in allowing a foreign prince to deputise for her so frequently. His greatest regret was that he had to leave Vicky behind, for the continuing disagreements with his father led him to value her love and advice increasingly. The King's jealous fears were correct; Fritz proved his English popularity beyond doubt when he opened the exhibition in May, in his capacity as President of the Exhibition Commission appointed to prepare Prussia's role in the display, and again a few days later when he was a special guest of the Royal Academy of Arts at their annual dinner. The other guests were impressed during his speech with his clear grasp of the English language, in which he dwelt on his genuine love of his wife's country. The Queen, in seclusion at Balmoral at the time, expressed herself in much simpler terms to Vicky: 'Dear Fritz's success is in everyone's mouth!'[18]

Vicky always regretted being prevented from attending Alice's wedding, held privately in the dining room at Osborne on 1 July with Fritz as best man, although she consoled herself as she looked forward to visiting her in her German home. On 14 August her third child, Henry William Albert, was born. The family expected that he would be called Albert in memory of the 'never-to-be-forgotten grandfather',[19] but sadly Vicky decided that to avoid confusion he would have to be Henry; he could be known as Albert by his maternal grandmother. Both parents were relieved that he was perfectly healthy in spite of the depressing months his mother had spent while carrying him — to her it was a miracle how he was 'there at all.'[20]

The baby was born during an approaching political crisis, the stormclouds of which had been gathering since before his father's visits to England. Early in 1862 the moderates in the ministry insisted that all government expenditure should be strictly accounted for in future, as extra funds had lately been fraudulently diverted towards the army. William panicked and dissolved the *Landtag* in March, blaming his ministers for not having exerted sufficient influence on the December elections and thus making possible such a large Liberal vote. The Liberal ministers resigned and were replaced by Conservatives, led by Prince Adolf von Hohenlohe-Ingelfingen. The new Minister-President was a moderate by Conservative standards, but this change was still applauded by the *Kreuzzeitung*. Further elections in May increased the Liberal majority and with it the government's difficulties. Still the King stood by his reform programme, and still the ministers advised him to give way.

His most resolute ally Roon suggested appointing Otto von Bismarck, his Foreign Minister, as head of the government. William shrank from this at first; the man had a 'reputation for wanton brutality',[21] and was unpopular with the other states in the Confederation. Would this not do more harm than good? Since 1848 Bismarck had served as ambassador to the courts of Paris and St Petersburg. He had been recommended for the Prussian Embassy in London the previous year, but the Prince Consort vetoed the idea at once; he had known that it was largely due to Bismarck's Anglophobia that the proposal of an Anglo-Prussian alliance during the Crimean war had been abandoned. Vicky did not know him personally, but had been told that he was 'a most unprincipled and unrespectable character'[22] and dreaded the consequences if he was appointed. Fritz knew him to be his mother's 'deadly enemy', and hoped at least for her sake that he would not be summoned. As for his own feelings, his distrust of such a future stemmed from Bismarck's own report of a meeting he had had in London with Lord Palmerston and the Foreign Secretary Lord John Russell, in his capacity as Foreign Minister. Bismarck found the English constitution totally alien to his philosophy in its insistence that the crown's advisers should come from the Parliamentary majority's ranks, as this allowed for what he considered to be excessive encroachments on the royal prerogative. The consequent despatch, Fritz wrote, was a grim forecast of what would come if such a man was to control the destiny of Prussia.[23]

As summer wore on it became increasingly obvious that King and ministry had reached deadlock; he would not concede on his reforms, particularly on the extension of two-year army service, and they would not accept them. The wearisome affair came to a climax on 17 September, when the *Landtag* was called upon to vote the measures en bloc; they were defeated by 308 votes to 11. William raged at his ministers, whose stubbornness matched his own, growling that anarchy was everywhere and he would sooner abdicate than yield. Roon held two trump cards; either they could stage a *coup d'état*, and authorise the illegal collection of the taxes that would not be voted, or he would call Bismarck to take over the government. On reflection the latter course of action seemed the safer, and next day he sent Bismarck a telegram urging him to return to Berlin at once.

That same day, 18 September, the King sent for Fritz. With tears in his eyes, William showed his son the deed of abdication and the draft of the speech in which he would announce his stepping down from the throne. It was a carefully-considered decision, he said as he paced slowly up and down the room, staring at the floor; God and his conscience would not allow him to do anything else. If the ministry refused to accept his reforms, he would make way for his son.

Fritz could not believe it. The shock he had had on being told of the plot to depose his father as Regent in 1860 was nothing compared to this. Threats to abdicate in the heat of the moment were one thing, but this was quite another. In his alarm, his sympathy for the 'poor broken old man' — William was nothing if not a good actor — he could not appreciate that his father was only doing this because he knew his son would never allow him to take such a step. He was right. Through no fault of his own, Fritz was not ready for the throne, and had the arguments at his fingertips. If a Prussian sovereign could be forced into abdication like this as a result of a Parliamentary decision, what precedent would be set for the future? What about the threat it would pose to dynasty, crown and country? Much as he respected the institution of Parliamentary government and the constitution, he revered the crown still more. If he had not been so overcome by his father's feigned distress, he would have suggested gently that William ought to concede over his reforms.

That evening, still reeling from the shock, he poured out the story to Vicky. It was appalling, as he had told himself all day. Or was it? Which came first — filial duty or Parliament? Could he accept the throne and begin his reign in the shadow of his defeated father? Would it be in the best interests of Prussia and Germany?

Vicky was just as taken aback as he was. What would dearest papa have recommended, she asked herself; she had little doubt. Why should they not take the chance? Why not make this sacrifice for their country, for their ideals? They must not think of themselves, but of the fatherland and of their children who would otherwise one day have to make good where they had failed.[24] But in her heart of hearts she knew it must be Fritz's decision, not hers. She guessed from his appeals to her that they must do nothing in a hurry, and from the look of pity in his eyes when he alluded to his 'poor father', what his answer would be. It made her feel so helpless, but she could only advise.

He might have thought differently had he known that Bismarck, stung into action by the threat of Parliamentary democracy, was on his way to Berlin as fast as he could travel. On 22 September he met the King at Babelsberg. William told him gravely that if they could not come to some understanding, the act of abdication would be published. Bismarck had only one answer: 'royal government or the supremacy of Parliament'.[25] William sighed with relief, and on the following day Bismarck was proclaimed Minister-President of Prussia.

Fritz's fears were confirmed; for the immediate future, while his father reigned, Bismarck would rule. It was an appointment which was to have unforeseen consequences on not only the hapless Crown Prince of Prussia, but also on both the map and the history of Europe for over half a century.

CHAPTER 7

Enter Bismarck, 1862-63.

Fritz had realised that the deadlock between King and ministry could not go on indefinitely, and he had foreseen the possible appointment of Bismarck. Yet he had persuaded himself that what he had envisaged during his darkest hours might not come true after all; surely the 'strong man' could not ride roughshod over all opposition without the combined weight of more moderate ministers restraining him. On the other hand he seemed just the man who would annihilate any arguments in his way. What would happen?

He soon found out. On 28 September the King sent for him again. No longer the sly 'broken old man', he was once again the bullying father ready to believe the worst of his son. Without mentioning the previous few days, he merely said that he was tired of sermons and would have no more of them[1] — with that Fritz was dismissed. Instinctively he had told himself that he should have thought twice about persuading his father not to abdicate, hard though it was to believe him so capable of deception. He shuddered on reading of a speech made by Bismarck later that week; the great questions of the time, thundered the Minister-President, would not be solved by speeches and majority decisions, but by blood and iron. For a moment he was ashamed of his military upbringing, and his eagerness to join the fray in Italy three years earlier; now he saw what the Prince Consort had meant by 'army mania'. Suddenly his homeland seemed utterly abhorrent to him — if ever he needed to leave it for a while, now was the time.

There was another reason for his discomfort; his popularity was facing a new threat. His brother-in-law's engagement to Princess Alexandra had just been announced. Not only Bismarck, but all German nationalists, frowned on it. The father of the future Princess of Wales was next in succession to the Danish throne, and on his accession the smouldering Schleswig-Holstein question would almost certainly flare into open controversy. The duchies of Schleswig and Holstein, of which the latter had a large German population, had been placed under Danish rule by the London Protocol of 1852. With the growth of German nationalist feeling, the inhabitants of both were growing increasingly restless. The death of the present King, Frederick VII, would invariably bring demands for recognition or self-government to a head. That Britain should as much as hint at a Danish alliance against Germany, by marrying her future King to one of the little country's princesses, was bad enough; but when it became known at large (probably through the indiscreet Duke of Coburg, who described the match as a 'thunder-clap' for Germany)[2] that Fritz and Vicky had been instrumental in bringing it about, their standing in Prussia fell accordingly.

Fritz was in despair. He felt powerless in the new political climate — what could he do about it? Ernest Stockmar told him sadly that he could do nothing; he had to maintain his position as Crown Prince, which meant avoiding getting caught up in party strife. As if by chance, Queen Victoria then told him that the Prince of Wales was borrowing the royal yacht for a Mediterranean cruise, while she invited Alexandra to stay with her in England. It would be politic, she went on, if he and Vicky joined the party on the *Osborne;* this would not only give them a pleasant holiday, but also remove them briefly from the threatening situation at home. They did not give it a second thought. As usual the King complained when they asked his permission to go, but secretly he was glad to see the back of them, and had never really intended to withhold his consent.

They left Coburg on 6 October, travelling through South Germany and Switzerland. Vicky spent the first few days in dread of the King changing his mind and suddenly calling them back, but as they climbed the Alps and whiled away the hours chatting with Bertie she forgot her worries for the time being. Fritz, however, could not help thinking of the crisis at home, and his birthday on 18 October was overshadowed by his wondering what would be the state of affairs on their return. Spending half the day in a railway carriage, imprisoned by pouring rain, did not improve his spirits.[3]

On 22 October they sailed from Marseilles, and there followed an idyllic few weeks of travel. He put his anxiety to one side as they explored the ruins of Carthage, picking up fragments of ancient mosaic to treasure in the years ahead. They visited the Bey of Tunis in his palace, who simply pulled out his Order in Diamonds from his pocket wrapped in paper, giving it to Fritz with no formality apart from a beaming smile and handshake. No longer was he a worried sleepless Crown Prince, but one of a party of tourists, whether lunching in the open air at Syracuse in a grove of orange and lemon trees, or sitting gazing at the bay of Naples while Vicky sketched beside him, or walking up the dormant Mount Vesuvius to be enraptured by the boundless view unfolding before their eyes. He relived his earlier visit to Italy as he guided her happily round the art treasures and churches at Rome, where the paintings by Raphael so admired by the Prince Consort brought tears to her eyes. The incognita they had preserved at Naples were relinquished as they went to see the Pope, who had not forgotten Fritz — he kept his hands firmly behind his back this time. The overwhelming magic of Renaissance art that greeted them at every turn made up for the squalor of present-day Rome, the atmosphere of which left much to be desired. The streets were dirty and full of beggars, they were driven almost frantic with itching by fleas, and they could have done quite well without the sight of a monk blowing his nose in an umbrella.[4] The most unfortunate note, however, was struck when they visited the house of Canitz, Prussian Minister to the Vatican, who was completely insane and spent most of his time in a strait-jacket. Fritz must have regretted that the same fate had not overtaken Bismarck.

After saying goodbye to the Prince of Wales on 21 November, Vicky's birthday, they left Rome for Florence and Venice — by which time they had spent so much on souvenirs and presents that they had to be very firm with themselves and resist the temptation to buy some of the beautiful but highly-priced mosaics — and on their return north stopped at Vienna. They were guests of honour at an imperial family dinner, where Francis Joseph put himself out to be a genial host, treating Fritz (one year his junior) like an old friend. Beneath the camaraderie lay political undertones; the Emperor, already looking aged and wrinkled beyond his years, distrusted Bismarck and suspected that his appointment would sooner or later prove to be at Austria's expense. When Fritz remarked that he wished the imperial cabinet could advise the central German states to tone down their hostility towards Prussia, his host did not answer. He longed to say that Berlin should drop her anti-Austrian attitude.[5]

On this uneasy note Fritz and Vicky arrived home. Only one shadow had lingered over the enjoyment of their travels — the news they received from time to time. The King was confounding public opinion with his 'imprudent and ill-judged' speeches,[6] but his behaviour was nothing when compared to that of Bismarck, who had driven like a steam-roller through all opposition. Under him the government was ruling without the military budget, collecting taxes and duties regardless of the fact that they had not been voted. Two or three years' military service was not an important issue to him in itself; what did alarm him was the dreaded democracy that could take such decisions against the sovereign's wishes. He had discovered a flaw in the constitution; the ministers were responsible for preventing the arbitrary collection of taxes, but no provision was made for their impeachment if they failed in or deliberately flouted their duties. Quite simply, constitutional power in Russia had one fatal weakness — it could not punish those who chose to break it.

Under the new regime, the winter in Berlin was even less bearable than usual. Vicky's descriptions of Fritz at about this time sound dangerously close to those used by Queen Victoria of the Prince Consort in his last months – 'looking ill, so pale, so fagged'.[7] Once again he had to accustom himself to seeing little of her in between his military duties, where the army had benefited considerably in discipline and morale since he had last seen it.

Sadly he had to acknowledge to himself that Bismarck, by allowing the King his own way over the reforms and thus providing extra expenditure for the forces, had succeeded where he through sheer dogged persistence on limited resources had failed. Weariness and his usual winter colds prevented him from getting the sleep he badly needed. As Vicky recognised, he did not have the necessary energy and freshness to meet new difficulties, at a time when there were so many of them.

The King, on the other hand, now looked much younger than before. When he invited his son and daughter-in-law to dinner one evening, they hardly recognised in their jovial confident host the bully they were accustomed to. For once the food, wine and hospitality were beyond criticism, but they could not enjoy it while he talked gleefully, and not without a desire to sting, of the improvement in the army — thanks to Bismarck. Fritz tried to persuade himself that his father did not realise he was playing with fire, but all the same he hardly dared think of the future. What outrages would the Minister perpetrate next?

Nothing fortunately could prevent Fritz from being best man at his brother-in-law's wedding. Vicky and Willy, now four, left for Windsor on 20 February, and he joined them at the beginning of March. As they stood in St George's Chapel, Windsor, on the day itself (10 March), they could not fail to remember their own wedding five years earlier — a little sadly, when they thought of the Prince Consort, to whom the occasion would have been so happy. They were so touched by the sight of the young couple smiling self-assuredly at everyone that they did not seem to notice the behaviour of Highland-clad Willy. Pulling the dirk from his stocking, he mischievously threw it on the chapel floor; when his uncles, twelve-year-old Arthur and nine-year-old Leopold, scolded him, he retaliated by biting their legs.

Fritz was cheered to hear that his father was not as yet totally under Bismarck's spell. Ignoring his Minister's protests, the King attended a dinner given by the British Ambassador in Berlin to celebrate the wedding. He had promised in advance that he would attend, and would not go back on his word.

But this did not stop them from considering Vicky's idea of asking Queen Victoria to persuade the King to let them spend half of every year in Britain. Despite the gloom which still pervaded Windsor in the aftermath of Prince Albert's death, it was still a veritable paradise after Berlin; the King made it obvious that he did not want them there. Reluctantly, however, they had to agree that the scheme was impracticable. Liberalism was in danger of being trampled underfoot; what would become of it, and the Prince's inspiration and legacy to them, if they shied away from keeping the fire alight at home? In any case, as Crown Prince and Princess, it would not look well for them to defect so openly. It was their duty to stay in Prussia, come what may.

Balmoral. Vicky could not stop herself laughing at Fritz in a 'little skirt'[26] —
a remark he bore with good grace for her sake, though it was an unpleasant
reminder of the first time he had worn the kilt twenty years earlier. Like the
Mediterranean cruise it was a badly-needed holiday, and as they walked up
to the site on Craig-na-Ban they relived the idyllic days when they had
become engaged. Queen Victoria was gradually finding peace of mind in
widowhood which was denied to her in London, and she was a model
grandmama to the children, even laughing at Willy's rather rude comment
that his English relations were pug-nosed.

The Prince of Wales invited them to Sandringham for his birthday
celebrations on 9 November, and they arrived in Norfolk a few days in
advance, having lingered on the journey south in order to compare the
provincial art galleries with those in Germany. But this was one family event
which could not shield them from the King's whims, for on 6 November
Fritz had a telegram ordering him home for the opening of Parliament which
was to take place three days later. Wearily he returned for the ceremony,
and while there the King at last gave him permission not to attend the
council meetings on condition that he avoided any more 'opposition'.
Having done his duty, he travelled back to England. A new shadow fell just
before he arrived; King Frederick VII of Denmark died. It was an event for
which Bismarck had been waiting.

CHAPTER 8

'Blood and Iron', 1863-66.

As Bismarck had written in July 1863, 'in ruling houses the nearest of kin may yet be aliens'[1]; the truth of that statement was very soon to be borne out. The tangled problem of Schleswig-Holstein* had given rise to Palmerston's immortal quip that only three people had ever understood it: the Prince Consort, now dead, a German professor, who had since gone mad, and himself, who had regrettably forgotten all about it. On the accession of Prince Christian of Schleswig-Holstein-Sonderburg-Glucksburg to the Danish throne as Christian IX, both duchies with their predominantly German populations demanded their own government. They belonged to the German Confederation; both Fritz and Augusta, like Queen Victoria, supported the claims of Duke Frederick of Schleswig-Holstein-Sonderburg-Augustenburg ('Fritz Holstein'), married to the Queen's niece Adelaide of Hohenlohe-Langenburg. With the support of several other German states, he promptly issued a proclamation announcing that he had assumed government of both on the death of King Frederick. Denmark, on the other hand, intended to maintain them herself.

The succession problem was on everyone's mind when Fritz rejoined Vicky and the children at Windsor. All was peaceful until the Prince and Princess of Wales arrived a few days later; the family had foreseen trouble, for as the eldest daughter of King Christian Alix defiantly declared that 'the duchies belong to Papa'. Both came into collision not only with the couple who had helped bring them together, but also with Fritz Holstein's mother-in-law Feodore, who was also staying there at the time. Not a meal passed without violent argument on the subject, until the harassed Queen Victoria took King Leopold's advice and forbade any further mention of it in her presence. It was the most unpleasant visit Fritz and Vicky remembered having paid to Britain, not just because of the family atmosphere, but also as there was talk of war on a scale considerably beyond the gathering at Windsor and Sandringham. They knew Bismarck to be against Fritz Holstein, who was not only closely related to Queen Victoria by marriage but also a confirmed liberal. Characteristically the Minister kept silent to all but a handful of close associates. He intended to take the duchies

*See above, p. 73.

for Prussia, whom he admitted had no claim, but their amalgamation would give Prussia added strength and size.

Fritz was in an awkward position. Like Bismarck he was a nationalist, who longed to see his country as more than just another German state. But he was a friend of Fritz Holstein from university days, and would have been glad to see him assume undisputed rule of the territories. At the same time he had no desire to go claiming them from Denmark for the sake of it, particularly as he knew and liked the new king and his family, to say nothing of having been best man at his daughter's wedding. All he could do was to sit back helplessly and see what move Bismarck would make next.

As he had expected, the Minister kept him in the dark until the last minute; on 16 January 1864, in league with Austria, he sent King Christian an ultimatum to evacuate and renounce all claim to the duchies within twenty-four hours. Opinion in the Diet of the German Confederation was almost as hostile to Prussia as it was in England, for Bismarck had acted without consulting the other states. He did not trust Fritz as he believed that, if the latter was told in advance, the secret would be betrayed to Queen Victoria. Already the 'strong man', distrusting Vicky's influence and dynastic connections, was punishing them both for the Danzig incident.

The protests of Vicky and Queen Augusta were futile; like it or not, Fritz was ordered away on active service. He went with reluctance, for it was ironic that the first war in which his services were called for should be against an enemy for whom he had sympathy, especially as the Danes would be so heavily outnumbered. They had hoped that England would come to their rescue in the event of war; Palmerston and Russell were all for going to their aid, but Queen Victoria was as pro-German as ever, and the nation remained uncomfortably neutral. On 1 February the allies marched into Schleswig, with Fritz humiliatingly as second in command under General Wrangel. Within a few days, however, he had to take the reins; Wrangel, he told Vicky, was 'half crazy', obstinate and stubborn, and at the age of eighty was hardly the wisest choice for a leader. Once in charge, he could not wait for peace to be declared. Despite the allied successes, there was much to worry him; he missed Vicky as badly as she missed him, he was depressed over Bismarck's hold on his father, and prayed that God would give him enlightenment to see through the man 'who has proved to be Prussia's undoing.'[2] Then he was ashamed to hear that the King had awarded him the Order of the Red Eagle with Swords. What had he done to deserve it, sitting in cosy boredom in his office at headquarters? How his soldiers would laugh at him — were orders no longer given for bravery in the field of battle? Vicky's letters were often the only genuine comfort he had; as the days turned into weeks, only the thought of her helped him to face the future with any optimism. From time to time, as he sat at headquarters waiting for the chance to prove himself, she sent him novels, champagne, cake and cigars.

At length his patience was rewarded. Within days of the start of the campaign the Danish army abandoned the Dannevirke, its line of defence in Schleswig, and retreated behind the fortifications at Duppel. The Prussian army marched towards the town at the beginning of March and Fritz, bored with doing nothing, and feeling his award might be justified if he took part in some genuine action, asked for and was granted permission to join the troops. It was not a request he made lightly, for he was still very much the reluctant enemy of Denmark and never ceased to feel sympathy for King Christian and his family, but he also resented being idle at headquarters and felt that duty would be better discharged on the battlefields. In April the fortifications were stormed and the Danes were driven back from their trenches onto the island of Alsen. His presence during the attack did much to inspire the Prussian troops, and he could not but share in the exultation of the princes and generals when the victory was theirs; but as he congratulated his regiment on their part in the success, his heart went out equally to the wounded on both sides, and he was thankful that the conflict would soon be over.

On 25 April a conference opened in London to discuss the consequences of the war; all neutral and belligerent powers were represented. The former proposed an armistice, which was arranged to last for six weeks as from 11 May, and later that week Fritz returned home. Vicky was overjoyed to see him again, although with his beard she did not recognise him at first as he waved to her from the window of his railway carriage. It was the longest separation — over three months — they had yet known, and during his absence so much had happened to her. She had had a spate of angry letters from England. Her mother had partly blamed them both for the war: 'you all (God forgive you for it) would have it.'[3] Bertie had condemned Prussia strongly, and in anxiety for her father Alix had given birth in January to a seven-months child, Prince Albert Victor. A welcome visit from brother Alfred had been spoilt by the sarcastic comments of *The Times*, which did not let the fact that the King had bestowed the Order of the Black Eagle on him go unnoticed without unpleasantness. When Vicky persuaded Augusta not to give up hope for Fritz Holstein's claim, the Queen snapped at her not to be so childish.[4]

It was during the war that she had to contend with her first taste of real unpopularity, which thanks to Bismarck gradually took root from this time onwards. As anti-German as ever, *The Times* chose to take the King and his 'mischievous cabinet' to task. With undoubted but tactless sincerity it congratulated Fritz on his stand on behalf of the Augustenburg claim, and also on having a Consort who shared his liberal views. It seemingly never occurred to the author that such articles would find their way across to Prussia, and subsequently Fritz and Vicky would suffer for it. They were music to the ears of Bismarck and his henchmen, who lost no time during the campaign in seizing on her divided loyalties and spreading rumours that she was unhappy at the success of the allied troops; everything she said and did was at once criticised as being in imitation of England, therefore anti-Prussian. 'I feel as it I could smash the idiots,' she wrote in May, 'it is so spiteful and untrue.'[5]

On his return Fritz was appointed to the command of the Second Army Corps by the King, who received him with some indifference. He would have been proud of his son, had Bismarck not continually whispered in his ear about the possible betrayal of state secrets the 'young man Absalom' could pass on to England. A few days' rest with Vicky elapsed before he began a tour of inspection, so he did not return to the front when the armistice expired in June and Prussian troops captured the island of Alsen. Unable to fight a losing battle any longer, the Danish cabinet sued for peace. Negotiations opened at Vienna in July, and three months later the treaty was concluded. Denmark renounced her claims to Schleswig and Holstein, in favour of Prussia and Austria. It was an ambiguous gesture which augured badly for the future.

What Fritz and Vicky had dreaded from the beginning, and what Queen Augusta and the angry English press had foreseen, was true. Bismarck totally ignored Fritz Holstein in the peace negotiations; he had sent his country to war in order to seize the duchies for Prussia, and was already boasting to his confidantes that war against Austria was now only a question of time. Fritz was disgusted at the part he had played in the campaign; who, apart from his wife, mother and mother-in-law, would believe that he had not wantonly taken advantage of Denmark's military isolation, subsequent British neutrality, and Fritz Holstein's lack of influence at Berlin, in order to further the territorial aims of his own country? His loathing of Bismarck, and his sympathy for his father 'in the centre of a web of lies'[6] increased accordingly. It was with unbounded relief that he returned to the comforts of the Neue Palais.

Gustav zu Putlitz and his wife were only two of several contemporaries who have left colourful reminiscences of their Crown Prince's domestic life. He would sit contentedly on the sofa in their drawing-room, a book on his knee and a pipe or tankard of beer in his hand, while Vicky would work at her spinning-wheel as she sang to herself, or at her easel painting subjects ranging from flowers to portraits and battle scenes, a set of the latter being made into prints to be sold in aid of Fritz's army funds. Her conversation, never banal, was remarkable for the way it touched on so many differing subject; a 'gay and smiling talk about bulbs' would suddenly switch to 'the serious discussion of the profoundest subjects of philosophy'.[7] Although her German had an English accent, Putlitz found it delightfully soft. The children would play gaily among themselves, uninhibited by the presence of adults, with none of the shyness which cast a blight over so many previous generations of royal infants.

Such glimpses of Fritz at home demonstrate how perfect his marriage was; 'the older I grow, the more I come to know of human beings, the more I thank God for having given me a wife like mine,' he wrote at this time. 'I trust that God will preserve our peace and domestic happiness. I ask for nothing else.'[8] In character both were so different, but it was an excellent case of two opposites complementing one another. Certainly she had the more dominant personality, but he impressed others by his quiet reflective attitude. While she won their heads, he won their hearts.

On 11 September 1864 Vicky gave birth to their third son Sigismund. That she was more fully her own mistress is shown by the fact that he was the first baby she was allowed to nurse herself; to this recent writers have attributed the intimacy with her five later children throughout their lives (two of which were tragically short) that she never enjoyed with the three elder, who on Queen Augusta's orders were entrusted to wet nurses. Before the birth she had wanted to ask the Prince and Princess of Wales to be godparents, but Queen Victoria advised that the time was not ripe for a reconciliation with the 'conquered party', so the Emperor and Empress of Austria were asked instead.

The Queen's wisdom was proved when Fritz took Vicky for a six weeks' visit to Switzerland after Sigi's christening. On their way back they met the Waleses in Cologne, but Fritz had unfortunately overlooked the fact that his uniform — which he wore because it never occurred to him to wear civilian clothes when meeting a fellow prince — was sporting the war decorations which he had accepted with such reluctance. Quite naturally they felt he was ridiculing them; Bertie wrote afterwards of 'a most objectionable ribbon which he received for his *deeds of valour???* against the unhappy Danes.'[9]

The incident was all the more painful for Fritz and Vicky as they privately agreed with Bertie's remark. On the King's orders, 18 December was declared a day of national thanksgiving for the victory throughout Prussia; church bells pealed at regular intervals, special celebratory church services and military parades were held, decorations were awarded, and a dinner was given in the evening for all princes who had fought in the war, and members of the war cabinet. Fritz's personal feelings overcame his nationalist pride, and he asked his father for permission not to attend. Prusso-Austrian victory over a small power like Denmark was nothing to make a song and dance about. The angry King would not listen to him, but he made his protest all the same. He cut Bismarck dead at the dinner, and sat still when the other guests raised their glasses to toast the Minister's health — a gesture which the cynic noticed with a certain cruel satisfaction.

With Bismarck's all-pervading presence hanging over them at Berlin and Potsdam like a dark cloud, Fritz and Vicky — particularly the latter — searched hard for a place where they could live more informally, away from the trappings of state and the prying servants, many of whom were spies in disguise chosen by Queen Augusta and Bismarck. Vicky discovered the little village of Bornstädt by accident during the autumn, when she was out driving and her coachman took the wrong road from Berlin. The difference between the countryside in which she suddenly found herself, and the busy tense atmosphere of the city, impressed her with the same contrast between London and the carefree Scottish Highlands which had struck her parents before buying their estate at Balmoral in 1852. Exploring the tangled wilderness, the rough track sheltered by woodland, the untrimmed grass and hedges, and the humble cottages which were dilapidated but strangely inviting, she found a little house for sale partly hidden by an avenue of poplars, with broken windows, flaking paint, and an untended garden. By Christmas she and Fritz had bought it, and in the following spring they converted it into a farmhouse. He looked after the management of the land and the labour employed to get it into shape, while she attended to the dairy, poultry-yard and garden. Little had Fritz imagined before his marriage that he would become a part-time farmer, and enjoy the life so much. Unlike the army, it provided something he could share with his family. Tears of joy came to his eyes as he watched the children ride their ponies, chase each other through the trees, or help their mother make butter, living not as princes and princesses but cheerful country youngsters.

It was only a matter of time before they made themselves quite at home in the village. Before they discovered it, its living standards were even more archaic than those at the Berlin Schloss in 1858. Time had stood still for the people who never undressed, tore food apart with their hands, and wrapped their babies in newspaper or rags before placing them on insect-ridden beds of damp straw. Meeting the challenge wholeheartedly, they set to work to show the villagers benefits of modern sanitation and hygiene. Soon they knew everyone, and it was not unusual to see Fritz dressed as an English country squire, strolling along the roads or riding on horseback. What Bismarck had done for the efficiency of the army, he could never have done for Bornstädt — or indeed cared to. For all his royal dignity Fritz possessed the common touch, and delighted in being a father figure to these people, always ready to stop and say good morning, or to enquire after the health of the sick.

Stories of the royal schoolmaster quickly passed into the realms of Prussian folklore. He often visited the village school to listen to the children's lessons, sometimes taking the teacher's place. On one occasion, touching a medal, he asked a little girl to which kingdom it belonged. 'To the mineral kingdom,' she replied. 'And this?' he asked, pointing to a flower. 'To the vegetable kingdom.' 'And I myself: to what kingdom do I belong?' Back came the answer: 'to the kingdom of Heaven.'[10] Another morning, as he was talking to the youngsters and looking at their work, the master was handed a telegram telling him that his mother was seriously ill. With the words 'leave the school to me', Fritz told him to go and look after her, and carried on the lesson until the clergyman arrived to relieve him.[11]

Among the guests who enjoyed hospitality at the cottage in Bornstädt were Fritz Holstein and his brother Christian, both of whom had been maliciously deprived of their property and army commissions by Bismarck. Fritz had championed their cause as long as he could, arguing with his former friend Duncker who had not the courage to stand up to the Minister's wrath, believing that the creation of a new state of Schleswig-Holstein under the Hereditary Prince's rule was the most satisfactory way of maintaining harmony between Prussia and Austria. But Bismarck had different plans; he dismissed the Augustenburg claim by saying that the army had fought for Prussia, not for Duke Frederick, and that to settle the duchies in his favour would encourage other pretenders. The convention of Gastein, signed in August 1865, agreed to the administration of Schleswig by Prussia, and that of Holstein by Austria — a temporary measure if ever there was one.

Fritz and Vicky longed to do something for this ill-treated family. As if by magic, a chance presented itself. Prince Christian, unlike his brother, was a bachelor and spent much of his time at Bornstädt as a family friend, playing with the children like an elder brother and sharing Fritz's cigars; their closeness in age (nine months separated them) and his ability to speak fluent English endeared him to them. Although a good-natured soul — to Vicky he was 'the best creature in the world'[12] — he was hardly the most eligible prince on the European royal market, being bald, rather ugly and penniless. While he pottered around in rustic unemployment at Bornstädt, Queen Victoria was earnestly considering the future of her third daughter Helena, who at nineteen was a girl of intelligence but no real physical attraction and 'wanting in charm'.[13] Such meagre qualifications and her mother's insistence on keeping a married daughter in England limited her prospects, until Vicky suggested Prince Christian. If the two — despite their age difference of fifteen years — liked each other, then he as a pauper would presumably not object to living under the eye of a mother-in-law.

It was arranged that they should 'happen' to meet, like the Prince and Princess of Wales had done at Speyer Cathedral in 1861, at Coburg in August. The anniversary of the Prince Consort's birth date had been chosen for a family reunion and the unveiling of his statue there. It proved a joyless occasion, although it was the first time that all nine brothers and sisters had been together since the wedding in 1858. Fritz and Vicky felt uncomfortable as the terms of Gastein — signed a fortnight earlier — amounted to ill-disguised Prussian plunder, made all the worse as they were helpless to do anything about it. The Prince and Princess of Wales were still smarting over the Danish defeat, and when introduced to Prince Charles Bertie managed to be outwardly civil but Alix defiantly tossed her head and refused to speak to him. Fritz could not blame her, but such incidents did not endear him to his uncles, who never tired of reminding him of his part in introducing a Danish princess into his wife's family. Then Queen Victoria was so incensed at the King's ignoring her letters that she would not go and call on him, or even visit Queen Augusta at Coblenz, let alone invite her to the unveiling. The latter was deeply offended at what she took to be a personal insult. Bismarck would have been beside himself with joy if only he knew how his policies had all but set the once-so-happy family at each others' throats.

Despite the unpleasantness on all sides at the gathering, Christian and Helena were sufficiently taken with each other to realise that if they rejected this chance of marriage they would soon regret it. Notwithstanding the Princess of Wales's pained incredulity at this partisanship of her father's rivals, it was not long before Queen Victoria announced their engagement. In Berlin, too, where it had been believed that Fritz's cousin Albrecht was to marry Helena, the news was received with amazement. Queen Augusta scoffed at the 'poor match', and Bismarck sneered; to him it was just another ridiculous gesture of what he disdainfully called the 'Anglo-Coburg faction'. The faction repaid his scorn. When Vicky wrote to ask what her sister would like for a wedding present, their younger sister Louise provided the answer: 'Bismarck's head on a charger.'[14]

After Fritz's autumn manoeuvres were over he and Vicky paid a visit to England, and on their way stopped at Brussels to see King Leopold. Bedridden, pale and looking all of his seventy-four years, but still as mentally alert as ever, he insisted on getting up to have lunch with them, although he had to lie on a sofa supported by pillows. He talked incessantly about family affairs and politics, glad that Christian and Helena were to be married, and angry with Bismarck's intrigues. He saw through the uneasy peace that Gastein was supposed to have brought, and could tell that it was only one rung of the ladder; where it would end he dreaded to think, but was glad that he would not live long enough to see it. Like the Prince Consort (to whom, they noticed for the first time, he seemed so similar both in looks and speech), he gave them his blessing for the future, seeing in them two greatly-matured honest young people who could do as much as anybody to preserve or restore Prussia's reputation for decency that Bismarck was destroying. Realising sadly that they had seen him for the last time* they continued on their way to London.

For once there was no welcome as they arrived; the country was in mourning for Lord Palmerston, who had just passed away, and the Queen was taking advantage of this excuse for seclusion to make arrangements for Helena's wedding. They stayed at the Prussian Embassy, before going with some trepidation to call on the Prince and Princess of Wales. After considerable pressure from the rest of the family they had become reconciled to the

---

*He died on 10 December, six weeks later.

approaching marriage, but there was more civility than fraternal affection shown. Sandringham was as informal as ever; an enormous stuffed baboon stood in the main hall holding a silver plate for visitors' cards, while acres of woodland and pasture provided a shooting-paradise for Fritz and Bertie, who were out with the guns every day dressed comfortably in their tweeds. But it was a relief for all four when the visit was over.

It was not until early the following year that Queen Victoria realised how dependent the King was on Bismarck, recently raised to the rank of Count. She wrote to William suggesting that Christian and Helena should be allowed to spend part of their honeymoon at Gravenstein Castle, one of the properties in the duchies which had been confiscated from the Augustenburgs. The King had fallen into the lazy habit of passing on all his correspondence, even family letters, to his Minister, and as often as not the latter dictated his master's replies. Such was the case in February 1866, and the Queen was furious at the rude reply she received. It was left to Vicky to defend him; as she pointed out, her father-in-law was 'by nature so kindhearted, easy and amiable'[15] before he fell into Bismarck's clutches. But the Queen did not pursue the question, for suddenly there were more pressing matters than honeymoon arrangements.

By March it was clear that Bismarck's boasts about war with Austria were no idle threat. Austria was traditionally regarded as the major European power, and he had secretly bided his time for the day when he could contest this. The vague terms of the Gastein convention would give him what he needed. Like Fritz, Francis Joseph was unhappy about the partitioning of Schleswig and Holstein, and after a few months' consideration he too suggested that they should be handed over to Fritz Holstein after all. The matter was referred to the Diet at Frankfurt, where the representatives endorsed the Augustenburg claim, thereby overruling the agreement of August 1865.

Bismarck was pleased, as events were playing into his hands. But would his colleagues support him in his desire for war? Roon and Moltke, now Chief of Staff, did, but they knew Fritz did not. Despite his voluntary absence from the council meetings, and the contempt in which many members of the Conservative parties held him, Fritz still had some influence left. The moderate and progressive groups had never ceased to applaud him since Danzig; only the *Kreuzzeitung* adherents and most fervent Bismarck-worshippers allowed their distrust of his liberal views to outweigh their respect for his military talents. This influence had to be destroyed as far as possible if Bismarck was going to wage war a second time, and the most effective way of doing this was the simplest. To all those who did know Fritz personally, and were therefore not in a position to know better, Bismarck set about ruthlessly denigrating him. His remarks to Count

Crown Prince and Princess Frederick William and family, 1865. Children l. to r.: Princess Charlotte; Prince William; Prince Sigismund (in father's arms); Prince Henry

Benedetti of France, that the Crown Prince 'occupies himself with politics which he does not understand, talks of things of which he knows nothing, and opens books which he does not read,'[16] were a typical example. To those who did know him the Minister callously drew the picture of a man henpecked by a power-drunk, ruthless wife. Much as he hated Vicky, he feared the liberal influence she had on her husband. The slander was a damaging one as Fritz had a reputation in his family for being mild and easily-swayed, and the distorted image of Vicky as a dangerous virago was therefore such a credible one that it has survived to the present day.

The King wanted peace so badly that he asked his son to write to Queen Victoria, saying that he would accept any offer of mediation her government would care to make. Fritz was overjoyed as he wrote to his mother-in-law, believing that war was good as averted. Vicky sent a letter at the same time, stressing that Austria had done nothing to offend the majority of Prussians, and that the only ones to want war were Bismarck and the *Kreuzeitung*. Bismarck did not know that Fritz was writing, she added excitedly. But she was too optimistic, for when he found out he was livid. So the King wanted peace; then his paternal and fraternal instincts must be overcome. The old man was fond of Fritz in his own way, but he was so used to quarrelling with his wife that there seemed to be nothing unusual in doing the same with their son. That their son never enjoyed rows, and grew to dislike them more as he became older, was quite beyond the horizons of William's limited imagination. Bismarck's solution was to rake up memories of Danzig, and lament Fritz's championship of the Augustenburgs, making out that he was working against Prussian interests, and therefore a traitor; how terrible, he would say with tears in his eyes, it must be for His Majesty to have such a son and heir. The Count had no scruples about resorting to such tactics when they suited his ends, and his cruel efforts to turn father against son had no little success. The King's reluctance to fight his fellow-sovereign Francis Joseph was no problem; was it not treachery of him to wish to make the duchies independent, a view totally contrary to both Prussian policy and the Gastein convention? He was so persuasive that the King, bristling at Austria's perfidy, was all for saddling up his charger and going to war at once. Bismarck had to restrain him — Prussia was not yet ready.

In the meantime Count Guido Usedom, the Prussian Ambassador in Florence, was taking advantage of Italy's dormant dispute with Austria over the ownership of Venetia, Habsburg domination of which was an obstacle to Italian unity. An alliance was signed in April, in which Italy had inserted a clause stating that, although the country would follow suit if and when Prussia declared war, the alliance would automatically expire if war was not declared within three months. Bismarck therefore had to act quickly. By the treaty he had effectively destroyed the German Confederation, the constitution of which forbade any of its members to ally themselves with a foreign power against another. If he did not strike at once, then Prussia would be taken to task for flouting the Confederation's peaceful co-existence.

Fritz and Vicky were living in a perpetual state of alarm and excitement; being informed of next to nothing through official channels, they could never be certain whether war would be declared or not, until the moment came. The suspense soon told on the latter. On the morning of 12 April she took the train from Berlin to Potsdam so that her confinement, expected in a week's time, could take place at the Neue Palais. On the journey her labour pains began. The train was unable to accelerate as there was another immediately ahead on the same line. She was taken from the carriage in a state of collapse by her ladies and hurried into the palace, where she gave birth to a daughter a few hours later. Nothing was ready, and the baby had to be wrapped in an old flannel petticoat. To the profound relief of all the little princess was none the worse for having arrived so unexpectedly, and a delighted Fritz telegraphed to his mother-in-law that Vicky was 'happily delivered from a strong and healthy daughter'[17] — an error of grammar which amused both proud grandmother and telegraph clerk. Princess Frederica Amelia Wilhelmina Victoria was christened on 24 May, and was always to be known as Princess Victoria in honour of the fact that it was the Queen's birthday.

By now war was just around the corner. In the first week of May Queen Victoria declared to Fritz that she had written enough to his father, and all her pleading and warning was having no effect. Lord Clarendon, the Foreign Minister, knowing that Bismarck wielded more power than his sovereign, insisted that the British government could do nothing; it was up to the Queen, if she so wished, to use her influence. The pacifist Liberal majority in the Prussian *Landtag* suggested an European conference, but the Queen said that neither she nor her government would take part in any proceedings which would allow Prussia to annex the duchies, and the idea collapsed.

It was a hard decision for her to take, for she wanted peace as much as Fritz and Vicky did. They all knew the war would divide the family far more thoroughly than the Danish conflict had done; already their German relations were taking sides. Supporting Austria were the Grand Duke of Hesse and his nephew Louis, Vicky's brother-in-law; the blind King George of Hanover and his family; and the Duke of Coburg, who in the end remained neutral. Ready to draw the sword on behalf of Bismarck was Louis's brother Henry, who had served with the Prussian army for several years, and was in command of the Second Lancers.

Looking at Vicky's grim expression, her ill-concealed trembling, and the anxious faces of the elder children at his daughter's christening in the

Friedenskirche at Potsdam, Fritz could not keep his mind on the ceremony. Inwardly he prayed that this new campaign would be short, and that his relations would be spared; how could he and Vicky ever look Alice in the face if Louis was killed? In command of the 120,000-strong Silesian army, he left for left for active service later that week. On 14 June, the same day as he and his army established their headquarters at the fortress of Neisse, the Frankfurt Diet voted for the mobilisation of the Federal Army to fight for Austria.

Four days later, just as Fritz and his troops were about to march south into Silesia, Queen Augusta journeyed to the front, her set white face contrasting strangely with her black dress. She had come to tell him that Sigi, at the age of twenty-one months, had succumbed to meningitis. He had been suffering from cerebral convulsions for a couple of days, but Wegner and the royal doctors had followed the forces to the front. Vicky had been driven frantic, and her grief at the loss of the 'little sunbeam in the house'[18] — the sight of his toys scattered around the cot, his clothes which she had lovingly made, the memories of his helpless struggle as he screamed for his distracted mother to soothe him — had touched even the cold-hearted Queen. In her undemonstrative manner she had been fond of her fair-haired grandson, and she sensed the loss that his father would feel.

The bereavement indeed hit Fritz heavily. For several hours, he was suddenly not just a commander about to lead his army into battle against a brother German nation, but instead a stricken father who had been called away on business and was denied the chance to rush home and comfort his weeping wife, which he longed to do. With a feeling akin to horror, he realised the tragic irony of the boy's death; it had happened just as he was about to attack the country of his godparents.

Suppressing his feelings, he busied himself in his duties, reconnoitring the ground and planning the route they were to take into Austria, but his soldiers could see the silent look of suffering on his face. On 27 June, the Silesian army won their first victory at Nachod. Fritz was a model commander, maintaining his composure under heavy enemy fire, and giving his men words of encouragement. At the end of the day, after the Austrian forces had been driven back, he overcame his physical and mental exhaustion long enough to visit the wounded in the field hospitals with words of comfort.

On 2 July, roused to enthusiasm by his son's success, the King arrived at Gitschin in Bohemia to assume supreme command. The combined forces of his men and the army of the Elbe, under Prince Frederick Charles, met the Austrian troops under General Benedek on the plain near the town of Königgrätz the following day, and a message was sent to Fritz to bring up his troops at once for an all-out attack. Until his arrival soon after midday, victory hung in the balance; by the evening over 40,000 Austrians had been killed, wounded or taken prisoner, and the remainder of the army was in retreat. On the Prussian side, the casualties were less than 10,000.

After the fighting was over, Fritz came face to face with his father — a moving moment for both, as the King presented him with Order *Pour le mérite*, an honour only conferred for personal gallantry on the field of battle. It was the first decoration he could honestly feel he had earned, and in his emotion he fell to his knee and kissed his father's hand, tears blinding his eyes. In the exultation of victory and the weariness at the end of a hard task well accomplished, both forgot the personal differences which had so bitterly divided them.

With such a decisive triumph behind them, Fritz was looking forward to peace. Spending up to thirteen hours a day on horseback and directing operations of the battlefield, with gunfire roaring in his ears and dead or wounded soldiers everywhere he looked, was not a life he relished. 'War is an appalling thing,' he wrote in his diary in the evening after Königgrätz, 'and the man who brings it about with a stroke of his pen at the green table little reeks what he is conjuring.'[19] He presumably had Bismarck in mind.

The war was now effectively over. The King intended Fritz and his men to pursue the defeated army towards Olmütz, where it was retreating, but Fritz regarded this as courting disaster; the more he became separated from the remainder of the Prussian troops, the less likely he was to win a battle on his own if cornered. There was nothing for him to do but to wait at his headquarters for the council of war, which was called on 23 July. The King wanted to continue the campaign, following the Austrian troops to Vienna and annihilating them there if necessary, until he found himself in a minority. He then capitulated — so peace was to be concluded, but what was the victor's prize to be? To him, victory meant one thing: gains in territory. He could not see Bismarck's point of view, that it would not do to antagonise Austria unduly by depriving her of land, in case she was needed to help fight France or some other power in the future. All the Count had intended was to expel Austria from the German Confederation, leaving Prussia as the undisputed superior power. When he saw the single-mindedness of the King threatening to undo his long-term plans he stormed out of the council chamber, growling with rage, threatening to resign one moment, to throw himself out of the window the next. In his fury he hardly cared what he said.

The situation was retrieved by Fritz, who placed his hand fraternally on the Minister's shoulder as he stood staring angrily out of the window. Reminding him that he had never wanted the war in the first place, he was ready to support any plans for peace. Bismarck inwardly cursed himself for having to rely on his personal enemy, but it had to be done. Fritz went at once to see his father, and in the course of half an hour's heated discussion won his case. The King gave in, compelled 'to bite into this sour apple and accept a disgraceful peace.'[20]

Having seen the preliminaries of peace signed on 26 July Fritz returned home. Physically and mentally very tired, he was pleased to be on his way. He broke his journey at the Friedenskirche in Potsdam, where nearly three months before his youngest daughter had been christened, and a month later his son buried; his tears flowed freely as he looked at the little grave. Already he was being feted as the hero of Königgrätz, but it was a title he would gladly exchange for the return of the little boy to whom he had never said goodbye. Victories could not compensate for the loss of a child, he wrote; 'in the midst of great events, the more sharply does such a piercing grief wound a father's heart.'[21]

Vicky had taken the children to Heringsdorf, a village on the shores of the Baltic, to escape an outbreak of cholera at Potsdam. It was in the woods nearby, as she watched the children playing under the summer sun, that he joined them. For both, it was a reunion of mingled feelings; both had changed. He had grown his beard again (which he now kept for good), and looked thinner and more serious, not to say older. Sorrow had aged her too, and so had the endless round of nursing into which she had plunged herself to stop brooding.

Happy as they were at being reunited, they could not be certain that peace would last. A few days before Königgrätz, Fritz had written to her that he heartily hoped it would be the last war he would experience. But he knew Bismarck too well not to be able to appreciate the foresight in her letter written on the day of the battle: 'Who knows whether we may not have to wage a third war in order to keep what we have now won?'[22]

CHAPTER 9

Peace With Uncertainty, 1866-69.

Peace was formally signed at Prague on 22 August 1866. The punishments Bismarck inflicted on the pro-Austrian states were severe, considering that he was now free to achieve his aim of annexing Schleswig and Holstein. To these he added Hanover, whose ex-King George had fled to England in June,* and the landgraviate of Hesse-Homburg, which had belonged to the Grand Duke of Hesse. It was only thanks to his having the Tsar as a brother-in-law that saved his title and the rest of his land. As Fritz had to admit, it was the sad consequence of going to war on behalf of the loser, but the fact that his relatives on the English side had suffered so badly placed him in a difficult position. His discomfort was made worse by the behaviour of some of the Prussian soldiers. The majority marched home peacefully, but an irresponsible fringe made the most of their victory. In Frankfurt, one of the towns gained from Hesse, soldiers treated themselves to free cab rides, clothes, jewellery and food, ordering them to be charged to the Hesse government account. It not only drove the little state into bankruptcy, but also the Burgomaster to hang himself in despair.

What alarmed Fritz more than anything else was the effect that Prussian — or rather Bismarckian — greed would have on his personal, as well as his country's, reputation with his wife's family. Queen Victoria understood; so did Christian Holstein, and therefore Helena; so, to a limited extent, did the Duke of Coburg. But would the rest of them believe that he was not among those who were acquiescing in the brutal plunder? As he rode on horseback in the triumphal entry of the troops into Berlin in September, his thoughts were less on the victory honours than on hope that his in-laws would not judge him by the Minister-President.

It was with both optimism and apprehension that he went to St Petersburg in October to represent Prussia at the wedding of the Tsarevich, later Alexander III. Vicky was glad to make the sacrifice of the temporary separation as she waved him goodbye, for the Prince of Wales was going as well. She sensed that the Russian court would make a fuss of her brother and encourage his dislike of Bismarckian Prussia, already begun so effectively by Princess Alexandra, if Fritz was not there. For the bride was none other

*Where he died in 1878, aged fifty-nine.

than Princess Dagmar of Denmark, Alix's younger sister. All King Christian's children had a strong sense of family loyalty, and never forgave Prussia for depriving him of Schleswig and Holstein.

On one count Vicky was right. Bertie was the more enthusiastically-feted of the two in Russia; the Tsarevich met him personally at the station on arrival, which he had not bothered to do for Fritz two days earlier. But the brothers-in-law got on much better than Fritz had dared to hope. The Prince of Wales had been to visit Vicky in Berlin on his way, and had observed something of her helpless position. Having always loved and understood his sister, he saw through the emotional letters that Queen Victoria showed him, with their vitriolic condemnations of Bismarck in one line and glowing praise for Prussian troops in the next. A brief visit to Berlin confirmed his suspicions; the quarrelsome family and the absolutist Count were impossible to live with and keep a cool head. Over champagne and caviar at the palace of Tsarskoe-Selo Bertie found in Fritz the same gentle, war-abhorring fellow who had acted as his best man, and whose medal-flaunting at Cologne the previous year had been no more than tactless oversight.

Fritz's success with one fellow-heir did not attend his meeting with the other. After the wedding he drove with the Tsarevich through the brilliantly-illuminated streets of St Petersburg. The latter, clad in Cossack uniform, 'never said a single sensible word, even when he did open his mouth.'[1] Although they were second cousins, Alexander was by nature a suspicious character who did not yet know his guest well enough to see through his relationship with Bismarck, against whom like his bride he bore a grudge for the conquest of Denmark. It was an uncomfortable ride which did not finish a moment too soon for either.

Soon after his return to Berlin, Fritz saw how fragile the state of peace was; by March 1867 the possibility of open conflict was looming once more. This time Luxembourg was the centre of controversy. The Grand Duchy was under the sovereignty of the King of Holland, at the same time belonging to the North German Confederation created by the treaties signed by the pro-Austrian states after the war, with the King of Prussia in control of all the armed forces. Napoleon saw it as a potential conquest for France, at a time when the Prussians had achieved victory in two short successive wars and were challenging the French for European supremacy. The inhabitants of Luxembourg did not regard themselves as Germans although the territory was used as a Prussian fortress, and King William III of Holland would jump at the chance of renouncing his sovereignty over it in return for the settlement of his debts. Bismarck was not concerned on his own account, as he did not consider the state worth fighting over. Its value as a fortress was minimal, and some other area could be found just as easily.

But Fritz was not to know this; he sensed that the Count was planning to go to war with France sooner or later. The King, still living in the twilight of his father's defeat at the hands of Bonaparte, would threaten to abdicate (seriously for once) rather than hand over one of his fortresses to France. Before long war was being talked of openly in Berlin, and experience had taught Fritz that rumour was more often than not followed quickly by mobilisation. Moltke and Roon were both eager for a new campaign, seeing a chance to nip Napoleon's European prestige in the bud just as his precarious Mexican empire, under Emperor Francis Joseph's romantically-inclined brother Maximilian, was crumbling. Fritz, like Vicky, believed with some misgivings that it would be more honourable to fight than let France take the duchy, but both of them joined in the sighs of relief when the sabre-rattling died down. With the new Confederation in its infancy, Bismarck was not ready for another war, and in the end an European conference agreed to the withdrawal of the Prussian garrison and the neutrality of Luxembourg; France was left with a feeling of humiliation and a bitter distrust of the Count.

Nevertheless peace was cemented, temporarily at least, by the congregation of royalties in Paris at the International Exhibition in the early summer. Apart from Fritz, Vicky, the King and Queen, almost everyone who was anyone was there. The Prince of Wales (leaving the rheumatic Princess behind), Alice and Louis, the Austrian Emperor and the Tsar, even the Sultan of Turkey, were among the more illustrious who examined wares displayed by over 50,000 exhibitors. Few sensed the shadows of the ominous Krupp cannon from Essen, each weighing fifty tons and capable of firing shells twice the weight of ordinary artillery. To those who did not suspect that they were witnessing the imperial sunset, Krupp's work was just one exhibit out of many. Only in the minds of Bismarck and Moltke, taking 'quiet strategic walks around Paris',[2] lay the key to the future. But their thoughts were unperceived by the other guests, who when not wandering around the stands in the Champs de Mars, sampled the weekly gala performances at the Paris Opera, mingled with the crowds enjoying the sunshine in the Tuileries, or whiled away the hours over a carafe of wine at the open-air cafés.

Fritz struggled to enjoy himself. Paris made a pleasant change from the ultra-martial atmosphere pervading Berlin, but he found it hard to treat the festivities as more than a rather superficial pantomime. Much as he liked the company of Napoleon and Eugenie, who were born hosts, he felt he could never really trust them. Their furtive alliances with Italy, and the recent Luxembourg affair, made many a German politician uneasy, and he suspected that the exhibition was a smokescreen for some further menacing activity.

But Vicky enjoyed herself even less; her heart was just not in the visit. The last time she had been in Paris as a guest of the Emperor and Empress, 'beloved papa' had been there as well. What would she not have given for him to be still alive, she asked herself bitterly, as she stoically endured the suffocating ballrooms till all hours. There were other reasons for her sudden depression. She was pregnant again, and in such a condition the agony of Sigi's death returned to her. Would he still be a chuckling, bright-eyed youngster, romping at home with his brothers and sisters, if the doctors had not been called away to the battlefront? Whose war had it been anyway? The sight of that jovial monster Bismarck, a glass of wine in one hand, an ostentatious cigar in the other, and a joke perpetually on his lips, made her blood run cold. This, and the criticisms from her in-laws — that she had brought a much smaller trousseau to Paris than any of them, that she found night after night of dancing exhausting, and that she showed more interest in the stalls displaying surgical instruments (fanned by her work for the wounded during the wars at home) — were more than she could take. One evening, just before another of those tiresome balls, she begged Fritz to be allowed to go home, With a heavy heart he asked the King who snorted that she could wait another few days. Defiantly she ordered her maids to pack and left for Germany that night, leaving Fritz to face his father's wrath alone.

He returned home a few days later to a Berlin that seemed even more unbearable. The 'long and apparently cordial' conversations[3] that he had in public with Bismarck were part of a facade that deceived everybody but a select few. The Count wanted nothing more than to have his future sovereign in his clutches, and to this end he managed to close in on him most effectively. King William argued with his Minister-President sometimes, but on the whole he was content to leave the details of government to him. At least they shared politically Conservative views as well as a sense of the greatness of Prussia and their clashes, such as the one over the victory spoils in 1866, were few and far between. Why, Bismarck asked himself, could the Crown Prince not be won over? They had some common ground, which was useful at the right time — for example, when Fritz had to explain to his father that Austrian friendship was worth preserving — but his respect for the constitution and his doggedly liberal views were disquieting.

When he discovered that what he regarded as Fritz's 'subversion' (such as the speech at Danzig) was no mere passing phase, he vindictively decided to punish him and carefully isolate him as far as possible from his political allies. In his eyes the prime culprit was Vicky, of whom he was secretly more afraid than he liked to admit. Before his rise to power he had heard her spoken of as a determined and curiously intelligent young woman, and it was with a sense of shock that he discovered she really was; her political acumen was extraordinary not to say frightening, and with her ability to argue she was a match for him, let alone anyone else. That she was a woman made it all the more unnatural, and he saw that it was largely her influence that prevented him from making a disciple of her husband. His smear campaign against her, one of the most thorough and long-lasting ever mounted against any historical figure, was his means of revenge, and also his way of destroying what little respect her in-laws had for her. By 1867 her children were universally pitied for having such a mother, with her 'unfortunate English ideas and unPrussian views'.[4] It was in addition an attempt to reduce her influence on Fritz.

At the same time he began a devious scheme of isolating them both from their most trusted friends in Prussia, namely those whom next to her he most feared. They included Morier, Prince Hohenzollern (still a generally-respected figure despite his resignation as Minister-President in 1862), and Baron von Roggenbach, the Liberal Prussian representative at Frankfurt who remained a staunch friend of Vicky in her widowhood years later. Bismarck's scheme was the simple one of planting spies in the Neue Palais; whenever a vacancy appeared in the household, he and his crony Moritz Busch found somebody to fill the position, after having groomed them to watch their employers carefully, and to report back faithfully on anything they saw or heard that might be of interest. By the time of the Paris Exhibition two of these trained 'servants' were established in the accounts department at Potsdam, and thus gave Bismarck the key to finding out just what Fritz and Vicky spent. The other staff reported obligingly on who visited the palace. Fritz had to stop inviting Morier, a tactful move which fostered the impression that the diplomat had fallen out with his royal friend. The only alternative was to risk his expulsion from Prussia on some trumped-up Bismarckian charge of interference; he was still a welcome guest at Bornstädt, where he came regularly with the utmost discretion. It was he who warned Fritz and Vicky to take the greatest care in all they did at the palace. They must be careful what they said to each other unless certain they were alone and nobody was listening at the door, he said, and must not write anything remotely inflammatory even in a 'private' diary except in cipher; Vicky had found her desk smelling of unfamiliar tobacco, or with the lock broken, too often not to know that dirty work was afoot.

Vicky gave birth to their youngest son on 10 February 1868, her mother's wedding anniversary. He was called Waldemar, after some discussion with Fritz who insisted on the name Joachim being added. He would have chosen it as the main name if she had not told him she could not bear it.[5]

In April, shortly after the boy's christening, Fritz was sent to Rome for the wedding of Crown Prince Humbert to Princess Margharita of Naples; he went reluctantly as he was recovering from influenza at the time. Knowing how much he liked Italy, Bismarck would have almost certainly chosen somebody else to go if Fritz had been in good health; he observed that the latter was prone to illness in the winter, and in a country where princes were expected to be spartan, recurrent attacks of bronchitis or pneumonia kept him in bed several days at a time in bitter weather. He was not as robust as the King, who was much less affected by coughs and colds than he pretended to be. Moreover it was part of his punishment, and a means of keeping him away from his wife's influence, to send him to all corners of Europe as Prussia's representative. If Fritz ever protested, Bismarck produced the trump card by appealing to his love for his father.

He therefore had to make the best of a bad job. His depression was soon dispelled by the rousing reception given him; everywhere he appeared there were cries of '*Evviva Prussia, l'angelo protettore d'Italia!*', while the press made much of his constant smile and martial bearing. As a result of her defeat Austria had been forced to cede Venetia to Italy, and a grateful King Victor Emmanuel conferred upon him the Grand Cross of the Military Order of Merit of Savoy, in recognition of his services to Italian unity. In every garrison town he visited on his journey, he passed along the lines of troops to thank the officers personally, dutifully ignoring his cold and braving the almost incessant rain.

When Prince Napoleon, the French Emperor's detested cousin 'Plon-plon' appeared, the cold reception given him underlined Fritz's popularity, for Italy like Germany grew to distrust French territorial ambitions more every year. Bismarck had known that Napoleon would also be at the wedding, and this provided him with another good reason for sending Fritz. Both princes had been friends for several years, and therefore would be seen together. What better way was there of giving an impression to the rest of Europe that the present peace between Germany and France would be a lasting one? It was a cunning trick that deceived the Italian press at least. They privately agreed that they wanted to preserve peace, although they knew that their countries' policies were beyond their control.

After the wedding Fritz attended a court ball, where another incident occurred that has become legendary. Princess Margharita was dancing with a banker's son, who accidentally stepped on her gown and tore the trimming. Gasps of horror which ran through the ballroom turned to astonishment as Fritz instantly produced a case from his coat pocket and took out a pair of scissors. Kneeling down, he cut off the torn strip of lace. The wide-eyed Princess held out her hand to take it back, but instead he pressed it to his heart, then folded it and put it back in his pocket with the scissors. 'He is a true knight,' murmured the amazed onlookers, but a Stuttgart press reporter was less poetic: 'These Prussians are sharp fellows, always armed, and ready for everything.'[6]

The following January Willy celebrated his tenth birthday. Like Fritz and his forebears, he was awarded the Order of the Black Eagle and appointed Lieutenant in the First Regiment of Guards. A photograph of him standing proudly in his uniform shows his left arm looking almost normal, the hand holding a glove with no apparent awkwardness. To a casual observer it might seem that he was physically sound. Only on probing deeper would one know that the picture was a tribute to both the work of the tailor who made the left sleeve slightly shorter than the right, and to the boy's tenacity in doing his best to overcome the handicap. By this time the arm had proved that all the medical treatment and machinery to which he had been subjected were in vain. He could not run fast, climb trees, or cut his food with normal cutlery. Because he had a distorted sense of balance, learning to ride — a necessity for a future King of Prussia — was an arduous process which in its early stages made him scream with terror as he struggled to keep his seat.

Yet his natal injury need not have made him the man he became, if it had not been for the disastrous choice of his tutor. On Morier's advice his parents appointed George Hinzpeter when Willy was seven. The diplomat recommended this stern, humourless disciplinarian with boundless confidence in himself and his ideas, who was to prove just as incapable of understanding children — let alone handicapped ones — as Baron Stockmar, who had cast such a shadow over the Prince of Wales's formative years. His reasons for putting Hinzpeter forward lay in the political and economic views the two men shared; that these had precious little to do with the upbringing of children appears to have escaped Morier. Hinzpeter's principles as a governor were based on what he termed Prussian simplicity, which Fritz and Vicky believed would stop 'that terrible Prussian pride and ambition which grieved dear Papa (the Prince Consort) so.'[7] They were wrong, for while condemning personal pride, he constantly held up to his charges* the example of their mighty country and her superiority to all others, at a time when Bismarck was making a mockery of the principles of democratic government and advancing her prestige with the sword. The tutor's other ideas make one shudder; the boys spent twelve hours a day at their lessons, with only breaks for meals and physical exercise. For breakfast they ate dried bread, and when entertaining visitors for tea they had to offer their guests cakes without taking any themselves. Henry apparently suffered no lasting ill-effects, but the spartan regime left its mark on Willy. It was also from Hinzpeter that he learnt to ride. The governor lifted him onto his horse without stirrups, time and time again, ignoring his wails and entreaties to stop, until he learnt to stay on. Yet the end scarcely justified the means; it is not too much to believe that this cruelty permanently warped the boy's mind.[8]

---

*Henry was also entrusted to his care at the age of seven.

How often it has been said or written that the future Emperor William's unstable personality was largely due to his mother's obstinate attempts to bring him up in the image of her beloved father. One recent example speaks of her 'fighting down her violent resentment of the undoubted fact that Willy had not turned out to be another Prince Albert'.[9] This argument has been given added weight by her less guarded outbursts to her mother that she hoped he would grow up as unlike the rest of the Prussian royal family — his father excepted — as possible.[10] Yet the finger of accusation should be pointed at Hinzpeter and Bismarck instead.

Were Fritz and Vicky really so blind to the tutor's faults? They knew him well enough personally, and although they found him a stiff and unfriendly character, it did not occur to them that his unbending attitude was anything but a praiseworthy quality in a princes' tutor. Fritz had been entrusted to a governor at the same age, and soon established a cordial relationship with him; so, strangely, did Willy in time. If he ever feared that he and Vicky had chosen the wrong man, he did not realise it until the damage was done. This stemmed not so much from their shortcomings in understanding Willy, who as a deformed child they found difficult to judge by normal standards, as from the isolation in which Bismarck had effectively placed them. They had very few people whom they could consult, firstly on the choice of a governor, and secondly on how good or how bad he was for the boys, once appointed. The only people they could trust enough to ask were Morier and young Stockmar, who had just resigned as their secretary. The latter was the more perceptive of the two, and had his doubts about the suitability of Hinzpeter, 'a hard Spartan idealist', but fear of being accused of meddling held him back from speaking his mind. If only he had had the courage to express his misgivings, Willy might have grown up into a very much better man and monarch.

In September 1869 Fritz was obliged to play pawn to Bismarck again, this time to attend the opening of the Suez canal. Having spent the summer on his tour of inspection, away from Vicky and the children — who needed a father's discipline as they became older — he would have preferred to spend the autumn at home. But Bismarck resorted to his usual devious tactics; he did not tell him to go in so many words, but stressing that it was either him or his father, he dwelt at length on Fritz's sense of duty, the old man's age, and the heat of Egypt — and Fritz had no choice. He guessed something of the political implications of his mission; Francis Joseph, the Emperor Napoleon and the Empress Eugenie would be there as well, and it was a heaven-sent opportunity of feigning Prussia's peaceful intentions, especially as he was known to be a man of peace. It was tasks such as this that made him clench his fists with anger as he realised how helpless he was when being used in such a way. Bismarck was using him as a symbol of pacifism whilst he was probably plotting the very opposite. That he was never taken into the Count's confidence only made his position worse.

Fritz departed for Vienna in October, leaving Vicky behind; she would have gone too had it not been for the extra expense, and the prospect of several months away from the children. With him instead went Prince Louis of Hesse. Bismarck knew that the Austrian Emperor was perpetually on Fritz's conscience, and saw a ready-made reconciliation within grasp between Austria and Prussia. Dressed elegantly in Prussian uniform, Francis Joseph received Fritz warmly and exchanged 'words of old friendship',[11] but kept off the subject of politics. Yet it was an encouraging sign seeing that he did not know Fritz well enough to realise how little influence he wielded at court, and found it commonsense not to trust either him or Bismarck too much after 1866. Nevertheless the Emperor's cousin Archduke Albrecht told Fritz they recognised that he had only done his duty as Prussian Crown Prince. Were the Minister-President's designs already being seen through by his neighbours?

After leaving Vienna distinctly cheered by the steps he had taken towards reconciliation, Fritz took the chance to indulge in some interesting travel for the first time since the autumn of 1862. The tourist in him came to the fore as he strolled around Brindisi, Corfu and Troy, pondering on their associations with ancient civilisations that were mere schoolroom legends to those less fortunate than himself. While doing so he picked up seashells and other keepsakes which he would always treasure. At Constantinople he was a guest of the Sultan, who had recently ceded to Prussia the site of a monastery belonging to the Knights of St John in Jerusalem, later converted into a German Protestant church and hospital. From there he went to Jerusalem early in November. As he rode through the narrow streets the brightly-robed monks and Jews lined his path, gazing at their visitor as though he was a deity. With fascination he followed a group of clergymen around the church of the Holy Sepulchre; among other things he was shown the sword that had belonged to Godfrey of Bouillon, the crusader elected King of Jerusalem in 1099, but to his escorts' surprise treated it less as a holy relic than as a weapon, picking it up and giving it 'a true military flourish'.[12] At sunset that evening he climbed the minaret of the Mosque at the Mount of Olives, an occasion he never forgot. Here 'that wondrous peace of Nature supervened which even in any other place has a solemn character of its own,' he wrote afterwards. 'To read over again one's favourite passages in the Gospels at such a place is in itself an act of worship.'[13] On the Sunday he received Holy Communion in the Christ Church, and then attended the ceremony which formally granted his country possession of the monastery site the Sultan had given. After the city governor had handed him the keys he gave orders for the Prussian coat-of-arms to be fastened to the entrance gate. This was followed by a short speech and the signing of the cession deed, officially witnessed by the Consul-General and the Pasha.

From Jerusalem he passed through Beirut and on to Damascus, one of the most attractive cities on his journey. Here the white houses, mosques and minarets, surrounded by a mile-wide ring of green groves with oranges and citrons, suggested to him the image of 'a pearl set with emeralds'.[14] He enjoyed himself walking around the bazaar, even though the merchants soon saw through his attempted incognito. For the first time on his travels he saw hardly anyone in European costume, or even modern Turkish dress; 'so that we feel ourselves in the East indeed!'[15] That evening he was paid a most unusual honour. He had just returned to his quarters when the master of the house asked him to act as best man at the wedding of his fifteen-year-old daughter, an invitation he felt most privileged to accept.

He reached Suez on 16 November to be greeted by the Empress Eugenie clad gaily in her naval officer's cap and blue veil, her dress looped up high enough to show off a pair of bright yellow leggings. The 'blessing of the canal', conducted with formal addresses from the Mohammedan Ullemah and a Roman Catholic priest, was followed a day later by the formal opening. The Khedive of Egypt led the procession with Eugenie, Francis Joseph, Fritz and Prince Henry of the Netherlands (in that order), on separate ships with their private suites, followed by a number of smaller vessels.

And what of the planned political fraternity? Bismarck could not have arranged it better if he had been there himself. After the opening the group of royalties was photographed. One picture showed Fritz between Francis Joseph and Eugenie, the latter with her hand on his arm. Bismarck longed to slap his Crown Prince heartily on the back as he smiled at the portrait — what a superb impression of Franco-Prussian friendship and goodwill. He ensured that it was printed in as many newspapers as possible.

The next week Fritz visited various ruins in the plain of Thebes, and with some amusement rode through the desert on a camel. In Cairo he laid the foundation stone of an Evangelical church which was about to be built, and ascended the pyramid of Gizeh. But unlike most Europeans of the age who visited Egypt, he found it an anti-climax; it belonged 'to those things that one undertakes for the sake of saying one has done them, but which otherwise makes no claim to utility or pleasure.'[16] To him there was something tedious about the ritual of being harnessed to a couple of Arabs and then being pulled up the staircase step by step. Perhaps he would not have been so jaded had Vicky been with him. His travels as far as Jerusalem and Port Said had given him pleasure, but now the canal was opened and he had done his duty. With every day spent in Africa he missed her more, and to each new place he went he found himself longing for her beside him, to share these strange new lands that would have had her perpetually at her sketching book.

From Alexandria on the North African coast he sailed to Naples, and then Cannes where Vicky had been enjoying the Mediterranean air with Alice for the last few weeks. Together they enjoyed the happiest Christmas they had yet known, with both Bismarck and Berlin miles away, and Fritz regaled them all with a day-to-day account of his travels. On 26 December they reached Paris and called upon the Emperor Napoleon, but were alarmed to find him 'changed and ailing and much dejected'.[17]

Had they been able to foresee the situation which would exist in the months ahead, they would have doubtless shared his dejection.

CHAPTER 10

Birth of The German Empire, 1870-71.

Ever since the treaty of Prague Fritz had lived in continual dread of a third war; he could see that Bismarck was just biding his time, allowing the North German Confederation and its mutual alliance to mature before drawing the sword against France. Being kept in ignorance as much as ever about political affairs, he could only guess at what the statesman was up to. After he and Vicky returned to Berlin at the beginning of 1870, they found themselves plunged yet again into the never-ending round of *soirees*. Standing in overheated and overcrowded rooms for up to five consecutive hours, night after night, left him looking persistently pale and tired.[1] Vicky was the only one with any sympathy for him; the robust King and Queen were blind to the strain it placed on his health, and contemptuous of all appeals to spare him a little. At length he was sent on medical advice to the spa at Carlsbad; while regaining his strength and drinking the waters in the bracing air there, he little guessed that the storm was about to break.

In 1868 the childless Queen Isabella of Spain had been forced to abdicate, and the Prime Minister Marshal Prim set his sights on Leopold, a younger son of Prince Hohenzollern. After the Prince had discussed his son's candidature with a few respected friends, including Fritz, he wanted nothing to do with such a potentially unstable throne in a country of which they knew nothing. As far as he and Leopold were concerned, Prim was now free to approach the Wittelsbach candidates next on his list. At this stage all negotiations between the Spanish and Prussian governments had been kept secret, and on Leopold's refusal in April 1870 Fritz believed that the whole affair was closed for good without ever having reached public or press.

He reckoned without Bismarck, who in skilful manipulation of the main characters saw the perfect means of picking a quarrel with France. Napoleon was old, ill, and almost as much a political simpleton as any of his advisers. Together they were no match for the crafty Junker, and could be easily provoked. To them the idea of a Hohenzollern on the Spanish throne would be blatant encirclement. Prussia had demonstrated her military prowess twice in the past six years, and Prince Leopold's brother Charles had been elected Prince of Roumania in 1866;* was there no stopping the family's

---

*The principality of Roumania, formed from the states of Moldavia and Wallachia, did not become a kingdom till 1881.

ascendancy? Like Fritz, the King was against the canditure in the first place, for a similar reason; it did not suit the dignity of his family to accept a throne after the previous monarch had been deposed. Queen Augusta openly pretended to side with her husband, but in private she relished the thought of her family adding another throne to its list of achievements, and she urged Leopold to accept after all. For once she was in agreement with her old enemy Bismarck.

Fritz and Vicky were at Potsdam, talking excitedly about their forthcoming holiday at Osborne, and congratulating each other on the birth of a third daughter Sophie, born on 14 June, when alarming news reached them — Leopold had accepted the throne after all. They were angry but hardly surprised to hear that negotiations had been re-opened several days previously; the King and his statesman had allowed the news to become public knowledge without bothering to inform their Crown Prince. But their shock was nothing to that of the government in Paris, who howled with rage — just as Bismarck had intended — and called upon Leopold to renounce the throne again. Wearily Fritz told Vicky that this could only end in mobilisation, and the immediate future would find him in command of his troops instead of enjoying himself at Osborne. Forcing a smile and an optimistic outlook, Vicky told him not to give up hope so easily — he should go and face the King, and demand to know just what was happening.

He accordingly went to Berlin to look for his father, but found the Count instead, and was sadly taken in by the statesman's mood. Pretending to take Fritz into his confidence, he adopted his most pleasant manner and said that he hoped the business could be settled amicably. Fritz did not share Vicky's acute perception; Bismarck was mild and ostensibly communicative when matters were playing into his hands, and his schemes seemed to be working, hysterical and destructive if they were not. If Vicky had been present at the interview she would have known better than to take him at face value, but Fritz was hoodwinked and went back to the Neue Palais profoundly relieved. The next thing he heard was what he had been hoping for; Leopold had withdrawn his acceptance for a second time. This announcement was celebrated by a family dinner laid on by the King and Queen, who concealed their differences and excelled themselves in hospitality as they raised their glasses with Fritz and Vicky in a toast to Prussia, peace and baby Sophie.

Fritz was as confident as his parents that they could forget the whole matter. Only Vicky, suffering from post-natal depression and taught by bitter experience not to be too optimistic, viewed matters in a less than rosy light. She dreaded the prospect of France, confident of military superiority, making capital out of the issue by declaring war. Like Fritz she believed Prussia to be outnumbered in terms of troops and not in the least ready to fight. She pressed him to sound out his family's opinions, but visiting uncles, cousins and brother-in-law soon showed him that he and his alarmed wife were in a minority. Next he went to Berlin, but his parents had gone on their summer 'cures', the King to Ems and the Queen to Coblenz. Bismarck, meanwhile, had retired to his estate at Varzin.

Not for some time did Fritz realise that he had been tricked into believing that the Minister-President did not want war. Moltke was partly to blame; in league with Bismarck, he had made sure that Fritz had only recently seen the incompetent Bavarians in their military training, thereby giving him the impression that many of the German forces were unprepared. He had also kept Fritz ignorant of his secret patrols along the complete Franco-German border by foot, where he had devised several methods of attack according to the lay of the land. In addition he and Roon had moulded the rest of the Prussian army into a compact, efficient fighting unit which was one to be reckoned with. If it had been so geared in 1867 then Bismarck would have found a way of provoking the French into war over the Luxembourg dispute.

There was another clever piece of stage management that at the time escaped Fritz's honest vision. The Minister-President's presence at Berlin would have been a sign that he was indulging in some underhand trickery to spark off the war for which he was waiting. That he was at Varzin, supervising the harvest for autumn and entertaining his cronies with the pick of his wine cellars, meant one of two things; either he had laid the snare and was waiting for France to walk into it, or the air was clear and everyone could look forward to peace after all. Fritz was one of the many who believed the latter.

But the trap was set; under the influence of his advisers, Napoleon and his government sent the King a telegram demanding that Leopold's candidature for the Spanish throne should not be renewed. Enjoying his stay at Ems, William was in no mood for belligerence, and he dictated a politely-worded message that he could give no guarantee one way or the other. Bismarck received it for approval while dining with Roon and Moltke, and on reading it shook his head; it was far too conciliatory. Setting to work with his pen he deleted about two-thirds of it; what was left read as an abrupt snub. On receiving this, the famous 'Ems telegram', the French government felt grossly insulted; on 15 July, less than a week after Leopold had washed his hands of Spain, France declared war. So skilfully had Bismarck played his role that Fritz and Vicky were not alone in believing Napoleon to be the aggressor.

Now that the die was cast, it was with a sense of weary relief that Fritz went to call on Bismarck a couple of days later. The Count's tone was just as it had been at their last meeting. Sadly, he said that there was no way of avoiding war; he would rather not have had it, but the honour of Prussia was at stake. Again Fritz was deceived by the actor in his father's chief servant; when the King, reluctant for a full-scale campaign against France, talked at the war council of partial mobilisation, he persuaded his father that this would not be enough. After the meeting was over he walked out gravely to the crowds assembled around the station at Wildpark, and announced the result in his clear resonant voice: 'War and mobilisation.'[2] The commanding sight of their Crown Prince, a tall Charlemagne-like figure in his uniform, bringing them the tidings let loose a wild burst of cheering.

How Vicky wished she could share their enthusiasm. The afternoon humidity, and the teasing of the excited children who sensed their mother's anxiety, made her restless as she sat in the sitting-room at Unter den Linden, looking mournfully at the crowded street below where the lusty strains of *Die Wacht am Rhein* told her she was alone in her thoughts. Unlike Fritz, who despite being kept in the dark by the other commanders had faith in Prussia's ability to organise her soldiers to advantage in battle, she believed the odds to be fearfully against them,[3] and wondered how many of the women would be mourning the loss of a husband or son by Christmas. Maybe England would come to the rescue, but Queen Victoria was in a difficult position. Much as she appreciated her family connections with Germany, she still had a corner in her heart for Napoleon and Eugenie, despite the Prince Consort's bitter railings in his last years against the 'arch-meddler of Europe'. Moreover, the Prussia of the 1850s that dearest Albert had treasured as a road towards an united liberal Germany had gone, to be replaced by an aggressive sabre-rattling Prussia in which liberalism was struggling. What would he have thought of it? True, France was the aggressor — or so it appeared — but Lord Loftus and Lord Bloomfield, present and former British ministers in Berlin, had warned Lord Clarendon at the Foreign Office of Bismarck's lack of scruples and his eventual ambition of unifying Germany. Once again Britain preserved uncomfortable neutrality but Fritz and Vicky did not give up hope that she might send troops to fight against France. Nor did the rest of the family; they felt that England 'would have had it in her power to prevent this awful war', if she had, like Russia, Austria and Italy, undertaken to punish the aggressor who dared to disturb the peace of the continent.[4]

On Sunday 24 July Sophie was christened in the Friedenskirche, a sad ceremony which brought back to her parents the bitter memories of little Vicky's christening. What should have been a happy occasion was overshadowed by 'anxious faces and tearful eyes, and a gloom and foreshadowing of all the misery in store'.[5] Nobody looked cheerful as they gathered round the font, the men in their uniforms and high boots serving as an uncomfortable reminder of the battlefields they would soon witness. The King, looking as though he had aged ten years overnight, was trembling so much that he had to ask the stony-faced Queen Augusta to hold their grandchild. Waldie and little Vicky, frightened by the array of unsmiling faces and the clergyman's deep voice, cried as they begged their mother not to 'let the man hurt baby'. Fritz had been given command of the Bavarian and Wurttemberg troops, and asked the respective Kings to stand as godparents.

On the following day, husband and wife took Ccmmunion together in the chapel. Both prayed that he would return victorious from the war, as he had the last time. Remembering the previous campaign, they also prayed that Waldie would be preserved. He was a delicate child like Sigi had been, and deep inside they were haunted by the fear that he would die, like the brother he had never known, just as his father was on his way to the front.

At half-past five on the Tuesday morning Fritz took his leave. Having agreed with Vicky that they would spare each other the heartbreak of a formal parting, he left a farewell note. He was in command of the Third army (the others being under General von Steinmetz and Prince Frederick Charles, with the King in supreme command), with General von Blumenthal as his Chief of Staff. It was not a force of his own choice; with men from Westphalia, Hesse, Thuringia, Waldeck and Swabia as well, about a dozen different dialects of German were spoken in the ranks. The Bavarians and Swabians had a reputation for being inefficient and undisciplined, their leaders more of a hindrance than a help. No wonder, he thought gloomily, they had been entrusted to him. His reception in Munich did little to alter his feelings. He attended a dinner-party and gala theatre performance with the neurotic King Ludwig of Bavaria, and while he recognised that the young monarch supported the national movement of Germany, there was something a little artificial about the festivities. It was with a sinking heart that he established his first headquarters at Speyer, about a hundred miles from the French border, on 30 July. After they had pitched camp he visited the Bavarian lines to speak to the soldiers in person, and spread 'that contagious enthusiasm which is worth so much on the eve of battle'.[6]

Four days later they marched south-west to Landau, where he issued orders that on the following morning they would cross the river Lauter onto French territory. On the opposite bank stood the town of Weissenberg, which witnessed the first open conflict. He arrived on the battlefield soon after nine in the morning to direct operations in person, and by midday the town was in German hands. The troops next concentrated on surrounding and attacking the French infantry on the Geisburg heights fortifying the town, and with an hour the latter surrendered. That afternoon he rode on horseback up the slopes, stopping now and then to speak to the wounded lying around him. To those who were not injured but covered with powder smoke and dust he addressed a few words of gratitude, embracing the tattered flag of the Royal Grenadiers and their wounded commander, Major von Kaisenberg.

Where was the leader he had defeated? General Douay had been killed in the fighting, and Fritz asked to be taken to see his body as it lay in a peasant's cottage in the town. It was one of the most poignant moments he had ever experienced. Only a few hours earlier both men had been bracing themselves for war; now one was victorious, and the other had paid the ultimate penalty of a soldier's life. None of the defeated men had stayed to mount a guard of honour over their commander and it was left to his dog, whining pitifully, to keep watch with his master.[7] Wiping the tears from his eyes, Fritz was filled with utter loathing of war as he gazed on the General's face — if only the dead man could know what he had been spared!

The next day he led his army towards the French stronghold at the town of Wörth, intending to attack on 7 August. They were forestalled by an exchange of fire on both sides early the previous morning, and battle ensued a day early. Within a few hours there were heavy losses in both armies, and the decisive moment came when the Germans captured the town and opened fire on three sides against the houses. Soon after midday the French commander, Marshal MacMahon, recognised defeat and ordered his men to retreat. By the bright light of the burning town Fritz congratulated and thanked his troops and their respective leaders. He then went to see the mortally-wounded General Roult, who lay on a stretcher in a house at the neighbouring village of Reichshofen, and asked if he could send any message to the dying man's family.

That evening as he sat at headquarters he poured out his heart to his friend Gustav Freytag. 'I detest this butchery,' he confided. 'I have never longed for war laurels, and would willingly have left such fame to others without envying them.'[8] But he had not lost his sense of humour. After viewing the scene of carnage the next morning he found a Bavarian soldier breakfasting in a farm garden, and addressed him with a few words of greeting. The man jumped to attention with his hand at the salute, exclaiming: 'If only we had had your Royal Highness to lead us in 1866, you would have see how we would have thrashed those cursed Prussians!' Fritz laughed that he never received a compliment that pleased him better;[9] he wondered what Bismarck would have made of the remark.

After the victory at Wörth, 'our Fritz' was the idol of his soldiers. With such a motley collection from so many different parts of Germany he had had grave doubts about turning them into an effective fighting unit, but his style of leadership had endeared him to them. His words of comfort to the wounded and thanks to his troops after each battle showed them that he took a genuine interest in their well-being, and the trust he placed in subordinates without petty interference was appreciated. It was with disappointment that he found the days of the Third Army's independent operations were numbered.

On 17 August he was given a message from his father inviting him to be present at a battle near Metz. He hesitated to do so, and instead continued to lead his forces through the state of Lorraine towards the town of Nancy. Only two days later, when he heard of the victory on the day before, did he go to meet the other armies; after embracing his proud but shaky father, he and Blumenthal were both awarded the Order of the Iron Cross. The next campaign was to be centred on searching out the retreating force of MacMahon, defeated but still comparatively intact. To this end a Fourth German Army, consisting of some of the corps from the Second, and placed under the leadership of the Crown Prince of Saxony, was formed to join Fritz's forces. They proceeded to march north and drive the French army into Sedan, near the frontier of neutral Belgium, to join the remaining French troops and the Emperor at his headquarters. With all hopes of retreat cut off Napoleon and his commanders fought bravely, but the well-organised German armies and their mighty Krupp cannon, ironically so admired at the Paris exhibition three years earlier, prevailed. Late in the afternoon the French surrendered.

Fritz's sense of triumph was short-lived. Much as he believed in the superiority of the hard-working Prussians to their licentious enemy nation, he could not forget that he had frequently enjoyed the Third Empire's lavish hospitality. Soon after the surrender he talked privately with Napoleon, whose crushing military defeat combined with disease of the gall-bladder made him a pitiful figure as he sat dejectedly in his headquarters, a rouged wrinkled face concealing his pallor. As they met he stretched out one hand to Fritz, while with the other he brushed away the tears falling down his cheeks.[10]

Once Fritz had enquired after the old man's health, their conversation shed new light on contemporary events. He learnt that Napoleon had never wanted to make war in the first place, and contrary to popular belief he was not the real aggressor. Fritz had been so busy in his position as commander that it had never occurred to him the declaration of war had been provoked by Bismarck's trickery. After this his first priority was to ensure that the ex-Emperor was treated well. On his son's request the King asked him to hand over his sword in private, and afterwards allowed him to retire to the late King's castle at Bellevue; he could join his wife and son, the fourteen-year-old Prince Imperial, in England after the war was over.

With the decisive victory at Sedan, the army's surrender, and the speedy declaration of a French republic, Fritz hoped for peace at the earliest possible opportunity. He had played the part of a conquering hero for long enough, and was too full of compassion for his defeated enemy to want to prolong hostilities. But Bismarck was not content; he wished to crush France underfoot. The strain of war made him impatient, and he snapped at anyone who dared disagree with him. His ideas were uncommonly harsh; he ordered mass hangings of the *francs-tireurs** and the shelling of towns even

*Men from the irregular light infantry corps.

after they had displayed the white flag. He clashed with Fritz on countless matters. The latter insisted that there should be no looting by the troops under any circumstances, an order which most of them obeyed out of respect for their Crown Prince; that French soldiers should be taken prisoner and treated with respect rather than summarily executed; that no towns should be attacked after surrender; and above all that those which offered resistance were to be spared as far as possible. For instance the Cathedral at Toul, a renowned masterpiece of Gothic architecture, was to be kept out of the firing line. Bismarck was contemptuous of such considerations: so, that mere figurehead of a Crown Prince thought he knew better.

As the armies marched towards Paris in the last two weeks of September, Fritz's thoughts turned increasingly to the wife and children whom he so longed to see again. From Homburg, where she was cutting almost single-handed through anti-English prejudice to improve the squalid nursing conditions, Vicky wrote to him in the few hours she could spare. In return he sent her his 'war diary'. recording the campaign as he saw it, combining factual accounts and his personal thoughts. It was in these pages that he noted, a few days after Sedan, that her presence in the hospitals was much appreciated, and how the doctors declared themselves astonished at her wide range of knowledge.[11] Her interest in the surgical exhibits at the 1867 exhibition, and the instruments she had bought there, were being put to good use. Unfortunately she was appreciated too much. The wounded soldiers, both German and French, were resigned to their doom as they were brought in to die on the floors of the makeshift huts; her concern for their plight deeply touched them. The crowded little shacks where men were dumped and left unattended in filthy uniforms for hours at a time revolted her, and she paid for a number of inexpensive purpose-built hospitals to be erected out of her own pocket. The walls were to be painted in cheerful colours, and each ward was to have its own bathroom and drainage. It was only a matter days before this hard-working, energetic little figure was too popular for the liking of others. Countess Bismarck and her band of lady-helpers, dressed unpractically in their best clothes, came to assist as well but they did not conceal their disgust of the *Engländerin's* eagerness to share her duties with 'low-class' women nurses; as long as they were willing to help, that was all that mattered to Vicky. Her patience worn thin by anxiety and fatigue, she politely but firmly dismissed the Countess and her throng, whose prime interests were in keeping their dresses clean and holding their distance from the other nurses. A violent letter went to the Minister-President in France, who ground his teeth as he vowed revenge on the Princess who dared to order his wife around. The last straw came when the Prince of Wales allegedly told the French ambassador in London, over dinner one evening, that he heartily hoped his country would win the war. Within a couple of days, a fuming Vicky was ordered back to Berlin by the King.

Back home for a much-needed rest, her temper cooled as she drew up plans for modernising the hospitals and nursing homes after the declaration of peace, whenever it should come. In her spare time she read with loving attention the diary by instalments as received, mentally following every movement and route as described by Fritz. It gave her less pleasure to see the German newspapers, which reported each victory without once mentioning his name. She knew he would not care, as long as his army received due recognition, but she could not but feel hurt when his homeland chose to ignore him so wilfully. It was all the more galling as the English press repeatedly extolled his heroic virtues and leadership.

On 19 September the siege of Paris began. The French armies at Toul and Strasbourg surrendered the following week, and by the end of October the fortress of Metz had capitulated after a seventy-day siege. The fall of these towns relieved the scattered German forces. They could now hold at bay the new French armies being raised by the republican minister Leon Gambetta to relieve Paris, which held out as the last remaining bastion of resistance against the invaders. Orleans, the second last town to give in, did not fall to the army of Prince Frederick Charles until 4 December.

Once installed in the royal headquarters on the outskirts of Versailles, Fritz soon found himself at odds with Bismarck. He insisted that Paris must be starved into surrender, rather than bombarded, for two vital reasons. Firstly it was more humane; secondly it was less costly in terms of German resources, both of men and artillery. Even if it did end successfully, it would still result in disproportionately heavy losses. Moltke and Blumenthal agreed; Roon was the only officer to share Bismarck's view. Being a politician and not a soldier, the Count wanted to solve the matter the quick way — shell the infidel city and have it surrender within a few days. It came as an unpleasant surprise to find that he was outnumbered. Even before he had Moltke's and Blumenthal's support, Fritz clung to his preference for no bombardment. It shattered Bismarck's conviction that the Crown Prince was easily swayed once out of his wife's clutches; promotion to the rank of General-Field-Marshal after the surrender of Metz must have gone to his head, he thought. Public opinion in Berlin was strongly in favour of an all out attack on the capital, not a few agreeing with Countess Bismarck's suggestion of shooting down every French civilian — adults, children and babies alike. On 28 November Fritz noted in his diary that she was telling all and sundry he was responsible for delaying the bombardment. He proudly admitted it; he did not intend to open fire 'till in the opinion of professional gunners and experts the necessary ammunition each single siege gun requires for an effective uninterrupted bombardment is there on the spot.[12]

But unknown to him the Count and Countess were about to get their own back. Throughout Berlin it was openly said that he was delaying action not on technical considerations but on 'petticoat orders'; the two old Queens, Augusta and Victoria, pestered by the Crown Princess, would not allow it. The mutual loneliness of Vicky and Augusta during the war had brought them closer together than ever, and this new friendship added fuel to the fire. It was Vicky who suffered the greater unpopularity; partly as Fritz's wife, partly as the Bismarcks saw more long-term value in a vendetta against Prussia's future Queen than against the present one, and partly because of English neutrality. As anti-French hysteria grew in Berlin, so did hatred of Vicky, and by December Fritz was exasperated at the continued vilification of his wife. Still his troops were not ready to carry out a bombardment of Pariss, and he was not prepared to give in to 'the war drones, who follow the course of the war without responsibility or knowledge'[13] 'sitting at home in comfortable, cosy rooms',[14] who had not the least idea what they were talking about.

Paris endured the siege stoically, despite Bismarck's cynical comment that the luxury-loving French would not survive a day without strawberries and cream. The aristocracy and wealthy middle-classes had to make few sacrifices, apart from finding that there was less to eat than usual, so it was the poor who suffered most. Horses, cats, dogs and rats found their way into the average Parisian casserole. At length the hard-pressed butchers had to buy elephants from the zoos for food, though the price to the consumer which their purchase dictated made them a special delicacy only the rich could afford. The lower classes had to witness the wholesale demolition of their houses so that the bricks could be used for barricades, and the homeless sat on the pavements in the howling wind and rain, clutching their last possessions and huddling together in a desperate effort to keep warm. Soldiers frantically cut down the beautiful avenues of majestic trees in an attempt to slow down the German advance through the city.

Fritz shuddered to think of the deprivations that innocent civilians, particularly women and children, were suffering because of a war they could not help. As an example to the troops, both he and the King confined themselves largely to a diet of dry bread and cheese, with very little meat. Characteristically Bismarck scoffed at the starvation of the people who had entertained him so unstintingly in 1867, as he uncorked the champagne to wash down his caviar and ham sent from Varzin.

Meanwhile a consideration just as pressing as the bombardment was occupying Fritz's mind — German unity. His thoughts frequently wandered to the triumvirate of the great departed: the Prince Consort, King Leopold and old Baron Stockmar, and their plans for a free German imperial state under a monarchical head to 'march at the forefront of civilisation and be in a position to develop and bring to bear all noble ideals of the modern world.'[15] A laconic entry in his diary for 18 July, just after the declaration of war, shows that this had never been far from his mind: 'General enthusiasm: Germany rises like one man, and will restore its unity.'[16] At the same time representatives of four South German states — Bavaria, Wurttemberg, Baden and Hesse — were discussing an alliance of some kind after the war, possibly under a reorganised German Confederation. Shortly after they had approached Bismarck for a discussion which settled nothing, Fritz came to see him one evening for a private talk. What did he think of an imperial Germany? Bismarck nodded his head, but stressed the difficulties; most of the states were agreeable but Bavaria was reluctant to let Prussia take the initiative, and without Bavarian approval Wurttemberg would withhold consent as well. King Ludwig of Bavaria, best remembered for his extravagant castles, was known to have extraordinary 'nationalist' ideas; a year earlier he had suggested that there should be two Emperors of Germany - one of Peace, himself, and one of War, King William. To commemorate the idea he had commissioned a golden cloak embroidered with white doves and the crown of Charlemagne, and paraded up and down his rooms in it.[17] When Fritz suggested that any states which resisted might be compelled, Bismarck snapped that he had no right to say such a thing. The nerves of both were frayed by the stalemate situation of the siege, and in the argument which followed the Count threatened to resign in favour of somebody who, he said sarcastically, would be more agreeable; until then, he would act as he and he alone thought fit.

Fritz guessed what lay in his mind; he was not in the least bothered by Ludwig's obstinacy — the politician in him would find a way round that. What really worried him was that dreaded personification of liberal opinion and constitutional rule, the North German Confederation Parliament or *Reichstag*. He had recently spoken to the leaders, who knew that in their Crown Prince was a champion not only of an empire, but also of majority rule, free elections, and more constitutional monarchy. If the *Reichstag* took the initiative in unifying Germany, then its authority and power would be considerably enhanced.[18] Bismarck fancied nothing less; if he did not act soon, then his political enemies at home in Prussia would be in the ascendant and his own career would be jeopardised. As two successive British Ministers at the Berlin Embassy had suspected, he cherished the idea of uniting Germany at the right moment, whenever it should come — as long as he could do it in such a way as to increase his own authority. The moment was now, before the next *Reichstag* meeting. After Fritz had gone, with angry taunts of *Kaiserwahnsinn* (Emperor-madness) ringing in his ears, Bismarck set to work. Loth to admit the superiority of Hohenzollerns over Wittelsbachs Ludwig remained obdurate, until the Count remembered that he was up to his neck in debt. Dangling before him the prospect of a healthy sum from the *Welfenfonds*,* Bismarck persuaded him, albeit reluctantly, to

---

*The infamous 'reptile fund' formed by Bismarck from the confiscated fortune of the ex-King of Hanover.

put his signature to the letter drafted for him inviting William to assume the imperial crown.

So it was that the old King believed the creation of the Empire to be at the request of the German princes, not the people, so carefully had Bismarck done his work. Even Fritz was taken in for a while, and thought that Ludwig had written the letter of his own free will. When be learnt the truth his estimation of the Count, already low, dropped still further.

It dropped again when Bismarck goaded the King into giving the order for the bombardment of Paris to begin on 4 January 1871. Bitterly Fritz wrote in his diary that the statesman had made them great and powerful, but he had 'robbed us of our friends, the sympathies of the world, and our conscience.'[19] For all the superiority of the German artillery the bombardment proved to be a comparative failure. Only 97 Frenchmen were killed, 278 wounded, and a mere 1,400 buildings damaged for an expenditure of 12,000 shells; the several hundred Prussian gunners lost to French counter-battery fire made their enemy's losses appear trifling.[20] Fritz's comment that the world's sympathies were gone was a revealing one. Anger abroad, especially in Britain, was provoked by reports such as those of the famous church of St Sulpice being damaged, and it gave way to fury with the news of a funeral for six small children killed by one shell. It was the kind of event which sickened him, but he had little time for compassion when it was all he could do to maintain reasonable relations at the front. Once fire had been opened on the city Bismarck felt that military matters as well as political decisions should be his responsibility. Moltke was angered by his interference and 'ruthless despotism',[21] and to prevent them from falling out completely Fritz had to act as an intermediary. It was a task to which he was becoming accustomed; the princes were so jealous of each other that they refused to mention their colleagues' acts of bravery in despatches.[22] The generals behaved equally badly and Bismarck threatened to put an end to the personal insults by hanging the lot.

The bombardment entered its third week on the same day as the proclamation of the Empire, which took place in the Hall of Mirrors at Versailles. Fritz tried in vain to impress upon his father that the elevation of three German princes to the rank of King by the first Napoleon, sixty years earlier, made it necessary for him to accept the rank of Emperor in order to assert his superiority. The old man remained as touchy and glum as ever, muttering goodbye to 'the old Prussia, to which alone he had clung and would always cling.'[23] Not for the first time he threatened to abdicate and let his son 'get on with it'. He was not even allowed his own way over the title, which he wished to be 'Emperor of Germany'; Fritz and Bismarck preferred 'German Emperor', or 'Emperor in Germany', which emphasised the merging of Prussia into something greater, and would be more acceptable to the other German princes. When Bismarck asked his master for an opinion on some detail of the ceremony, the King burst into a towering rage which alarmed even the thick-skinned Count.

Both men were in a thoroughly bad temper when the proceedings began shortly after midday as the new Emperor entered the hall, filled with the crowd of princes, officers and deputations from army regiments. Mounting the dais decorated with brightly-coloured regimental banners, he addressed the throng brokenly before handing over to Bismarck, who read the imperial proclamation in an expressionless voice. It was left to the Grand Duke of Baden to try and inject some enthusiasm into the ceremonies as he stood on the dais, requesting three cheers for the Emperor, his father-in-law who stood crossly beside him. Finally, to the strains of the Hohenfriedberg March, William stumped out without even glancing at the angry statesman.

Fritz was left with mixed feelings. How he would have revelled in the pageantry of the proceedings, so befitting the new imperial era, which his father would enjoy 'only for the evening of his days'[24] (or so everyone thought at the time). Yet it had been spoilt for him by the quarrelsome atmosphere which had lasted days, and the childish behaviour of the new Emperor and Bismarck. Moreover, he had been defeated in his aim to help the *Reichstag* in presenting unity as a popular cause, as he had hoped. What would his father-in-law have made of the way in which his dream was fulfilled, by the very opposite means from which he had envisaged?

On the military front a few more days of shellfire convinced the Parisians that they had had enough, and on 28 January an armistice of three weeks was arranged between Bismarck and the French Foreign Minister Jules Favre. It was extended twice to allow peace negotiations to be completed. The terms were harsh; France had to cede the greater part of Alsace and Lorraine, including the fortress of Metz, and pay an indemnity of five million marks. Fritz and the Grand Duke of Baden protested that such humiliation would leave the country thirsting for revenge, but Bismarck and Moltke insisted that their enemy's spirit must be broken, and the King was greedy for the spoils which his Minister-President had denied him after their victory in 1866.

At last the return home was in sight, and only the thought of seeing his family again made Fritz endure the hideously gloating formality of a triumphal march into Paris on 1 March. With his father he left Versailles six days later, and their headquarters were transferred to Nancy on the homeward journey north. On 17 March they set foot on Prussian soil again, as they alighted at Wildpark station. With Vicky and Louise of Baden on the platform was Augusta, who received her husband icily. He had not even bothered to inform her of her new rank, and she only found out when her footman addressed her as Empress. Knowing how proud she was of her imperial status, William thereafter took pleasure in teasing her by speaking to others of 'the Queen', never 'the Empress'.

As Fritz drove back to the Unter den Linden with Vicky in an open carriage, waving to the cheering crowds who lined the route with cries of *'Unser Fritz'*, he felt at home once more. The longest separation they had yet endured — and were ever to know — had seemed more like eight years than eight months. It was an unforgettable moment as they stepped out of the vehicle and he set eyes again on his children, assembled on the palace threshold to welcome their conquering father who was the toast of the city. Still the crowds cheered, to break into a deafening roar when a window opened to reveal the smiling family of eight, Fritz fondly holding nine-month-old Sophie in his arms.

Endless festivities at home to commemorate the victory, combined with the formalities of day-to-day business, denied him the rest he wanted and needed. The first *Reichstag* of the Imperial age was opened in the Schloss on 21 March. Bismarck was raised to the rank of Prince, a title he sneered at but did not decline. It put him in a better humour than the Emperor, who was still harping on the loss of the old Prussia he had known so long, and flew into a temper with anyone who stepped out of line. When the Grand Duke of Baden innocently dared to compare the new triumphs with the events of 1848, his father-in-law shouted at him so loudly that he could be heard in the streets outside.

As for Augusta, victory celebrations meant more court balls, drawing-rooms and the like. Brushing aside Fritz's and Vicky's protests, she insisted that they should take part and accompany her. Her 'orders' were peppered with bitter attacks on the pro-French sympathies of England, and particularly on a speech made by Queen Victoria at the opening of Parliament in February referring to the belligerent powers as 'two great and brave nations', which she interpreted as being a snub for Germany. Vicky was amazed that the Emperor and Empress could indulge in so much activity and emerge unscathed, apart from wear and tear on their tempers; 'all other mortals get knocked up.'[25]

On 16 June the victorious army entered Berlin through the Brandenburg Gate, an occasion for more waving of flags and handkerchiefs, cascades of flowers and wreaths, and hearty cheering which by now was becoming tiresome. A statue of King Frederick William III was unveiled, mainly thanks to Fritz who had to lead his absent-minded father to it, and help him raise the sword high enough to cut the cord which held the cloths together.

The procession held a sinister note for Vicky. As she rode through the gate beside Fritz, resplendent with his new Field-Marshal's baton, she casually turned round and caught sight of Willy, following on his small dappled pony. She was alarmed at the look of pride on his face, the knowledge that one day this victorious heritage would be his. An unstable child, he was susceptible to flattery, and she was afraid of the courtiers who tried to 'nurture a mistaken pride' in him, believing it to be patriotic.[26] She could not help wondering if the events of the last few months had not turned his head. The summer's day on which they left for England came not a moment too soon.

CHAPTER 11

Imperial Representative, 1871-78.

During their stay in England, Fritz and Vicky regained some of the peace of mind they could not find in the endless carnival atmosphere of Berlin. After a few days they discovered to their relief that the anti-German feeling, which had increased as reports of brutality against France had multiplied, was not directed at them personally. The Liberal Foreign Secretary Lord Granville expressed the general opinion when he wrote to tell Queen Victoria that her son-in-law had distinguished himself not merely by his victories against the French, but also 'by his humanity, his moderation and his large political views'.[1]

The holiday was also a good opportunity for repairing frayed family relationships. The Waleses had not made much allowance for some of Vicky's less rational comments, written at the height of anxiety ('dear Bertie must envy Fritz who has such a trying but such a useful life'[2]), but when they were reunited at the Prussian Embassy all was forgiven and forgotten. While relaxing in the sunshine and seclusion of Osborne, Fritz could speak his mind to his mother-in-law, and warn her that it would not surprise him if one day Bismarck declared war on England.[3] At a time when the Queen was frequently involved in arguments with her elder children, perhaps nothing bound her closer to them than a loathing and fear of the newly-elevated Imperial Chancellor.

The feeling was mutual. The statesman had little reason to fear their Imperial Highnesses, but he paid back their hatred with interest. It made him see red to think that the Emperor had allowed them to go to England and lap up the popularity which he felt was his by right. His grievance over British neutrality reasserted itself, and he never tired of reminding all who cared to listen that it was the Birmingham factories which had supplied the French with many of the rifles and cartridges which had killed scores of Germans. He conveniently chose to forget that the Queen had sent her daughter linen for the bandages that had been used in nursing countless wounded back to health.

Just as Vicky's popularity had rebounded on her during her nursing at Homburg, so did Fritz's quietly enthusiastic reception in his wife's country prove harmful to him at home. Well-intentioned but tactless eulogies in *The Times* on the 'constant friend of all mild and Liberal administration', with whose accession the main obstacle to Anglo-German friendship would disappear,[4] found their way to the ears of the main obstacle himself. While in England Fritz contracted pneumonia, partly as a result of the exhaustion he suffered after returning from the war, and on his way home he stopped at Wiesbaden for a few days' convalescence. There he received a paternal letter from the Emperor at Ems telling him to take his time and not to hurry home. He took the message at face value, thinking nothing more of it until he and Vicky reached Potsdam some weeks later. Bismarck had taken advantage of his prolonged absence to expel him from both the Council of State and the committee for military affairs, to which he had been elected just before his visit to England. He could not believe it at first. It would have suited him as Crown Prince not to think too badly of his father's chief minister, much as the two men differed in character and politics, but his magnanimity was clearly wasted on a man who took every conceivable underhand step to undermine his authority. His motto 'I often forget, I never forgive,'[5] was no idle boast. He had certainly not forgotten Danzig or *The Times*'s sympathies, and even if he could do so it was not in his nature to forgive.

From his own point of view Bismarck had one very good reason for keeping his relationship with Fritz a cool one. It lay in his position as Chancellor, which according to the new imperial constitution was above and independent of the *Reichstag*. No matter how radical the Liberals in the chamber, or whatever the size of their majority, he could remain in his position as long as he had the Emperor's approval. William was seventy-four, and despite his considerable energy which enabled him to dance at social functions with the stamina of a man half his age, he was beginning to feel his advancing years. The possibility that he could suddenly succumb to a stroke or some ailment at any time was never far from Bismarck's mind. Then what would happen? The Chancellor knew only too well — his new Emperor would spare no effort in persuading him to resign. The thought made him shudder, and the best thing he could do under the circumstances was to consolidate his popularity at Fritz's expense. Unwittingly it was Vicky who provided him with ammunition. Her interest in education led to her founding several girls' schools, one of which had an Englishwoman as headmistress. That she should interest herself in matters such as schooling was bad enough, thundered the Chancellor and his henchmen, without her making the English element so prominent. He attacked her publicly for this as he did her disregard for etiquette when she renewed her acquaintance with poets, painters, scientists, who were invited to the Neue Palais — mockingly referred to as the 'the palace of the Medicis' by the Conservatives — regardless of rank. There was no reason why she should not entertain whom she wanted in her home, for the days had gone when her in-laws had almost fainted with horror at the news of the young Princess consorting with 'low' people. That she did was common knowledge, but Bismarck used it to her disadvantage, making sure that it discredited Fritz at the same time, blunting the edge of the imperial hero's popularity.

With an active military career apparently behind him, and deprived of his council positions, Fritz's chief connection with the army now lay in the annual inspections of the military contingents in the South German states. It became in time a wearisome formality which he undertook without protesting out of a sense of duty, but the only pleasure it gave him was the reunion with soldiers he had known during the campaigns against France. Otherwise he found it a tactless reminder of the war, like the ostentatious celebrations each September on the anniversary of Sedan, or at worst a shabby substitute for the political experience he should — and would but for the grace of Bismarck — be receiving as the next Emperor.

Over the passing years he had become more and more a man of peace. Just as his illusions of glory on the battlefield had faded at the hands of bitter experience, so had his fondness for hunting and shooting. He dutifully attended the autumn hunting-parties in the Hanoverian forests with his father and their royal guests, and he taught Willy how to handle a gun with his right arm. But unlike most of his male relatives, his devotion to animals did not go hand in hand with a delight in what he regarded as wanton butchering. An official visit to Madrid some years later was almost spoilt by a bullfight laid on in his honour. The competitive element in hunting left him cold, for apart from swimming sports had never appealed to him. Such factors made him appreciate home and family life all the more. His last child, a daughter, was born on 22 April 1872, just over a year after his return from Paris. She was named Margaret (later known as 'Mossy') in honour of Crown Princess Margharita of Italy, one of the godparents.

As the official world grew increasingly oppressive, he took more pleasure in his career as a patron of the arts. It was unusual to say the least for a Hohenzollern to busy himself in such a field, in an age when most royal art patrons were only superficial dilettantes; the two prominent exceptions, apart from him and Vicky, had been the Prince Consort and King Ludwig of Bavaria. Fritz was appointed Protector of Public Museums, with special responsibility for raising the standard of the royal museums and galleries and acquiring new exhibits. His role was an important one, for none of the family had previously taken any serious interest in art since the late King. Now that Prussia had risen from the status of a small military kingdom to the centre of a new imperial power it was only fitting that she should take her place alongside the cultural centres of Dresden and Munich, and compete with other countries in the arts as well as in industrial and commercial expansion. One of the first instructions he laid down was that every report to the Minister of Education regarding the museums should be initially submitted to him, and that a copy of every order from the ministry should be transmitted through him. It was largely due to his influence and work of William Bode, Director of the Berlin galleries, that collections such as that of the industrialist Barthold Suermondt, comprising a priceless group of seventeenth-century Dutch paintings and drawings, were bought for the state.

His patronage was not confined to the administrative aspects; he and Vicky made a point of visiting the studios of painters and sculptors both at home and abroad. Anton von Werner, who had accompanied him on the Franco-Prussian campaign and painted the famous group portrait showing the imperial proclamation at Versailles, owed his position as a leading historical artist and his presidency of the Fine Arts Academy to Fritz's patronage, while the versatile painter Adolf von Menzel and the sculptor Reinhold Begas were only two of many talented men who came to know their Crown Prince well and appreciate his keen interest in their work.

In order to develop a sense of appreciation in the children as they grew up, Willy and Henry were frequently taken on weekend excursions to see the art treasures of the Empire. Fritz never tired of taking his family to the cathedrals at Brandenburg and Magdeburg or elsewhere, but he had been there so often during his younger days that the long explanations of the guides, learnt by heart, bored him intensely. He usually managed to cut them short with a joke or what he hoped would be an awkward enquiry, but on one such visit he failed. Their host at the Marienberg cathedral was treating them to a tedious description of the ancient temple on whose site they were standing. Suppressing a yawn he asked if they could obtain a photograph of the temple idol. The guide promptly answered: 'It shall at once be procured!' and carried on from where he had been interrupted.[6]

It was in the year following his new appointment that Fritz learnt something of Bismarck's capacity for distorting the truth to suit himself. He had had a crowded few months; shortly after Mossy's christening he had undertaken his annual tour of military inspection. After that he and Vicky had held a fete in the park of the Neue Palais in September to commemorate the meeting of the three Emperors (German, Austrian and Russian) at Berlin, resulting in the *Dreikaiserbund* or alliance of the three powers. This was followed by a visit to Dresden in November to celebrate the golden wedding of the King and Queen of Saxony. He intended to go directly from the festivities to join Vicky and the children in Switzerland, but on the journey he was taken critically ill with an internal inflammation. After a slow convalescence, most of which was spent at Carlsruhe with the Grand Duke and Duchess of Baden, he went for a cure at Wiesbaden. It was at this time that the right-wing *Reinische Kurier* quoted him as telling Vicky that she might be called upon to act as Regent for a time in view of the gravity of his illness, his father's old age, and their eldest son's minority. In the event she must promise him 'to do nothing without Prince Bismarck, whose counsels have raised our House to an undreamed-of power and greatness.'[7] So used had he become to the Chancellor's behaviour that it did not arouse him to anger, for it was useless to protest in any case, but it irritated him that a statesman should resort to such methods to strengthen his position.

In April, a few weeks after his return from Wiesbaden, he and Vicky were invited to the International Exhibition at Vienna. On their arrival they were received more effusively than they had ever been before, thanks to the new Austro-German alliance. For once his Field-Marshal's uniform did not remind his Habsburg host so vividly of the defeat at Königgrätz, while Vicky's bubbling enthusiasm contrasted sharply with the stentorian presence of the Empress Augusta, whose loud voice very soon earned her the nickname of 'Foghorn'. The shy Empress Elizabeth found her 'pompous and boring like everything that comes from Berlin,'[8] although she quickly found good reason to exempt Fritz and Vicky from this verdict.

The most fertile contact Fritz made in Vienna was with the painter and professor Heinrich von Angeli. After seeing his portraits in the exhibition he and Vicky visited him in his studio and invited him to Potsdam. This was not only the beginning of Angeli's career as the most prominent portrait painter to the royal European courts (replacing the ailing Franz Xaver Winterhalter, who died that July), but also of an enduring friendship between the Austrian and his patrons. He came to the Neue Palais nearly every year from 1873 onwards not just to paint and instruct his sitters, but also as a trusted companion who enjoyed the company of the continent's most enlightened heir and his consort. After a few visits to Potsdam he compared their palace to the house of a private citizen, where the hosts and children made up a 'simple and charming family picture'. He was impressed by Fritz's quiet character, 'never speaking a word more than is absolutely necessary in family conversation,'[9] and not once mentioning military or political topics. He was pleased to notice Fritz's interest in Vicky's progress at sketching under his tutelage, for until then her favourite medium had been sculpture, painting and drawing usually taking second place. Very soon the fond husband began to work in charcoal and colour, although lacking his wife's aptitude. It was while entertaining men of Angeli's calibre that he could forget the trappings of imperial power and the distasteful world of the Chancellor.

After leaving Vienna in May they stayed at Venice, Milan and near the Italian lakes, before returning to Potsdam. Here they prepared to receive the Shah of Persia, one of most unusual guests that an European court could expect. Nobody in Prussia had ever met him, but his arrival was preceded by colourful rumour. He was apparently touring the Western world like a travelling circus complete with a suite of ministers, attendants and a harem, which must have caused alternate relief and disappointment among the female German population. When he arrived he lived up to his eccentric reputation, and despite their initial doubts Fritz and Vicky were quite taken with him. He had no sense of time, and invariably kept everybody waiting three-quarters of an hour before appearing at the military inspection and other functions arranged in his honour. Being unable to manage a knife and fork he tore food apart with his bare hands at meals, spitting it out after chewing so he could examine the remains. It was whispered that lambs were slaughtered and roasted in his rooms, and pieces distributed to each member of his suite — a story which had the distressed royal children weeping bitterly.

In spite of this the latter were equally fascinated by him, and he showed great interest in them. Nevertheless the rest of the family found him undignified and a great bore; the papers marked his visit with 'disparaging anecdotes, some very funny and mostly all untrue', though his 'perfect adoration for England and everything English'[10] and dislike of Russia doubtless did much to colour his reception at court. Appropriately he left Germany for Windsor, where his presence once again caused a sensation.

It was at this stage of his life that Fritz owed a good deal to his happy domestic background with his wife and children, his love of travelling to meet other sovereigns and princes throughout Europe, and interests in every field from art and literature to science and agriculture, which were often due to Vicky's influence. Philippson's description of him as 'the representative of the Empire in whose existence and power he was less part than the smallest official and the least important officer'[11] was an accurate summary of his dilemma. To somebody without his interests it would have been a mortifying role. To him it was often an invidious position, but fortunately he adapted himself with a fair measure of good grace. Count Alfred von Waldersee, a member of the Bismarckian clique and later Chief of General Staff, whose subsequent behaviour and memoirs did much to distort his and Vicky's posthumous historical reputation, quoted him as saying in 1873 that he thought it unfair of Providence to let his father live so long.[12] That he could ever have made such an unfilial remark is completely out of character, and its authenticity is even more dubious in the light of other statements by Waldersee, but the Crown Prince would have hardly been human if he had not thought such a thing in private. The Emperor himself would not have disagreed. 'Don't you think one can live too long?'[13] he wistfully asked a courtier one day.

For a while Fritz's life was little more than a chronicle of foundation-stone-laying, travelling to weddings and celebrations in all corners of the continent, and family visits to his wife's relations in England, or alternatively to her sister Alice at the humble palace in Darmstadt. It was on their visit to Russia that Bismarck found an opportunity to keep their popularity in check. In January 1874 Queen Victoria's second son Alfred, Duke of Edinburgh, was to marry the Tsar's only daughter Marie, and they were among the royalty invited to St Petersburg. Wearing the sable coat bought for her by Fritz, Vicky was captivated by her first sight of the legendary country. She got on extremely well with Alexander, who made her a present of a glittering diamond and ruby bracelet. Several months after their return Bismarck circulated the rumour that she had gone simply to conclude an Anglo-Russian alliance against her husband's country, and a grateful Tsar had presented her with the jewellery for this very reason. The story was an obvious falsehood. If the bracelet had been given her for 'services rendered', then she would hardly have been so indiscreet as to wear it on her wrist at every court reception she attended; and if such an alliance had been brought about, it would have been at the instigation of the Prince and Princess of Wales, who were also at the wedding, not on the initiative of the German Crown Princess, whatever her family connections. Nevertheless the smear campaign against her was so firmly established among the Anglophobes and anti-liberal court circles that it was believed. When left to himself, the Emperor was prepared to be pleasant towards his daughter-in-law. But, with tears rolling down his wrinkled face, he was forced by his Chancellor to admit that he regretted having allowed her to accompany Fritz to the wedding. When he was chosen to go on an official visit to Spain in 1883 his father forbade her to be with him, as he did not want a repetition of the scandalous tittle-tattle. It was a double triumph for Bismarck in not only embittering relations between William and Vicky, but also in securing approval for keeping husband and wife apart.

The malicious gossip was also encouraged by that least dependable of allies, the Empress Augusta. The new bond of confidence between her and her daughter-in-law during the Franco-Prussian war was short-lived, and peace had not long been declared before she became her familiar bickering self once more. The barrier was reinforced by a well-intentioned but ultimately disastrous legacy of the old Dowager Queen Elizabeth. She had been completely disarmed by Vicky's solicitude at the passing of her husband, and on her death in 1873 she left her magnificent jewels to her niece instead of bequeathing them to the Prussian crown, as had been the custom. The incident illustrates the affection that Vicky could inspire in those who knew her closely, and that the Queen had been one of her bitterest enemies at first is significant, but the Empress was insanely jealous and never forgave her daughter-in-law. Like her political foe Bismarck, she could be cruelly vindictive and took a merciless pleasure in seeking revenge by poisonous chitchat, which apart from making Vicky unpopular in court circles discredited Fritz as well.

The cloudy atmosphere of Berlin drove husband and wife increasingly to Bornstädt, away from spiteful gossip and the all-pervading aura of the Chancellor, to the joys of country life and friendly villagers who formed their impressions of the couple not on Bismarckian calumny but on what they saw at first-hand. It also helped them to enjoy their visits to Britain even more, whether huddled around the hearth at Windsor or strolling across the Scottish moors around Balmoral, Fritz cutting a striking figure in his kilt. Even the unpolitically-minded Princess of Wales gradually understood the cruel position in which her brother-in-law lived. Whether she really believed that on his accession he would restore to her father all or part of his territory is uncertain, but in her blind hatred of Bismarck she learnt to judge the future German Emperor more fairly than she had in the past.

The children were always welcomed by their English grandmother, who took far more interest in them than Augusta ever did. Yet it was on one of their visits that Queen Victoria had the fright of her life. Working in her room one evening, she looked up from her papers to see the beady eyes of a small crocodile leering at her; her screams brought the whole household running. They were equally terrified and order was not restored until Waldie, helpless with laughter, took 'Bob' away. His love of animals did not stop at dogs and horses, and Bob was his favourite pet.

The Queen did not always show the same affection at this time for the children's parents, and it is revealing that on several of their visits to England after 1871 they stayed at the Prussian Embassy, at Sandringham, or elsewhere. Fritz was criticised by her in a letter to her secretary in 1874 as being 'rather weak and to a certain extent obstinate . . . as all his family are, thinking no family higher or greater than the Hohenzollerns.'[14] Nine years later, writing to her granddaughter Victoria, Alice's eldest child, she castigated both him and Vicky; they were 'not pleasant in Germany', and 'high and mighty'.[15] Although she never liked to admit it, she was envious in the knowledge that her son-in-law and daughter were destined to succeed to an imperial throne while she was a mere Queen. It still rankled after her declaration as Empress of India in 1876, and not until the final tragedy of Fritz's life did her jealousy recede.

The happy family circle was not destined to remain so much longer. Unknown to his parents, the forces that were to set Willy against them were at work. They took on a definite substance in January 1873, although they had begun earlier, when the ex-Emperor Napoleon died in exile at Chislehurst in Kent. Remembering the happy times she had known at the glittering French court, and touched by his pathetic downfall and disease-racked last years, Vicky was deeply upset. Willy could not understand her emotional outbursts, for he recalled that she had been reduced to floods of tears when his father had gone to fight the same infidel. .Puzzled, he took the matter to Hinzpeter, who by choosing his words carefully made his charge believe that his mother was indulging in treason by mourning one of Germany's enemies. The idea took root in the impressionable boy's mind, and over the next few years he took all his confidential problems to the governor, whom he regarded as his best friend. This pleased Hinzpeter as, like many other German men with old-fashioned views, he disliked Vicky because she was a woman whose brains made him feel inferior. In common with Bismarck, it suited his personality to find ways of scoring off her.

Why did Willy not go to his father? They had been close to each other in the past. Like his brother-in-law the Prince of Wales, Fritz was distressed by the arguments which had prevented him from enjoying an easy relationship with his own father, and with this in mind he had vowed to try and establish harmony with his sons right from the start. The pre-empire days when father and son had sat on the floor in the Neue Palais, turning the pages of the richly-illustrated *German Treasures of the Holy Roman Empire* which evoked the glorious past, were not so far behind them. But another of Bismarck's schemes was bearing fruit; in sending Fritz on every representative mission possible, he was keeping him away from his son. The less Willy saw of his father, the more he would look upon him as a stranger as he grew up. In due course this would make it easier for the Chancellor to turn the lad against his parents and their politics. It would also foster the impression that Fritz was an ineffectual father, completely ruled by his wife when it came to bringing up the boy. The cruel legend has persisted to this day.

To be fair to Bismarck, however, it must be said that he was not the first to poison Willy's mind against his mother, and therefore indirectly his father too. Augusta had petted and indulged him as a little boy because as a future heir he was the only child of her son in whom she took an interest. In order to curry favour, she had told him that his mother could not bear to nurse him as a baby because his injured arm was repugnant to her.[16] It was a disgraceful lie for which there was no valid excuse. To the first German Empress, therefore, belongs the distinction of being probably the first person to drive a wedge between mother and son. In doing so she laid the foundation stone on which Bismarck built, for anyone who set Willy against his mother set him against his father as well.

Just as Fritz's university education had seemed little short of revolutionary in the 1840s, so did the proposal to send Willy to the Cassel *Gymnasium* (grammar school) in 1874 for three years astound the court. Contrary to popular belief, the idea was not Vicky's. It had been the brainchild of Hinzpeter, who wanted to bring the boys further under his control and therefore away from their parents, but he had cunningly submitted it in such a way that she soon believed it to be of her making. She fully agreed with the ostensible motives; it would surely prevent 'that terrible Prussian pride' from ensnaring Willy. He must not grow up with the idea that he was of 'a different flesh and blood from the poor, the peasants and working classes and servants.'[17] So enthusiastic did she become about the scheme that she accepted all responsibility. How Hinzpeter must have smiled to himself at not having to take the blame, or bear the wrath of those who did not care for the idea. For the Emperor was deeply affronted; the boy was his eventual heir, so why was he not consulted first? He wanted him to stay in Berlin, to appear at manoeuvres and reviews like his father had done at the same age, and to be in the public eye as much as possible. This was just what Fritz and Vicky did not want. Yet it had been an error of judgment on their part to keep the plan to themselves, and not let the Emperor know until so near the time. Vicky did herself a disservice at the same time by not being completely honest and telling them that it had been Hinzpeter's idea in the first place, since the old man had the same unbounded faith in the governor that she did. It can be explained by one of two reasons: either the thought of defying her father-in-law for the sake of what she believed to be right for her son carried her away ('I enjoy a pitched battle'[18] as she had written after Danzig — and her youthful impetuosity had not died in her yet), or else she knew William to be so completely under Bismarck's influence that he would not believe her if she denied perpetrating such a radical idea. The Empress took their part, which only hardened the old man's opposition.

Willy's confirmation on 1 September 1874 at the Friedenskirche took place in the shadow of the row between Vicky and the Emperor. It was left to Fritz and the Prince of Wales, who had come to stay specially for the ceremony, to calm her down. Her eyes were red and she made a great effort to keep herself from trembling as she watched her son calmly listening to the long tedious addresses, and answering the forty prepared questions without hesitation or embarrassment. She managed to regain her composure by the time it was over, and the four of them — Fritz, Willy and Bertie and herself — took the sacrament together. Later that week she and Fritz saw her brother and the boys depart; Henry had been scheduled to attend the Naval Academy. They would live in a nearby castle under Hinzpeter's surveillance, and attend their schools as dayboys. The *Gymnasium* had a reputation for being progressive in the best sense possible, with staff who were both humane and highly qualified. Fritz went there at the beginning of Willy's first term, and again in November. On both occasions he was pleased with what he saw, and on the latter he watched some of the lessons in progress.

After the cold winter of 1874-75 they needed a change of climate, and went to Italy in the spring. Visits to King Victor Emmanuel and Crown Prince Humbert made their holiday a pleasant one, and Vicky's artistic talent thrived under the guidance of Anton von Werner, who was staying in

Venice at the time. It was a rude shock for them when they returned to Berlin in May to find Germany apparently on the verge of war again.

France had made an astonishing recovery from the conflict, paying off her indemnity by September 1873, eighteen months before the date specified in the treaty. The subsequent departure of the last German soldier from the occupied territory was soon followed by reorganisation of the French army, and representatives of every political party in the country were talking of revenge. When Bismarck was told that the government in Paris was purchasing thousands of cavalry horses from German stables, he published a decree suspending the export of any more. Shortly afterwards a meeting between Victor Emmanuel and Francis Joseph at Venice gave rise to rumours that an Austro-Italian-French coalition was in the making, and Bismarck's recent persecution of the Roman Catholic church and Catholic party in the *Reichstag* made the supposed alliance look like a threat to Germany. In April 1875 the *Kölnische Zeitung* published an article commenting on the threat to European peace posed by the French army and the Venetian encounter. Two more right-wing papers took up the theme, and stock exchanges all over the continent were shaken by the scare. Few were more concerned than the Emperor, whose attention was drawn to the inflammatory articles by his daughter Louise. Anxiously he wrote to his Chancellor, who disclaimed any connection with them. The excitement died down after Fritz came home, but after the prelude to the Franco-Prussian war he knew better than to place his trust where it did not belong. At the beginning of June he met Bismarck, who assured him eloquently that 'he had never wished for war nor intended it' and blamed the panic on the press. He wished he could believe the Chancellor, but as Vicky said, 'as long as he lives we cannot ever feel safe or comfortable.'[19]

The affair cast a shadow over Fritz's activities during the summer — his visit to Vienna for the funeral of the Austrian ex-Emperor Ferdinand, his opening of a Horticultural exhibition at Cologne, and another round of army inspections. He was sufficiently soured for once to complain about having to dash 'from one (German state) to the other by rail, like a State messenger' when he wrote to Prince Charles of Roumania that autumn. He was willing to fulfil his duties, 'but there are limits, especially when one is no longer as young as one was.'[20]

Did his hollow existence as a representative at Bismarck's beck and call have another sinister purpose, previously unforeseen by himself and Vicky — to make him feel old and weary before his time? Even allowing for his delicate health, for him to complain of feeling his age at forty-four, when his father had ascended the throne in his sixties and showed no sign of relinquishing it on the threshold of eighty, was disturbing. In a mood of depression at this time he told Hinzpeter that he felt he would never rule; the succession would skip a generation.[21] He was nothing if not a dutiful

Crown Prince and Princess Frederick William and family, 1875. Children l. to r.: Prince Henry; Princess Margaret (standing at back); Princess Victoria (seated at front); Princess Sophie; Prince Waldemar; Prince William; Princess Charlotte

heir, as Bismarck knew and had mercilessly used to his advantage. Surely he would not have objected to travelling hundreds if not thousands of miles a year if only he had been rewarded with the political role and confidences which any heir apparent deserved. Well might he have agreed with the words written by his dejected father-in-law in 1858, when comparing himself to the donkey in the treadmill at Carisbrooke Castle near Osborne: 'small are the thanks he gets for his labour.'[22] For the Prince Consort, life lost its savour because he toiled too hard; Fritz's misfortune was that he was given the wrong work, and the knowledge that the wrong work was deliberately given only made it harder to carry out with good grace and enthusiasm.

The following year produced yet a further war scare which made him wonder if he would ever live to see another year of unclouded peace. This time the threat came from the Balkans. In the summer of 1875 Slav nationalists rioted in Bosnia and Herzegovina, and ministers representing the members of the *Dreikaiserbund* agreed to draw the sword if necessary in order to deter the rebels. Russia particularly favoured armed intervention, and the alliance would as likely as not draw Germany and Austria into any conflict which ensued. With outward calm Fritz braved himself for the order to mobilise, which fortunately did not come. It was a war which he had dreaded fighting far more than the others. The Slavs and Turks were dangerous enemies who thought nothing of stabbing their opponents in the back and torturing rather than taking prisoners; and, worst of all, it could have brought him face to face with British soldiers. Both Queen Victoria and her Tory government, under Benjamin Disraeli and the Marquess of Salisbury, distrusted the 'terrible man' Bismarck as much as they did Russia, whose threatened expansion in the Balkans would be at the expense of British trade routes to India and the far east.

With cautious relief, Fritz tried to forget about the Balkans as he devoted himself to another plan under his aegis as patron of the arts — the Hohenzollern Museum. His inspiration had come from a visit before his marriage to the Rosenborg Castle at Copenhagen, a museum containing souvenirs of the Danish monarchy arranged in chronological order, and he wanted to establish a similar collection in Berlin commemorating his own dynasty. Portraits, weapons, furniture and similar items, accompanied by captions and explanations, resulting from hours of painstaking research, all found a place in the new museum which was opened on 22 March 1877, the Emperor's eightieth birthday.

While his father was developing Germany's reputation as a *Kulturstaat*, Willy was finishing his education at Cassel; had his parents but known it at the time, they would not have judged the experiment an unqualified success. His regular placing as tenth in a class of seventeen did not cure his passion for boasting, and far from treating him as 'one of the lads', his fellow-pupils looked up to their eventual ruler and flattered him endlessly. Moreover, he had gone there with misgivings about the liberal notions of his parents. Bismarck was to him the great god whose policies of blood and iron had made Germany great; liberalism, so it seemed, had contributed nothing to the birth of the Empire. His history lessons at the *Gymnasium* had reinforced his faith in the Chancellor, and this was to have disastrous consequences for his parents, if not for country and continent, in the future. Hinzpeter had contributed his share by encouraging him to speak out. The boy had found fault with everything — the headmaster, the curriculum, the 'lack of Germanism' — largely for the sake of it. Both pupil and governor had become visibly more aggressive; the latter, proud of what he had made of the prince, was twice as arrogant as he had ever been, and no longer afraid of treating Vicky as his intellectual inferior — which she certainly was not. With anguish in their hearts, she and Fritz realised too late that they should have thought twice about Morier's partisanship of the man.

For the time being, however, the volcano lay dormant, and nobody was more eager to help fight Willy's battles than his parents. He was to come of age on 27 January 1877 and enter the First Regiment of Guards as a lieutenant, wearing the highest decorations that Russia, Austria and Italy could offer him. Britain did not follow suit at first, and not without good reason. Queen Victoria had invited him to stay at Windsor during the previous autumn, and did not like what she saw very much. Without preaching she tried to 'discourage his pride' as gently as possible, and told him that he should mix more with ordinary people — not a very constructive piece of advice, as his experience at Cassel had not produced the required effect. It was because of this that she decided on sending him only the Grand Commandership of the Bath. Willy sulked when he heard, and bullied Vicky into pressing her mother to send the Order of the Garter instead, the best that she could bestow. Precedent, as well as the examples of the other countries, were on his side. His grandfather had awarded the Queen's three elder sons — the Prince of Wales, the Duke of Edinburgh, and Arthur, Duke of Connaught — the Black Eagle. Lamely Vicky wrote that he 'would be satisfied with the Bath, but the nation would not'.[23] The Queen saw through this excuse, but the last thing she wanted was to provoke a family quarrel from which she might emerge the loser, so reluctantly she gave way; her grandson got the Garter. Wearing his new decorations with a hauteur that would have made his late grandfather turn in his vault at Windsor, Willy collected the ultimate accolade, the Black Eagle, from the doting Emperor. Fritz watched the ceremony sadly but would not admit defeat as he prayed for his son to be 'true upright, and honest.'[24] After receiving his Guards commission, Willy followed in his father's footsteps and went to study at Bonn. Unwisely it was decided that he should read no less than eight subjects, covering everything from history and science to philosophy and art. It was probably because of this impossibly wide curriculum that he never really mastered the art of concentration. According to his lecturer Rudolf Gneist, he was a typical prince as he knew everything without having learned anything.[25] The only tangible result of his university days was increased admiration for Bismarck.

Willy was not the only tiresome member of the family; in her own way Ditta was just as worrying. As a child she had been a disappointment, her parents' letters frequently referring to her as being naughty and backward. She had got her mother into trouble with Queen Victoria at Balmoral by refusing to shake hands with the Highland servant John Brown: 'Mama says I ought not to be too familiar with servants.'[26] Nor did she improve as she grew up, largely due to the Empress Augusta's influence. Although her grandmother took less notice of her than of her elder brother, she still petted and encouraged her — by the sly method of not discouraging — to make spiteful remarks against her parents. By the age of sixteen she was a typical Hohenzollern princess of the mould so dreaded by Vicky on her arrival in Prussia; vain, discontented, with an insatiable appetite for malicious gossip and all-night socialising. Her waywardness was seized on by the Empress's clique, for her endless moaning about her parents, which was really nothing more than ordinary teenage rebellion, was just what they wanted to hear. In April 1877, shortly after she and Henry were confirmed, the Emperor announced her engagement at a family dinner to the Hereditary Prince Bernard of Saxe-Meiningen, son of Fritz's childhood friend. He and Vicky were very pleased about the betrothal, and doubtless relieved to see her gain her independence, but Catherine Radziwill was more perceptive. To her the foolish and frivolous girl could not have been in love with anyone at the time, and was only marrying in order to escape a family life that was becoming irksome.[27] Bernard was a sycophantic college friend of Willy, and in the spring all three were enjoying a ride on the switchback railway in the Pfaueninsel, the royal pleasure-park on the Isle of Peacocks in the river Havel at Berlin, where Fritz had often played both as a small boy and as a father. Bernard was standing behind her when Willy accelerated the controls for a joke. Ditta was terrified and held on to her brother's friend; this led her to imagine that she was in love with him.

A few weeks after the engagement was made public, Fritz and Vicky went to Kiel to see Henry enter the German navy on board the training ship *Niobe*. Just as Queen Victoria's second son had chosen a naval career, so did her daughter's second son follow suit. So far Henry was a good son and gave no cause for alarm, though he had been tainted to some extent by Hinzpeter's upbringing. Frequently at the mercy of his bullying elder brother, he later turned against his parents. Being a weak character he tended to sail with the wind, although he was always closer to them than Willy or Ditta.

Before the end of April war had at last broken out between Russia and Turkey in the Balkans. Fritz and Vicky had hoped for peace throughout the year — 'there has really been enough war!' — but the latter's fears that 'the Russians will have their own way, and that they only mean to wait until spring comes, and brings them a more convenient opportunity for fighting' were soon realised.[28] Despite Bismarck's pro-Russian policy, he was restrained from intervention largely through the Emperor's reluctance to see his country at war again. Fritz took great interest in the course of the fighting because his cousin Charles of Roumania was at the Russian front. The Prince had been his orderly officer during the Danish war, and sometimes Fritz half-wished that he was in the army as he followed Charles's role in storming the fortifications at Plevna, for which his experience at Duppel in 1864 had been an useful initiation. In January 1878 the Turkish army was forced to surrender, and it was to a background of fragile peace that Fritz turned his attention once more to the immediate family circle.

Royalties from all over Europe including his brothers-in-law from England, the Prince of Wales and the Duke of Connaught, flocked to Berlin in February to attend a double wedding on the 18th; that of Ditta and Bernard, and of Prince Frederick Charles's second daughter to the son of the Grand Duke of Oldenburg. It was an exhausting ceremony lasting for over six hours, but according to her uncle Bertie Ditta, looking 'like a fresh little rose'[29] in her silver moiré train, emerged from it all with the vitality of her seemingly ageless grandparents. Fritz and Vicky were surprised by the grace and lack of emotion their daughter showed at the signing of the register and the endless *Fackeltanz*.* The excessive solemnity of the programme was lightened for them not so much by the girl's outward calm and smiling face as by the presence of the Prince of Wales. Having visited the court of Berlin more often than the rest of his relations except Alice (who was too ill to come this time), he understood a good deal of the wearying atmosphere in which his brother-in-law and sister had to live. He realised that his cheerful manner and merry compliments to even the sourest of the German princesses were just what they needed to lend a ray of sunshine to their rigid existence. Bringing into play the diplomatic attitude which was second nature to him, he was an immediate success with the Emperor, who was flattered by the way in which his son's guest had a good word for everything and everyone.

The following month the Sultan of Turkey concluded peace at San Stefano, by which a large amount of territory was ceded to Russia. In

---

*A torchdance held at German weddings in which the bride and bridegroom danced with every member of the royal family in turn.

Britain, Disraeli and Salisbury insisted that Europe would not recognise the treaty as it stood, and on the initiative of the Austrian Foreign Minister Julius Andrassy a congress at Berlin, under Bismarck's presidency, was summoned to discuss the Eastern problem. For once the Emperor had to suggest that his son and daughter-in-law might like to accept an invitation from Queen Victoria to go and stay in England. Like his Chancellor he was normally impatient with them for visiting the country as often as they did, but Bismarck had been incensed by the improving relations between Vicky and his master. His solution was a simple if obnoxious one; the Crown Princess, he asserted, whose vehement hatred of the Russians was well-known, would undoubtedly use her pernicious influence to stir Disraeli into making some sort of trouble when he arrived. Could His Majesty send her out of the country before the Congress opened?

It was a veiled order to which William could hardly say no. With pleasure not untinged by bitterness, Fritz and Vicky boarded the train at Wildpark for their 'home from home'.

CHAPTER 12:

Regency and Tragedy, 1878-81.

The English summer of 1878 was as fine as any which Fritz and Vicky had ever remembered spending together. He was always moved by the welcome which family, public and press alike gave him, while her love for her mother country was reinforced a little more on each visit by her increasing unpopularity in Berlin. After returning a visit to the Prince and Princess of Wales at Marlborough House they went to spend a couple of days at Hatfield House in Hertfordshire with Lord Salisbury. The other guests included Prince and Princess Christian and Disraeli, and on the first evening no less than forty-two sat down to dinner. On the following day Count Münster, the German Ambassador in London, handed Salisbury Bismarck's official invitation to Britain to take part in the Berlin Congress. It was at once taken as a 'hopeful message of peace',[1] and Fritz felt particularly relaxed as they went out driving in the countryside that afternoon.[2] They had reached Panshanger House, the home of the Cowper family, and were enjoying the magnificent collection of paintings there, when a servant came from Hatfield with grim news from Germany: an attempt on the Emperor's life.

On 11 May the Emperor was driving in an open carriage through Berlin with the Grand Duchess of Baden when a plumber's employee Max Hödel fired at him from behind a cab. Bullets hit the vehicle and William stopped his journey to watch the police chasing the man, with a nonchalant 'Were those shots fired at me?'[3] Three weeks later, on a similar excursion, he was not so fortunate. A Doctor of Economics with suspected socialist sympathies, Karl Nobiling, fired at him from the upper window of an inn overlooking the street. This time he was severely wounded; bullets penetrated his helmet and went into his neck, back and arm. With blood pouring down his face he was hastily rushed back to the Schloss in a dead faint, and over thirty grains of shot were removed from his body. The surgeon Dr Langenbeck was amazed that he had survived such a vicious attack, and could not believe that he would last the night. Momentarily he recovered consciousness, and in a weak voice asked for someone to call his son back home.

It was with considerable trepidation that Fritz and Vicky reached Calais shortly before midnight, within hours of the outrage, and they stepped onto the yacht with the gloomy news that the old man's life was despaired of. As they drew nearer to Berlin, where anxious men and women were expecting the imminent proclamation of their second Emperor, one prayer was on Fritz's lips — that his father would be saved. Although he had long awaited his accession, the last thing he wished to do was to inherit it by the hand of an assassin. Besides, he and Vicky had heard rumours of anarchist plots to kill them all, and she had personally received threatening letters saying that she would be shot as well if she appeared in public;[4] would they be the next?

The day after their return Fritz was commissioned to take temporary control of the government. Yet his hands were tied; shortly after regaining consciousness the Emperor had signed a bill ensuring that affairs of state would continue as before. Unlike the regency of 1858 to which William had been appointed as a result of his brother's derangement, Fritz was empowered to act just as a deputy until his father's return to health, if indeed the latter did not succumb to his injuries and loss of blood. Needless to say, it had not been totally the Emperor's idea; Bismarck was taking no chances.

Fritz was sickened if not surprised. He and Vicky knew who was the real Emperor in all but name, and had rather expected it, but after all he had done for country and empire it was a disheartening gesture. The worst aspect of it was that he was nominally Regent while being powerless, and he had to rule — or rather reign — in accordance with Bismarck's policies. To the European statesmen who did not know him well personally, it would show him up as a turncoat who had suddenly deserted his principles for the sake of good terms with his Chancellor. He would rather not have been made Regent at all; the reins by which he was held made a mockery of him.

As if to demonstrate who was the ruler and who was the figurehead, Bismarck promptly scrapped a plan which had intended to make Fritz Governor-General of Alsace-Lorraine. It was a project which had been discussed earlier in the year, in order to give him a worthy official position. Since 1871 the provinces had been governed by a dictatorship from Berlin, but after a few years the Conservatives in the *Reichstag* felt that they ought to have some degree of independence in the hope of uniting them more firmly to the empire. The question of appointing an officer to govern them, answerable only to the Emperor, was raised; the Crown Prince was the obvious choice.

Bismarck was averse to anything which might give him undue prestige, but then he reconsidered. Making him ruler over territories which he had helped to conquer in war was a subtly-disguised punishment for a political enemy who must have been thirsting for responsibility. Afterwards he had second thoughts; Fritz had been a reluctant aggressor, and he possessed the gift of endearing himself to almost anyone who was not of a reactionary political persuasion. To the jealous Chancellor the risk was too great. The Crown Prince was quite popular enough already, and the Emperor's incapacity gave him the right excuse for calling off the idea. Instead Marshal

Manteuffel was appointed to the post. Not content with this, he dissolved the *Reichstag* in Fritz's name in order to hold elections that would hopefully reduce the number of Liberal seats, giving the reason that the party was indirectly to blame for the assassination attempts by not voting recently for a very repressive anti-socialist bill, and making much of the fact that Hödel had once belonged to the Social Democratic Party. The elections resulted in — for Bismarck — disappointingly small gains for the Conservatives, but it pleased him to make what small gestures he could to try and show up the new Regent as a Judas who no longer stood by his allies.

The Congress of Berlin opened on 13 June, and was dissolved a month later. Fritz took no part in it beyond welcoming the foreign representatives to the city and addressing them at the gala dinner on the opening night. He was not altogether sorry to see Russia's aims of territorial expansion thwarted, chiefly due to Disraeli's and Andrassy's adroit protection of their own national interests; England took possession of the island of Cyprus, and Austria was permitted to occupy Bosnia and Herzegovina.

In August, while on holiday at Homburg, Fritz was faced with the most agonising decision he had yet been called upon to take. Nobiling was in prison awaiting trial, only to die a few weeks later of wounds self-inflicted before his arrest, but Hödel had already been arraigned and sentenced to death. According to Prussian law, executions had to be ratified by the sovereign before being carried out. The Emperor was opposed to the death penalty and had commuted every sentence passed to him for approval. After the verdict on Hödel, Berlin could only talk of one thing: would Fritz take the same point of view? Malicious tongues suggested that if he spared the wretch's life, it would be due to the influence of his consort who wanted to encourage future attempts on her father-in-law so that she and her husband could come to the throne sooner. Fritz heard the rumours, and found himself in an unhappy situation. He shared his father's humane instincts, and shrank from sending a man to die. But weighed against this consideration was not the hostile opinion to Vicky, but the popular view that it would be foolish to show leniency to one would-be assassin who had struck within so short a time of the other, especially as one attempt had so nearly succeeded and it seemed the time for stern measures.* After several days of hesitation and worry he signed the death warrant, but few people realised what an effort it cost him. His friend General von Albedyll, head of the military cabinet, saw how much Fritz took the matter to heart, and was

*European crowned heads and their heirs were frequent targets for anarchists in the closing years of the 19th century. Conspirators killed Tsar Alexander II in 1881 after several unsuccessful attempts; in 1898 the Empress Elizabeth of Austria was stabbed in Geneva, and in 1900 King Humbert of Italy was shot dead in Monza only three months after a bullet had narrowly missed the Prince of Wales on a visit to Brussels.

certain that he could not sleep on the night of the execution.[5] He was obviously relieved on hearing it was all over, and a warm smile spread across his face as he read a letter from his father thanking him for having spared him the ordeal.

By now it was apparent that the Emperor's health was defying popular expectation and he was going to pull through. For Fritz it meant more years of waiting, but he was deeply thankful that his father had survived the attack. He was at the review at Cassel in September where the semi-invalid, trembling but looking much fitter, appeared in horseback in public for the first time since June. After the soldiers dispersed at the end of the manoeuvres he felt cheered, and in a matter of weeks he was restored to full health. On 5 December Fritz relinquished the hollow regency and the Emperor returned to Berlin, sobered by the thought that 'this trial' had been imposed on him in his own capital and by a fellow-Prussian,[6] but apparently none the worse for his ordeal.

It was generally believed that Fritz would be given some special position in the government — or perhaps the proposed Governorship of Alsace-Lorraine — in recognition of his recent duties, but this proved to be unfounded. The day after stepping down, he received a formal letter of thanks from his 'affectionate father', which was impersonal enough to be published in the papers, and nothing more. To give William his due he was certainly grateful to his son for having deputised for him, and had it been in his power he would most likely have tried to give him something more substantial in return. Yet the shock of his attack had weakened what little resistance to Bismarck the infirmity of old age had left him, and he no longer had the stamina to argue privately with his Chancellor. Far from attempting to disagree with him, as he frequently had before, he was more than ever in the statesman's clutches. Shortly after the end of the regency he became concerned that Germany had been unfairly treated at the Congress, and that Fritz was responsible. He failed to realise that his son had not played any part in the negotiations, and when a guest at one of the Empress's parties pointed out that Bismarck alone was to blame for what had taken place, he retorted that his Chancellor was 'only human. It was but natural that he should try and make himself pleasant to the Crown Prince.'[7] Two years later Fritz discovered to his horror that his father signed everything the Chancellor passed to him without bothering to read it first. His protests were silenced by a curt 'Prince Bismarck knows what he is doing.'[8]

Outwardly patient, but inwardly embittered, Fritz resigned himself once more to years of interminable waiting. Unknown to him, fate was to deal him and Vicky two severe blows within three months, as half a year of frustration was followed by a winter of double family tragedy.

For several years their visits to Alice at Darmstadt had been tinged with anxiety over her ill-health. Childbearing and endless charitable works had overtaxed her strength, and when diphtheria struck the Grand Ducal family of Hesse it claimed the life of her youngest daughter May and, just as the rest were recovering, hers as well. Coming on the anniversary of the Prince Consort's death, it was a sad Christmas in Berlin for her sister and brother-in-law, who were forbidden by the Emperor to attend the funeral for fear of infection. Maliciously the Empress commented at a tea-party a week later that it was just as well for Alice's children that she had died because 'like all English Princesses, she was a complete atheist'[9] — a spiteful judgment on her friendship with the controversial theologian David Strauss.

In March 1879 Fritz and Vicky went to stay with the Waleses at Sandringham and to attend the wedding of Louise, daughter of Prince Frederick Charles, to the Duke of Connaught. Despite the temporary suspension of mourning for Alice, it was not altogether a happy occasion. Little had been done by Prussia in the last few years to make the match popular in England, and the bride's father distinguished himself by his bad manners. He behaved rudely to his son-in-law's family, complained that his daughter's house did not have enough rooms, and told everyone that he had confidently expected his previous visit to England to be his last. Trying not to blush with shame at his cousin's haughtiness, Fritz in his Cuirassier's uniform envied Louise a little as he led her down the same aisle that he had trod twenty-one years earlier, thinking how she would relish her escape from a miserable family life and the sour Berlin court.

Within a day or two of returning to Berlin, the curtain rose on the second act of the tragedy. Fritz and Vicky were watching the younger children rehearsing a pantomime one afternoon when Waldie complained of a sore throat. The court official who had noticed him playing in the cold March air with a fringe of icicles on a stable roof in the palace yard, trying to swallow as many as possible in the shortest time, was under a delusion when he attributed to this the boy's illness.[10] Nevertheless, for all his love of practical jokes and often unruly behaviour, in which he was far more like his uncle Bertie than his late grandfather (whom Vicky thought he so resembled), he was a thin undersized child who had inherited his father's delicate health. A cold broke down his resistance to the dreaded diphtheria which had killed his aunt and cousin, and ominous white patches appeared on his throat. On 27 March, two weeks to the day after his parents had attended the wedding in England, their youngest son died.*

---

*Contrary to the assertions of some writers, he did not die of, or even suffer from, haemophilia, the 'bleeding disease' which Queen Victoria's daughters Alice and Beatrice brought into the royal families of Russia and Spain. None of Fritz's and Vicky's children were affected until Alice's daughter Irene, who was a 'carrier', married Henry and it was transmitted to two of their three sons.

This second untimely death was probably the worst tragedy that Fritz and Vicky had yet to suffer. The death of the Prince Consort, though unexpected, was easier to bear after the initial shock had passed; the loss of their faithful adviser and father figure was mitigated to some extent by the realisation that a parent was not immortal, although the Emperor seemed determined to prove himself an exception to the rule. Sigi's death had been painful for them; as Vicky had told Catherine Radziwill, to lose a child was not just a dreadful sorrow, but an unnatural one too — 'we don't bring our babies into the world in order to survive them!'[11] She and Fritz had loved Waldie especially because his birth filled the gap left by his dead brother. Now there would never be another to take his place, and for a while they were distraught with grief. Not even the birth of a first grandchild, Charlotte's and Bernard's daughter Feodora, born on 12 May, could shake them out of their misery.

Fritz probably suffered the more, because he not only mourned the loss of his son, but at the same time had to comfort his wife whose prostration resembled that of her mother in 1861. Both he and his close friends would say afterwards that Vicky was never the same again. 'Ours is indeed a grief which must last a lifetime,' she wrote to Lord Napier. 'We can hardly realise yet that we have the lost the darling boy who was our pride and delight, who seemed to grow daily in health and strength, in intelligence and vigour of character. We had fondly hoped he would grow up to be of use to his country, and his family — we had planned and dreamt of a bright and useful future for him — of all that we dare not think now and will not repine, but the wrench is too terrible and Life can never be the same again. He is missed every hour of the day, and the House has lost half its life.'[12] To Charles of Roumania, Fritz wrote that with Waldie's death life had 'lost what remaining joy it still had to offer us, and we can only gather satisfaction from the execution of our tasks and duties.'[13] The resemblance to his world-weary father-in-law in his last years was growing stronger. Vicky writhed with agonised fury when she read that an Orthodox Protestant minister, on hearing of their bereavement, said that he hoped it was a trial sent by God to humiliate her.[14] Then her mind took a different turn. Why was diphtheria so nearly always fatal? How could it be cured? Could defective drainage be connected with the spread of the virus? The inner faith in her which would not admit defeat, and which sustained her in her belief that one day she and Fritz would inaugurate an era of constitutional monarchy in Germany, led her to search out books on biology, chemistry, medical science, even drainage construction. How she longed to do something about the terrible disease in order to save other mothers from going through the same tragedy. For a while nothing else mattered, as she spent sleepless nights reading till her eyes ached, longing for her son who was dead and for his elder brother who had seen him for the last time without realising it, before going to face life on a German warship.

While his parents were mourning his youngest brother, Willy was choosing himself a consort. His first love was his cousin Elizabeth ('Ella'), Alice's second daughter. His parents had encouraged visits to his aunt and her family during his Bonn university days, hoping that the homely atmosphere he found at Darmstadt would be a good antidote for the over-adulation which surrounded him everywhere else. Unfortunately it did not work; he was so restless that his cousins found him impossible. Having settled that they would spend a morning riding or playing tennis, he would suddenly rein in his horse or throw his racket aside and call them to gather round while he read to them from the Bible.[15] He only stopped talking when Ella was speaking, and hung on to her every word. But the feeling was not mutual, as she had already lost her heart to the Grand Duke Serge of Russia.

In the best romantic tradition he strove to bury his disappointment by looking elsewhere, and his next choice fell on Princess Augusta Victoria of Schleswig-Holstein-Sonderburg-Augustenburg, 'Dona' to the family. Her dynastic connections were impeccable; she was the daughter of Fritz Holstein, the niece of Prince and Princess Christian, and granddaughter of Queen Victoria's half-sister Feodore who had died in 1872. Fritz and Vicky were delighted when their engagement was announced in February 1880. At first the news was received coldly in Berlin. Dona was not considered particularly aristocratic, rich or beautiful, and the Emperor threatened to forbid the match until he heard that Bismarck had withdrawn his objections after hearing of her father's death. In fact the more he saw of the girl, the more the Chancellor approved. She was simple, unambitious, and without a trace of cleverness; there was no fear of her following in the tradition of intelligent Hohenzollern consorts. If she ever begrudged Bismarck his dispossession of the Holstein fortunes after the Danish war, she kept it to herself.

Fritz and Vicky welcomed the betrothal for several reasons. They felt that an alliance between their dynasty and the Augustenbergs was a kind of atonement for past wrongs. Secondly, they admired Willy for his determination to marry Dona in the face of public disapproval; love had overcome pride. Thirdly, it was their belief that marriage would soften him; university life and experience of the barracks had turned his head and given him too many airs and graces — the domesticity of married life ought to cure him of this. It was left to Queen Victoria to sound a note of warning. Ella was a girl of character and would have been a restraining influence on him; Dona was 'so gentle and amiable and sweet'[16] — would she be able to tame him?

The Queen's forebodings were right. Under Dona's blind worship, her future husband's vanity reached epic proportions, as became apparent on a visit to England in the autumn. While staying with Prince and Princess Christian at Cumberland Lodge, he visited the Waleses at Marlborough House and accepted their invitation to stay and celebrate Bertie's birthday a few days later; then without any warning, he packed his bags and returned to Cumberland Lodge the day before the birthday. The Prince of Wales did not complain; he was privately thankful that his nephew was not going to be there to spoil the day, but no word of explanation was offered, and Christian and Helena found his behaviour rather embarrassing. It was simply a gesture of contempt for the Prince who had been so unpopular in Berlin since the Franco-Prussian war; Willy had been told repeatedly to regard him as an anti-German meddler, and made it plain that he would rather have as little as possible to do with this 'wicked uncle'. The Prince of Wales did not realise this as yet, for he had written favourably of the young man after his confirmation, and wanted to establish a cordial relationship with him. It was perhaps this offer of an olive branch which made Willy regard him as a patronising old fool.

His parents tried not to read anything into his bad manners as they made arrangements for the wedding. It took place on 27 February 1881, the long ceremony proving as wearisome as Ditta's three years earlier. Both parents were quite 'knocked up' by the end; Fritz had been unwell, and Vicky had worn a heavy diadem on her head for over six hours. They never ceased to marvel at how the Emperor and Empress could retain their vitality throughout.

The marriage was still being talked about at court two weeks later when the horrifying news of the Tsar's assassination by the nihilists burst upon Europe; he was riding in a carriage through St Petersburg when a bomb literally tore him open and he was taken back to his palace semi-conscious to die. Bismarck did not hesitate to send Fritz to the funeral, smiling callously at the anonymous letters that he and Vicky had received assuring him that if he went he would be the next victim. Even the Prince of Wales, who was going as well, urged him to resist the order. He had heard from his sister-in-law Marie, now Tsarina, that the family were living in a state of virtual police siege so as to shelter them from the wave of street-fighting and stone-throwing that had followed the fatal 13 March. Fritz's protests were to no avail; the Emperor would not listen either, dismissing him with a shrug and a *'Faisons notre métier'*. Thanks to the strict security precautions which all but made prisoners of the visiting royalties, the obsequies passed off without incident, but it was the gloomiest representative mission he had ever undertaken. It was a Russian custom that the dead Tsar's face had to be kissed by all the family before he was placed in his coffin; his features had been hideously distorted by the bomb, and decay set in well before the funeral which took place a fortnight after his death. The guests' relief after the last service was unbounded, for there had been rumours of mines underneath the church and torpedoes embedded in the ice of the frozen river.[17] Although he was glad to have survived safe and sound, Fritz felt bitterly on the train back to Germany that Bismarck and his father were just waiting for a bomb or a bullet to get rid of him. The way they fussed over Willy made it painfully clear they would much rather see him follow his grandfather on the throne.

Yet at least his friends were not blind to the miserable position into which he had been forced. Lord and Lady Odo Russell, British Ambassador in Berlin, had seen at Christmas the previous year how 'low and out of sorts' he always looked; when they went on a shooting-party with him, his father, and King Albert of Saxony, he seemed lost in thought and took no part in the general conversation. They sensed something of the problems which would face him if his father and the Chancellor suddenly died; the situation would 'impose a hard and ungrateful task on the Sovereign, who (would) have to find and appoint the Ministers capable of re-establishing constitutionalism in Prussia.'[18] The ministers and the desire were both there; what was sadly denied was the opportunity.

CHAPTER 13

Silver Wedding and the Battenbergs, 1881-86.

Fritz's moods of increasing depression made him thankful for his protectorship of the arts, in which he and Vicky could do something together that not only gave them pleasure but was useful and would give similar joy to others in years to come. After the Hohenzollern Museum was opened he accepted the patronage of the German Anthropological Society, the President of which, the pathologist and Progressive Liberal member of the *Reichstag* Professor Rudolf von Virchow was to play a vital part in the closing drama of his life. The society's collections, which were formerly very weak, rapidly increased under his encouragement and the guidance of his old tutor Ernest Curtius, and his influence was paramount in persuading the ministry to finance excavations in Greece and Asia Minor. He helped to draft plans for their display in the *Volkervünde* (Ethnographical Museum) in Berlin, although they were still in the process of arrangement when he died. But his proudest achievement was the *Kunstgewerbe* (Arts and Crafts Museum). This was inspired largely by the Victoria and Albert Museum at Kensington, a favourite London gallery which he visited with Vicky nearly ever time they were in England. It had started as a small collection of the industrial arts in 1867, but after the Franco-Prussian war they both added their own priceless collection of tapestries and porcelain. Queen Victoria gave it her blessing with a large consignment of rare Indian vases, ivories and lacquer articles from the Kensington museum. From the latter also came the prototype of the inner court for the new building erected to house the *Kunstgewerbe*. It was opened on 21 November 1881, Vicky's birthday, and after the ceremony they threw a party for all the architects, advisers and scholars who had contributed to its success. Fritz felt as much at ease as his wife, moving among the guests and discussing the arts as if he was a museum curator himself. It was a delightful contrast to the interminable and pompous *soirées* which the Empress so loved.

There was another reason for Fritz's good spirits at the celebration; the elections of the previous month had resulted in a large Liberal return. He and Vicky were very pleased, although they had lived through too many disappointments to be unreservedly optimistic. Was a new day about to dawn? They had nothing but contempt for the less committed National Liberals who had sided with Bismarck in his persecution of the Catholics and Jesuits, but there were many members of the *Reichstag* with whom they were on excellent terms, on the rare occasions when they could meet without giving rise to suspicion. Among them were Virchow, Edward Lasker (who had condemned a measure to ban Jesuits from Prussia), and the leader of the Catholic Party Ludwig von Windhorst. With the increased Liberal majority some of these talented men, thought Fritz, might find it possible to exert more influence.

Had he been in a less elated frame of mind, he would have guessed that Bismarck had his own solution for dealing with what he saw as a threat to his authority. At the end of November he retorted that he did not intend Germany to be ruled after the English fashion[1] — an unsubtle reference to his long-standing feud with Vicky — and in January 1882 he issued a decree against parliamentary government. Not content with this he proceeded to dismiss Fritz's Court Marshal, Karl von Norman. The latter had arranged a supposedly secret meeting in his own apartments between his master and Eugen Richter, one of the Progressive Liberal leaders. But nothing could remain secret from Bismarck's network of underhand espionage for long, and the Marshal's defiance was rewarded by removal on a trumped-up charge of having accused the Chancellor of coming between the Emperor and his people. Fritz suffered for weeks afterwards, partly because he felt himself to blame. Sometimes it seemed as if he was to be isolated from all his friends. Only one faithful servant who was not a carefully-groomed spy, Count Gotz von Seckendorff, remained to him and Vicky, and he kept his place merely because he was so circumspect in his behaviour. His devotion to Fritz was well-known, and Bismarck never ceased to look for reasons to oust him. He never found one, but not for want of trying.

What had become of liberalism in general during the previous few years in which Fritz had helplessly watched Prussia move further towards absolutism? The strongest parties in the *Reichstag* after the first elections under the imperial constitution were the National Liberals, the Free Conservatives and the Progressives. The National Liberals were ready to compromise on most measures with Bismarck, not because they agreed with his policies so much as because they saw that his power was so firmly entrenched, and in their view it was better to vote in support of his legislation rather than risk another constitutional conflict and thus threaten the stability of the Empire. It was the more radical Progressive party which usually resisted the Chancellor, and with whom Fritz found himself most in agreement, although he and they had differed in their views on nationalism and unification. After the 1881 elections in which the Conservatives and National Liberals joined forces, the Progressives and Secessionists (the radical Liberals) amalgamated to form an united Liberal party to be known as the *Deutsche-Freisinnige* * Partei*. Among its leaders were Richter,

*Literally 'German free-thinking'.

Ludwig von Bamberger and Max von Forckenbeck, all of whom were keen supporters and friends of Fritz. Bismarck looked upon the new party with anxiety, not because they formed a powerful opposition to his Conservative-Liberal minority alliance, so much as their obvious support for the Crown Prince. Not for nothing were they soon nicknamed the *Kronprinzen Partei*, and it seemed certain that they would stand by him when the Emperor died. The Chancellor's security depended on driving a wedge between the new coalition, or what he sneeringly called the 'Gladstone ministry', and the heir to the throne.

He found the answer, or believed he did, in the colonial issue. The *Freisinnige* policy was opposed to German colonisation, on the grounds that it would not only prove of no practical use to the Empire, but also bring it into collision with other European powers, especially Britain and France, who already had the lion's share of territory in other continents. Somehow Bismarck came to think that Fritz was an ardent champion of such a policy, although it is hard to discover what gave him this idea; it was possibly a red herring thrown down by one of Fritz's friends in the *Reichstag* to put the Chancellor off the scent. The one who really had colonies on the brain was young Willy, already looking forward to his reign and 'a place in the sun', when Germany would raise her prestige to undreamed-of levels by massive colonisation in Africa. Fritz agreed more with the *Freisinnige* policy, but Bismarck did not realise this and thought he could used the supposed difference to keep Crown Prince and party apart. Moreover the annexations made by Germany in Africa would provide an excuse for conflict with England in the next reign if one was needed.[2] Nothing really came of it in the end; the Chancellor's judgment was weakening under the strain of indigestion, ill-health and old age — he was now nearing seventy — and like the war scare of 1875 it was a failure which emphasised his weakening powers.

While Bismarck was attempting to make political capital from the colonial issue, Fritz and Vicky were celebrating their silver wedding. The day itself, 25 January 1883, was declared a public holiday. Gifts poured in from corporations and guilds throughout Germany, including paintings and sculpture by living artists, ivory and ebony cabinets, and from the *Reichstag* came a magnificently-carved oak dining-room suite. Everything was later put on temporary exhibition in the *Kunstgewerbe*. In addition to these presents, collections were made both nationally and in Berlin amounting to over one thousand marks, and presented to them by an official deputation for distribution to whatever charities they wished. A large proportion went towards founding a children's hospital in Vicky's name.

Yet both would have certainly foregone part of the avalanche of congratulations if only their family situation had been a little more harmonious. The *tableaux vivants*, arranged at the request of Vicky who had so eagerly participated in dressing-up as a girl to entertain her parents on anniversaries, and the Venetian ball to follow, were both postponed for a few days by the sudden death of Prince Charles. When they took place they were spoilt by the numerous petty quarrels which were becoming so common. Dona was the chief offender; rather inappropriately representing the Queen of Love who was to offer her parents-in-law a bouquet of flowers with a few words of thanksgiving as they sat on a dais between the Emperor and Empress, she wore a tight dress which showed up her pregnant figure, her pallid face, and bright scarlet arms. For the ball she refused to wear a dress which Vicky had given her, simply to show that she did not take kindly to what she considered to be her mother-in-law's interference.

Dona was proving herself to be the right wife for Willy, not only in his estimation but also in that of his grandparents and the Chancellor. Only with her parents-in-law did she not get on; besotted admiration of her husband led her to resist their efforts to establish a warm relationship. She kept her distance from Fritz so pointedly that he felt he hardly knew her at all. Vicky gently tried encouraging her to buy some attractive dresses instead of the frumpish garments she usually chose, and to wear tight underclothes in order to restore her figure after the birth of her first son William in May 1882.* But she replied coldly that there was no point in getting her figure back only to lose it again, as her husband intended to safeguard the imperial succession.[4] Apart from rejecting the advice this was quite possibly an unkind, or at best tactless, reference to the premature deaths of Sigi and Waldie; if so, it goes a long way to explaining the antipathy between both women. Beneath the bland exterior lay not only a mind 'devoid of any individual thought or agility of brain and understanding'[5] — the verdict of the contemporary diarist Daisy, Princess of Pless — but also a stubbornness which made her reject all offers of help from the woman so hated in official circles at Berlin. Her mother-in-law supposedly enjoyed meddling in and managing other peoples' lives; Dona had been warned and had no intention of following in her footsteps. From this grew a barrier between her and Fritz and Vicky which was never broken down.

If Dona was a disappointment to them, her husband was becoming down-right incorrigible. With marriage increased his sickening air of self-importance, his admiration of Bismarck, and the taunts that his parents were 'not German enough'. His arrogance brought contemptuous remarks from the English court. When made a present of a Highland costume he had himself photographed in it and distributed copies with the caption 'I bide my time'.[6] He rarely visited Fritz and Vicky, and when he did it was usually with an enormous suite which made it 'conveniently' impossible for them to talk to him alone unless he so wished; when he did, there was always trouble.

*She later became famous for her dowdy attire; on a visit to Russia as Empress her host, Tsar Nicholas II, described her hats as 'particularly impossible'.[3]

Crown Prince Frederick William, 1883

While Fritz remained calm, regretting his son's excessively self-opinionated manners but consoling himself with the hope that he would soon grow out of them, Vicky refused to accept what she regarded as the young man's insults without giving as good as she got.

Matters came to a head during a father-and-son exchange shortly after Fritz's fifty-second birthday. Asked how he could justify his behaviour, Willy told his father he had shown quite openly for a long time that he could not bear him. Taxed with the perfectly fair accusation that he kept everything from his parents, his answer was simple: 'Mama always gets angry when I express opinions on politics which are contrary to her own.'[7] Insolent as the remark was, it was not far from the truth. It was beyond Willy's powers of consideration to take into account that the more he praised the reactionary policies and poured scorn on the ineffectuality of contemporary liberalism, the more vehemently she attacked his 'superficial rubbishy political views — rank retrograde and chauvinist nonsense.'[8]

Vicky was fortunate in a sense as she could relieve her passionate feelings, both in her quarrels with Willy and in letters to her mother. Fritz suffered far more for his abhorrence of family rows led him into keeping his temper under control, which imposed a great strain on him. He was certainly used to them, as the conflicts which kept him apart from his father in the first few years of his marriage showed. Yet if he ever had the desire to quarrel with his son, it is questionable as to whether he still had the energy to go with it. He had helped to defeat the armed forces of Denmark, Austria and France, but the same success did not smile on his attempts to conquer the forces which were driving the monarchy into increasing absolutism. Moreover, German society was now developing along lines which would make it increasingly difficult to introduce the methods of rule which he desired.[9] That his son and heir was swimming with the tide made the wound worse. The frustrated years of waiting were telling on him. His winter illnesses left him progressively weaker, a perpetual *Weltschmerz* (world-weariness) always holding back his recovery, and aggravating the strain on Vicky who was hard-pressed to keep the flame of optimism from dying in him. He lost weight, looked pale, and streaks of grey began to appear in his auburn hair and beard. The princely bearing which had won the admiration of many an European journalist was beginning to fade. For his brother-in-law and fellow heir apparent in Britain, likewise denied any commensurate political responsibility, life was equally bitter at times but the Prince of Wales's consolations of an engaging social life were unmarred by the spectacle of his country's government pursuing such alien trends. By comparison Fritz's apprenticeship and role as a family man and protector of the arts was far from being a rosy one.

In the circumstances, it was a credit to him that he never deviated from his convictions. When one of his servants wanted to cancel his order for the radical *Volks-Zeitung*, Fritz ordered him to do no such thing. To the man's horrified assertion that it was 'a regular revolutionary paper', he replied that he knew what the government thought; he wanted to be informed on others' opinions as well.[10]

In September 1883 King Alfonso XII of Spain appeared at an army review in Homburg as the Emperor's guest, and Fritz was chosen to return the visit a couple of months later. To his annoyance, his father and Bismarck forbade Vicky to accompany him in order to prevent her from 'causing mischief' at the court of Madrid. It was therefore with mixed feelings that Fritz boarded the *Prince Adalbert* that November, but the people greeted him loyally as he landed at the harbour of Valencia. King Alfonso and Queen Christina were unsparing in their efforts to entertain him, though he would rather have gone without the 'repulsive spectacle' of a bullfight ordered in his honour. 'If I had not been officially obliged to stay there,' he wrote, 'I would gladly have departed at the end of the first victim.'[11] He enjoyed inspecting the troops and the arrangement of their barracks, and paid several evening visits to the theatre, but nothing impressed him more favourably than the city's museums. The Spanish entourage were rather surprised that their guest should return so often to the paintings in the Prado, 'but I employ these leisure moments in the contemplation of treasures that I shall probably never see again in my life.'[12] He found it hard to tear himself away from the masterpieces of the Italian and Spanish schools, particularly the works of his favourite artist Velasquez. On his other free mornings he marvelled at the displays of armoury in the royal palace, the unique collection of Gobelin tapestries, and the Escorial, which he considered essential 'in order to appreciate the past glories of Spain.'[13]

It was with regret that he said goodbye to both Madrid and his hosts. He felt nothing but admiration for the young King, who he was sure would win new respect for the tarnished Bourbon dynasty. It came as a great shock to him when Alfonso died of consumption two years later.

How thoroughly had Fritz been defeated by the years of waiting? Very few historians and biographers have failed to quote the momentous conversation he is supposed to have had with Bismarck in 1885, shortly after the Emperor's fainting fit at Ems made it appear that his reign might be imminent. According to this, the Chancellor was called to the Neue Palais and asked if he would be willing to remain in office after William's death. To this he replied that he would, on two conditions: no parliamentary government, and no foreign influence in politics. To these, so it is said, Fritz wholeheartedly agreed.

Unfortunately the story has been accepted at face value by many without due consideration for the authenticity of its source — Bismarck's own reminiscences. These are totally consistent with the character of their author; incidents are distorted by lies and personal spite, and the tone is coloured by what he or his sycophantic assistant Lothar Bucher (to whom parts of the three-volume work were dictated) wished the world to remember of him and his era. Like some of Shakespeare's plays, which he admired, they may well constitute first-class literature but this does not bestow upon them the mantle of authentic history. There is no way of knowing whether the interview did take place in any form or not, since all accounts which record it acknowledge the same source. Yet two points are certain. Firstly, Fritz knew that it would be impossible to dismiss his father's chief statesman on his accession, and the best he could do was to wait until they clashed, then rely on the support of the radicals and the *Freisinnige* to press for his resignation. Secondly, as Catherine Radziwill makes clear, he would not have accepted the conditions without strongly resenting the reference to 'foreign influence', an obvious slight to Vicky;[14] Bismarck was one of the last people from whom he would have tolerated such disrespect. However, the story may be true in some form or other. Daphne Bennett comments that the Chancellor intended to safeguard his position in the event of Fritz's sudden accession, because he knew the Crown Prince to be a man of his word;[15] and for him to accept the conditions offered would be consistent with the view that he no longer had the stamina to fight against the reactionary tenor of German politics as they stood in the last years of his father's reign. Nevertheless the incident must be regarded with extreme scepticism, if it is to be accepted at all.

When this conversation ostensibly took place, its protagonists were wrestling with a problem which divided the family far more bitterly than any dispute in the past had ever done. In 1851 Prince Alexander of Hesse had married a Polish countess who was lady-in-waiting to his sister Marie, then the wife of the Tsarevich, and for this he was dismissed from the Russian army. Under his new title of Prince Battenberg, little did he realise that the horror which greeted this morganatic match would be a storm in a teacup when set against the storms generated by two of his sons' marriages.

The first caused scarcely a ripple of discontent; the eldest, Louis, married Victoria of Hesse, Alice's daughter in 1884, and Fritz and Vicky were among the wedding guests at Darmstadt. It was the second one which strained relations between the courts of England and Prussia in 1885, the engagement and marriage of Beatrice, Vicky's youngest sister, and Louis's brother Henry. Once the Queen had forgiven her daughter for falling in love, she defended the match as vehemently as she had — for maternally selfish reasons — opposed it, and stood her ground against those in Berlin who looked down their noses at the Battenbergs. Vicky was her only champion. For once Fritz was inclined to disagree with her and take the same view as his father; no matter what the Queen might say, there was no disguising the fact that Henry was only a minor German prince. For this his mother-in-law took him to task when she next wrote to Vicky — fancy Fritz speaking of Henry 'as not being of *Geblüt* (stock), a little like about animals.' She reserved a more pointed attack for the Empress Augusta, with whom her old friendship was fading. How could the Empress object, when the father of her son-in-law was the son of 'a very bad woman'? If one enquired too deeply into the background of all the royal and princely families on the continent, 'many black spots would be found', and anyway fresh blood had to be infused occasionally, or the race would degenerate physically and morally. But nobody took the full force of the matriarch's outburst more than Willy and Dona, and justifiably too — the latter, 'poor little insignificant princess', was in no position to talk, for she had been frowned on at first as a future Empress because the Augustenburgs were hardly of more noble birth than the Battenbergs. Finally, to everybody she addressed one unchallengeable question: if the Queen of England thought someone good enough for her daughter, 'what have other people got to say?'[16]

They might have said nothing if only the issue had not been complicated by the threat of a Battenberg-Hohenzollern marriage, which by the time of Beatrice's engagement had already ruffled feelings severely. It could be traced back to 1878, when the Balkan state of Bulgaria was created as a result of the Berlin congress and the choice of ruler fell on Henry's elder brother Alexander ('Sandro'). While his liberal uncle Tsar Alexander II reigned in Russia Sandro had few worries, but the former's assassination brought his suspicious reactionary son, yet another Alexander, to the throne. When the young Prince of Bulgaria showed that he had no intention of knuckling under to the influence of St Petersburg, his throne began to look increasingly insecure. Then in 1883, while on a tour of Europe, he was presented to Fritz and Vicky at Potsdam. Like his brothers his eminently handsome looks were complemented by a vivacious personality which, at twenty-six years of age, made him a most eligible bachelor. Not surprisingly it was in Germany that he found himself a wife, or so he hoped. His choice fell on his hosts' eldest unmarried daughter Victoria, nicknamed Moretta, a very attractive seventeen-year-old. Described by Lady Ponsonby (the former Mary Bulteel) as 'a kind of wild, Scandinavian woman, with much of her mother's impetuosity and her eldest brother's eccentricity',[17] the prospect of being Princess of Bulgaria appealed to her. Whose heart was the first to flutter is not known, but the origins of the romance were soon lost in the controversy which later broke over the heads of the unhappy pair. It has been suggested that Sandro was not so much in love, as merely looking for a pretty consort who would provide him with sons and thereby help him to secure his position. This seems feasible, but whether Vicky really stage-managed their first meeting in order to try and encourage the affair or not (as some writers assert without a scrap of evidence) must remain a matter for conjecture.

One factor makes this unlikely: Fritz's disapproval. Unlike Vicky he could appreciate that Sandro was tending to bite the hand that fed him, and — as the British press had written gloomily about his own marriage in 1855 — he wished for his daughter some better fate than as the wife of an exiled ex-sovereign prince. Herein lay his main objection to the match, but it seems there were others. Was his pride genuinely insulted at the prospect of the son of a morganatic marriage becoming his son-in-law? Judging by his comments on Beatrice's engagement just over a year later, it most probably was. Then there is the theory that he was merely anxious to avoid another family row;[18] he knew that his parents, who argued on so many points, would be united in opposing the match. Whatever their views, to him it was a 'monstrous idea' and a weight on his mind. Hoping that the whole business would die a natural death, he suggested to Vicky that Sandro ought to 'keep away until we are in a position to see our way more clearly.'[19] According to his disdainful mother-in-law he was 'very angry' with his daughter 'and tried to put it out of her head.'[20]

After Vicky's initial enthusiasm had died down, he might well have persuaded her gently into seeing the affair in a more realistic light had it not been for the reactions of those two Tartars Bismarck and Queen Victoria. Sandro's interview with the Emperor, asking for the hand of his grand-daughter, ended violently with William — who no doubt recalled his family's opposition to Elise Radziwill long before — trembling with anger and the Prince threatening to leave Bulgaria if he was thwarted. On the other hand Bismarck, who refused to countenance the match as it would offend Russia, behaved more calmly. He suggested that the young man would do better to marry a millionairess; his throne would be far safer if he could strengthen his position by bribery. Then a few months later, when Sandro accepted an invitation to Balmoral, Queen Victoria was delighted with him. His stubborn resistance to Russia won her admiration, but she was no less taken with his good looks and compared him several times to 'beloved Papa'[21] in letters to her children — no mean praise. With her mother, the self-proclaimed 'Doyenne of Sovereigns'[22], on her side, and with Bismarck whispering words of corruption into the Prince's ear, Vicky championed him as a son-in-law more strongly than ever.

Fritz's passive role in the plans for his daughter's future can only be taken as a reflection of both his weariness and his perception that events were getting beyond his control. He was extremely fond of his three younger daughters, the *Kleebatt* (trio), whose affection for their parents was in marked contrast to the irksome behaviour of Willy, Ditta, and sometimes Henry. Moretta's statement in her memoirs, written in the late 1920s, that her engagement was approved of by both her parents at this stage,[23] was probably the consequence of no more than an understandable desire to avoid reopening old wounds. For once it is almost impossible to refute the charge in this case that he was influenced by Vicky somewhat against his own judgment. It is inconceivable that they could have quarrelled over the question of their daughter's marriage to a comparative commoner as they had done over the matter of Vicky, pregnant for the first time, going to Coburg to see her father. Not only had their mutual love and understanding, coupled with shared family tragedy and increasing isolation from contemporary politics, brought them closer together, but Fritz was too bowed down by the blows of the passing years to quarrel with anyone, let alone his wife. The Prince of Wales's approval of Sandro as his niece's husband weakened his resistance even further. He himself admired Sandro greatly, in his own reserved way; as a person he though him most suitable for Moretta, and in time it appears that his wife and brother-in-law reconciled him to the morganatic element, but he knew that it would be folly to encourage them in the face of combined opposition from his father and Bismarck. If — and when — he was Emperor it would be a different matter entirely, but as Crown Prince there was very little he could do.[*]

Bismarck naturally had his own ideas as to the girl's suitor; surely she would accept anyone who was eligible as long as he was manly enough? How about the Crown Prince Carlos of Portugal? However, she refused to consider him worth changing her religion for; he had none of Sandro's good looks and was colossally fat. She had even less time for the Chancellor's coarse and thoroughly-disliked son Herbert, whom he had attached to the German Embassy in London, and who considered he fancied the princess. Yet one thing was certain; Bismarck intended to thwart Fritz and Vicky by preventing Moretta from marrying Sandro. He did not need to condemn the match to the Emperor and Empress, whose own marriage stood as a witness to political expediency without love, and he won Willy and Dona over to his side by stressing the morganatic element of the family. When Queen Victoria sanctioned the marriages of his brothers into her brood and gave her support to this one as well, the Chancellor's blood boiled. It was her intention, he seethed, to bring about a permanent estrangement between Germany and Russia, to British advantage. Moreover, being 'fond of matchmaking, like all old women', she was so unaccustomed to contra-

---

[*]Enquiry has revealed that the Royal Archives at Windsor hold relatively few letters from Fritz to Queen Victoria written after 1883, and even these make no mention of the Battenberg affair. However, knowing the Queen's insistence on destroying any family correspondence she found in the least painful after reading it, it is not hard to imagine that he clearly expressed his opposition to the marriage in rather forthright terms that aroused her wrath. The absence of any letters he might have written in January 1885 appears to support this theory, for her remarks quoted on p. 159 above were evidently in retaliation for comments on Princess Beatrice's engagement in a presumably missing letter.

diction that she would arrive at Potsdam with the parson in her travelling bag and the bridegroom in her trunk, in order to perform the wedding on the spot.[24] Neither did he spare the Prince of Wales, whom he told on a visit to Berlin that the affections of princesses counted for nothing when weighed in the balance against national political interests. For once he had found an ally in his old and equally vindictive enemy Augusta, whose disdainful attitude virtually administered the death-blow to her friendship with Queen Victoria. The Empress had set her heart on Ella of Hesse marrying her grandson Prince Frederick of Baden, but when Ella pledged herself to Grand Duke Serge of Russia the Queen was blamed. When the latter so warmly championed the Sandro-Moretta romance, Augusta regarded it as an insult to herself and her family; her old friend was deliberately encouraging the marriage of a Prussian princess to a morganatically-born prince while 'plucking the finest fruits', the Romanovs, for her own relations. That the Queen was the grandmother of Moretta just as much as of Ella, and vehemently opposed the latter's engagement on acount of her distrust of Russia, was apparently ignored. Then when the *Almanach de Gotha,* the directory of royal and noble status and genealogy, suddenly demoted the Battenbergs from Part I to Part II, containing the lesser aristocracy (including the Bismarcks, of all people), the Queen was 'furious and indignant beyond words'.[25] She immediately believed the Empress to be responsible.

Fritz soon came to curse the day that Sandro entered their lives. Meanwhile his wife and daughter, braving almost total ostracision by the Empress, watched events in Bulgaria with ill-disguised admiration for her ruler. During the autumn of 1885 he faced a Serbian invasion of his territory, supported by Austro-Hungary, and trounced their combined forces at the battle of Slivnitza. Wild with delight, Vicky's emotions ran away with her as she sent him a twenty-eight-page letter of congratulation. So glowingly did she sing his praises that Bismarck and his cronies whispered it was really she and not Moretta who was in love with him. It was certainly easier for them to attack her than Queen Victoria, who applauded Sandro just as vigorously in her own way, and never missed an opportunity of inviting him to stay with her. Nevertheless she foresaw Russian jealousy at his sucess and knew that the Tsar's patience was wearing dangerously thin. So did Sandro himself; by April 1886 he was a worried man. The popularity he had won as a result of his victory the previous year was strongly resented at St Petersburg, and only one thing could save his position — immediate marriage to Moretta. But no amount of fervent love and admiration on the part of the three Victorias could save him from the undying hatred of his cousin. Early one August morning a gang of over a hundred Russian officers burst into his palace at Sofia, forced him at gunpoint to sign a hastily-improvised deed of abdication, and sent him under arrest to the Austrian frontier. Public opinion in Bulgaria demanded his return a week later but, embittered and aged by all he had gone through, he wearily ratified his deed of abdication. 'Seldom did so much injustice and ingratitude fall to any man's share,' wrote Vicky. 'He did his duty from first to last, and deserves the approval of all honest men and good soldiers.'[26]

While Vicky tried to comfort her hysterical daughter, and Queen Victoria railed against 'Russian villainy and monstrosity',[27] Fritz was preoccupied with family troubles of another kind — Bismarck's attention to the insufferable Willy. Having won the young man over to his reactionary way of thinking and turned him almost completely against his parents, the Chancellor proceeded to treat him as if he was already Crown Prince.

Fortunately one of Willy's missions had an unforeseen side-effect which brought him down to earth. On being sent to Russia in the autumn of 1885 to represent the Emperor at the Tsarevich Nicholas's coming-of-age celebrations, by which time the anarchist threats had subsided in the face of vigorous repression, Willy took it for granted that the court at St Petersburg had no tender feelings for his parents in the light of their attitude towards the Battenbergs. His mother completely ruled his father, he assured the Tsar, and his uncle, the Prince of Wales, was not to be trusted. If he had realised the respect that Alexander had for family life he would have kept his mouth shut, but the Tsar had worshipped his own mother and was on good terms with Bertie, who after all was his brother-in-law. He never forgave Willy for such unfilial talk and cold-shouldered him for the rest of his visit, later dismissing him as '*un garçon mal elevé et de mauvaise foi.*'

Bismarck's next plan, however, was more serious. In the following year he arranged for Willy to enter the Foreign Office at Berlin and gain some experience in international affairs. That his young disciple had no genuine enthusiasm or ability for hard work, and far preferred to act the part of a well-informed prince for show, was of no account; the Chancellor's main intention was to insult Fritz. It succeeded, and he wrote to Bismarck protesting that the appointment was dangerous 'in view of his tendency towards overbearingness and self-conceit.'[28] He himself had never been allowed to see a single foreign despatch in quarter of a century as Crown Prince, but he had endured too many years of humiliation not to be wise to Bismarck's motives, and was less surprised than hurt when the Chancellor did not bother to reply to his letter. It was a bitter pill to swallow — but a trifling one when weighed beside that which was yet to come.

Yet another cause of deep concern to Fritz at this time was the still barely dormant European tension. As he learnt much less from his father's ministers than from hearsay and the press, he was led to believe enough to appreciate that war could not be too far away. Once again French hostility was largely responsible, this time complicated by Anglo-French rivalry for the control of Egypt. France's refusal to cooperate against European intervention in North Africa left Britain to defend her interests alone, but the resulting bitterness led to Jules Grévy's government threatening to induce Germany to promise neutrality in the event of Anglo-French conflict. If Germany agreed then France would guarantee her friendship, but if Bismarck refused then the French government would accept Russia's constantly-renewed offers of an alliance. Fritz and Vicky considered such a prospect unlikely as Bismarck still apparently distrusted France, but they knew that as long as Germany did not give the French a formal declaration granting her a free hand towards England she would not move a step. They therefore felt that England should take 'some energetic step in Egypt to her own advantage' in order to assert her superiority and control.[29]

In January 1887 Fritz spoke to Bismarck. Exaggerating the threat to peace posed by the fiery French war minister General Boulanger, whose desire was for immediate revenge on Germany, the Chancellor dwelt grimly on France's renewed purchase of horses and building materials for the construction of barracks near the frontier fortresses, and spoke in vague terms of hopes for an 'understanding' with England and Italy. 'Matters are fast coming to a critical point here,' Fritz wrote to Queen Victoria, 'and if this unfortunate inexcusable war breaks out, how much the interests of the Great Powers, and England's in particular, will have to suffer.'[30] As in 1875 the scare soon lost its impetus, and French hostility towards Germany simmered for another generation. But within a few months, Fritz was preoccupied by worries infinitely greater than another war.

CHAPTER 14

The Shadow of Disease, 1886-87.

By any standards Fritz's programme for the summer and autumn of 1886 was a full one, particularly as he had not been well that spring. Moretta was taken ill with measles in March, Sophie and Mossy in turn catching the infection; just as they were recovering, their father went down with it. After a few weeks of convalescence at Homburg, he and Vicky attended the opening of the Jubilee Art Exhibition in Berlin, commemorating the twenty-fifth anniversary of the Emperor's accession to the Prussian throne. In June he was sent to Munich to represent his father at the funeral of ex-King Ludwig of Bavaria, who had been deposed on the grounds of mental instability only to drown with his doctor in strange circumstances. One of his last orders as King to his servants — fortunately ignored — had been to go and seize Fritz, chain him in a cave, and keep him on a diet of bread and water.[1] A few weeks later, he and Vicky entertained the haughty Duchess of Edinburgh at Potsdam. In August he was present at the quincentenary festival at Heidelberg with the Grand Duke of Baden, followed by a service and march past at Potsdam to mark the death centenary of Frederick the Great. As summer merged into autumn he attended the Wagner festival at Bayreuth, and then manoeuvres at Strasbourg.

With the added strain of continual worry about both Sandro and Willy, he thus thoroughly deserved the rest which his holiday visit to Italy in September allowed him. Vicky and the younger girls, still suffering from the shock of Sandro's ill-treatment, had left Potsdam first, and he joined them at the little village of Portofino near Genoa. It was a quiet spot, the simplicity of which recalled the pleasures of cosy Bornstädt, and they decided to return the following autumn; so might they have done if he had not caught a heavy cold there. One evening they went out driving with King Humbert and Queen Margharita, and the coachman lost his way. There was a chill in the air, and Fritz had not brought his greatcoat; when they arrived back later than intended he was shivering. Not only did his cold and catarrh remain with him throughout the winter after returning to Berlin, but when he spoke an uncomfortable hoarseness was evident. At the beginning of the new year 1887, Vicky wrote prophetically to a friend that she had reached an age when she no longer thought herself secure from the blows of fate.[2] Yet she could not have foreseen the heaviest one of all.

The symptoms continued for several weeks without any sign of improvement and Dr Wegner, baffled, decided to seek specialist advice. Early in March Fritz was examined with a laryngoscope by Professor Karl Gerhardt, lecturer in medicine at Berlin University. He discovered a small swelling on the lower portion of the left vocal cord, a matter which he said could be put right with some simple though painful treatment. Fritz accepted with fortitude the professor's agonising attempts to remove the swelling daily with a wire snare, but became uneasy after this proved unsuccessful and attempts were made to cut it out with a circular knife. This too failed and after a couple of weeks Gerhardt resorted to cauterising it with red-hot platinum wire. But every time the swelling was removed, it reappeared the next day. The professor was undoubtedly doing what he considered to be the best for his royal patient, but his method of cauterisation was in those days a risky one which no trained laryngologist would have attempted. In fact, such treatment in these early stages poses the first of several hypothetical questions about Fritz's illness: did the professor's methods turn a potentially harmless growth into a malignant one?

On 22 March a tremendous gathering of royalties at Berlin, among them the Prince of Wales and Crown Prince Rudolf of Austria, sat down to dinner in celebration of the Emperor's ninetieth birthday. Everyone noticed the hoarseness in Fritz's usually resonant voice as he made a speech congratulating his father.

For a while, however, anxiety mellowed in an aura of domestic bliss. Following his address came the announcement of Henry's engagement. The young sailor prince was not a strong personality; all too conscious of the shadow cast by his elder brother, while at Berlin he was susceptible to Bismarck's influence, siding with his brother and elder sister, but alone with his parents it was a different story. As Vicky wrote, he was 'always nice when he has been with us for some time, but not when he has been set up by others, and his head stuffed full of rubbish at Berlin.'[3] While Willy usually came to see his parents only to pour scorn on their ideals or to sneer at the Battenbergs, it was Henry who — in the face of strong opposition at court — had travelled to Osborne in July 1885 with his cousin Irene of Hesse for the wedding of their aunt Beatrice. It was to the same cousin that he became engaged less than two years later. Fritz and Vicky were not too keen on the intermarriage of cousins, but they gave the couple their blessing; wedlock might have the effect on Henry that had been lost on Willy, especially as Alice's daughters possessed a strength of character that was lacking in Dona. The engagement was celebrated after the Emperor's birthday dinner with a short theatrical performance staged by Henry and Moretta for their parents. It proved to be one of the last happy evenings that Fritz was ever to spend with his family.

Meanwhile Gerhardt was continuing to subject his royal patient to the painful and ineffective treatment. When the swelling failed to heal he suspected that he was dealing with a cancerous growth instead of a simple tumour, as he had thought at first. Early in April he decided to send Fritz for a cure at Ems where a change of air and rest from medical attention, apart from inhalations and douches for the nose and throat, ought to prove beneficial. Accompanied by Vicky, the three younger girls, and Dr Wegner, he left the cold air of Berlin for a few weeks. On his return in May he felt so much better that he was ready to believe himself cured, apart from continual hoarseness. Only on medical diagnosis did Gerhardt discover that the swelling was not only still there, but larger than before. Another opinion was required and he prevailed upon Professor Bergmann, one of his university colleagues. Bergmann was only a surgeon and could not use the laryngeal mirror, thus having to rely on Gerhardt's diagnosis — an example of teamwork which was common practice in those days. On the basis of this he recommended an immediate external operation on the growth, which he was convinced was malignant; to accomplish this successfully he would have to split the larynx in order to remove the swelling once and for all. In the eyes of subsequent medical opinion — and in the light of the rest of the case — he did not appreciate the seriousness of what he proposed, saying that it was no more dangerous than an ordinary tracheotomy (excision in the windpipe).[4]

By now Fritz, thoroughly alarmed, suspected that something was seriously wrong with him. He remembered with a shudder that his cousin Prince Frederick Charles had died in June 1885 of a cancerous tumour in the face. Already he began to speak gloomily of his numbered days and of the probability that his father would outlive him. Vicky was terrified, 'more dead than alive with horror and distress',[5] when Bergmann talked of operating. Her burden was all the heavier as for once she could not share her worries with him. Bravely she feigned an optimism she did not really feel in order to try and shake him out of his depression.

The gravity of the news shook Bismarck as well. When he first heard that Fritz was unwell he and his clique scoffed that he was simply out of sorts because of his father's longevity, and impatient for him to die. When it became obvious that the ailing Crown Prince had something rather more than the usual winter influenza, and that he was on the point of undergoing a serious operation, the statesman began to feel the earth move under him. At

Dr Morell Mackenzie

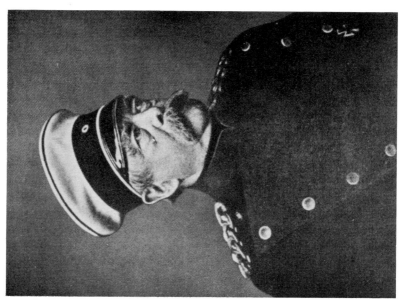

Otto von Bismarck

once he stepped in; no such operation, he insisted, could be undertaken without the consent of the patient himself and, since the patient was heir to the throne, the Emperor's consent would also be necessary. He proceeded to call in three more doctors — Dr Schrader, Fritz's own Surgeon-in-Ordinary; Professor Tobold, a semi-retired but very experienced Berlin laryngologist; and the Emperor's physician Dr Lauer. On 18 May all six (including Wegner) held a consultation and agreed that he had cancer; four were in favour of operating immediately. Gerhardt and Schrader objected as they placed more weight on the realisation — known to all — that it would as likely as not prove fatal, and that even if Fritz survived then he would certainly lose his voice altogether. The proceedings were reported to Bismarck, who agreed that no operation should take place without the consultation of another specialist.

The Chancellor came personally to tell Vicky of his intervention, and she was surprised to find him 'really very nice'.[6] In her anxious state she did not appreciate until he made it clear to her that one thing united them: growing apprehension of Willy. His arrogance was already quite intolerable; if he was to get it into his head that he might become Emperor before his time, the consequences would be equally unpalatable for parents and statesman alike. Already cancer was being openly discussed in Berlin, and some of Bismarck's less restrained disciples were saying among themselves that the Prussian constitution forbade the reign or accession of a sovereign who was mortally ill; it was a rumour which suited Willy and Dona very well. A worried and indignant Bismarck had to tell them that this was nonsense; even if Fritz did feel inclined to withdraw from the succession — which he certainly did not — it was not a choice for him to make. For Willy no longer worshipped the Chancellor so fervently, and the old man had a not unfounded fear that, once the young prince succeeded to the throne, his dismissal would not be very far away. It was therefore imperative that Fritz should follow his father, for even if his reign was only a short interlude it would still leave him time to secure his position. For Fritz, he knew, realised that it would be politically dangerous to dismiss Bismarck on his accession, while Willy knew well that it would be constitutionally possible, regardless of the consequences.

So who was 'the other specialist' to be? The doctors put forward several names from outside Germany, and after Bismarck had stressed for obvious reasons that he should not be French or Austrian the Scotsman Morell Mackenzie seemed the most eligible. His qualifications were impeccable, and he was the author of a textbook on nose and throat diseases which had been translated into several different languages and was used in German medical schools. Moreover Gerhardt already knew him, and he spoke fluent German.

But there were more sinister reasons for his choice. The German doctors were puzzled by their heir's illness, and while they assured Vicky that the operation they proposed was almost harmless, being 'undertaken without hesitation in the case of children and old people',[7] they were privately far from confident. The decision to consult a foreign specialist was nothing less than a deliberate example of handing on the torch. If the disease did take a turn for the worse and prove fatal — and they had no reason to suppose otherwise, particularly in view of Fritz's rather weak constitution — it would vindicate them if a foreigner was left to shoulder the blame. So why not an Englishman (the fact that Mackenzie was a Scot, though his practice was based in Harley Street, was of course academic); it would be a triumph for the Anglophobes at court if the death of their Crown Prince could be laid at the door of the country from which his unpopular wife came.

What added further weight to the case of German medical science and intrigue was that Mackenzie entered the case with a handicap; although well-known for his skill, he was not popular in his own country. However, on 19 May, at the other doctors' request, Vicky telegraphed to her mother to send him at once. This the Queen did but, knowing that her daughter's instincts of loyalty could be as passionate as her own, she added a note of warning from her own physician Sir William Jenner; the Scot was clever but 'greedy and grasping about money and tries to make a profit out of his attendance'.[8] On the afternoon of 20 May he arrived in Berlin and was driven to the Neue Palais, where rooms had been prepared for him. Fritz shook his hand warmly, and with a sad smile whispered gruffly that he was sorry for the trouble his throat was causing to everybody. He offered to let the doctor examine him at once, but the latter suggested that he should confer with the others in attendance first. After consulting them he examined Fritz's throat, which he was interested to note gave him no pain when breathing or swallowing — an encouraging sign. He removed a small portion of the swelling and passed it to Virchow, at the Berlin Institute of Pathology, for scrutiny under a microscope. His opinion was that an operation, which would as likely as not prove fatal, must be avoided if possible, and that a thorough examination should be made first to establish whether the growth was cancerous or not. Virchow considered that he could not make a conclusive diagnosis from such a small amount, and Mackenzie removed a larger sample two days later.

It was at this stage that the quarrels, which survived the unhappy patient, began. With tension on all sides it was inconceivable that trouble would not arise; now it flared. According to Gerhardt, when Mackenzie removed the second portion of the swelling he injured the healthy right vocal cord and made it bleed. The new portion still did not prove that the growth was malignant, but Gerhardt was suspicious. Not having Mackenzie's experience or skill, he was not in a position to know better, but he probably mistook the appearance of the right vocal cord and an excited imagination did the rest.[9] Mackenzie later felt that his own success on the first occasion 'had mortified him, and he was glad to find fault';[10] a rather self-justificatory but nonetheless credible remark. Whatever happened, it was the spark that set the fire alight and began the quarrels which overshadowed the rest of the patient's life, to continue long after he was in his grave. The German doctors maintained that the only course was for them to operate immediately, while Mackenzie insisted that Fritz would die if they did. Subsequent history as good as proved him correct. Less than two years later, after Fritz's death, when the controversy was at its height, Bergmann announced that he was going to vindicate German medical science by performing a similar operation on another sick man who had the same trouble, without 'relying on the delusions of a foreign doctor'.[11] Having begun to operate he discovered that his diagnosis was wrong, and the man died within a couple of hours; needless to say the incident was carefully hushed up. In 1896 yet another unfortunate was committed to Bergmann's hands, and the same thing happened. Writing to her daughter Sophie, by then Crown Princess of the Hellenes, Vicky said how thankful she was that she had listened to Mackenzie, 'and that dear Papa was not murdered in this fashion.'[12]

In the midst of the arguments, Bismarck intervened to remind the doctors that they were dealing with no ordinary patient. The life by which he had set so little store in earlier years, he thundered, was too precious to be considered like that of an ordinary man.[13] Vicky was distraught, hardly knowing who or what to believe. Yet she supported Mackenzie, and not just because of his nationality — although she would have been justified in so doing, after Willy's dangerous birth and her experience of German inefficiency and narrow-mindedness at the start of the Franco-Prussian war — but because she like him was optimistic. Her determination to look on the bright side, however, was no weak-kneed attempt to avoid facing up to the worst that could happen; it was vital for Fritz. Already weakened by years of bitterness and frustration, his sufferings exceeded the physical agony of his daily cauterisation. Two of her closest male relatives, her father and eldest brother, had been severely attacked by typhoid fever; her father had succumbed to it largely as he did not 'cling to life' and did not have the strength of will or the desire to survive. On the other hand the Prince of Wales had been far more seriously ill in 1871 but pulled through because, quite simply, life had plenty to offer. What had it left to offer Fritz if he recovered — a few years of rule, and subsequent inauguration of a new era, or more waiting on the threshold of the throne while the reactionary clique continued to fete young Willy? Vicky knew she owed it to him to keep his spirits up, an increasingly hard task. If he was allowed to believe that his illness was fatal, she understood, then he would wither and die almost at once. If she showed him that there was still hope left, perhaps he would recover. What other wife so devoted to her husband would have acted differently?

Unfortunately it was not only their enemies who distrusted Mackenzie. Few went as far as Willy and Herbert Bismarck, who both called him a deliberate fraud, but some of Fritz's liberal supporters were uneasy. Baron von Roggenbach declared that he was a shrewd man merely out to advertise himself and did nobody any good by his over-optimism. There was nothing wrong in looking on the bright side, with reservations, and one cannot criticise Vicky for doing so. She was no medical expert herself, and she was not to know who was right, Mackenzie or the German doctors — at this stage, the question was hypothetical. But in her unrelenting admiration for the man she overlooked his faults. He had left Harley Street in such a hurry that he did not bring his own surgical instruments and had to have them sent to Potsdam later, a lapse which seems nothing short of unprofessional; he consequently had to buy a pair of forceps made to an unfamiliar French pattern before examining Fritz for the first time. Secondly he was far too optimistic. When the German doctors told Vicky — and there is no reason to doubt it — that the disease was in its early stages and little harm had been done, Mackenzie went one giant step further and promised a complete cure within weeks, subject to favourable conditions. Even if he believed in his heart of hearts that this was possible it was foolish of him to say so, since if things were to go wrong the German doctors would have every justification in holding him up to ridicule. The stormy Anglo-German relations of the previous few years should have taught him to tread carefully, if indeed Vicky had not warned him himself; the more vocal German opinion of the day was only too ready to criticise a Briton.

Yet another reason for their standing by Mackenzie and his talk of a cure was the imminent celebration of Queen Victoria's Golden Jubilee in London. They had both set their hearts on going, and the Queen was expecting them. Not so Willy. In the spring he knew for certain that he would be invited, and when his father's illness became common knowledge, he took it for granted that he alone would be representing Prussia. At the end of May he came to tell Vicky that his grandfather had consented to this, and with typical presumption he immediately wrote to Queen Victoria and told her. Angry as Vicky was, she knew that it would be unwise to prevent him from going at all; it would only be another opportunity for the reactionaries to 'use' him against his parents. In ordinary circumstances the Queen would have welcomed her grandson with open arms, but she was not at all pleased with the latest reports of his disrespectful behaviour at such an anxious time. Moreover, she was thoroughly angry with nearly the whole of the Berlin court; at the same time the Battenberg affair flickered again. Moretta had entreated her grandparents to let her follow Sandro into exile, and a blank refusal was the least of the results. Then the Empress Augusta got it into her head that her son, believing himself to be dying, was about to give his immediate consent to the marriage. Undeterred by her old friend's taunts about the parentage of her son-in-law, she threatened to disinherit both Moretta and Vicky. The furious Queen could not 'find words to express her horror and indignation.'[14]

No matter what, Vicky was determined that she and Fritz should go to London for the festivities. They had both been looking forward to going, and she knew that it would be far better for his morale if they went — despite any physical discomfort that the journey overseas might produce — than if they stayed in Germany, where they would be surrounded by more clashes between Bismarck and the doctors. They won the day; Mackenzie suggested that Fritz should come to England and be treated as a private patient in his London surgery. On being told the forced smile he had assumed for weeks became a genuine one, and Vicky had to turn her face away hurriedly to prevent herself from breaking down in front of him. The German doctors on the whole were pleased as well; their patient's absence would relieve them for a while of their responsibility for a valuable life, and place the burden more squarely on Mackenzie's shoulders. Bismarck stood by the Emperor, who muttered that he could not prevent his son, a grown man, from making such decisions. The only proviso laid down was that at least one German doctor, and preferably two, should accompany them in order to have a say as to how far Fritz could safely be allowed to exert himself in the celebrations. Dr Wegner, as his physician of several decades' standing, and Gerhardt's assistant Dr Landgraf* were chosen. The only note of dissension came from Willy, whose pride took a heavy blow when he was told that he would be travelling to London as a mere guest among the many other royalties and not as the sole Hohenzollern representative.

The news that they were going to England aroused more than a little protest in Berlin. The Emperor was suffering from a recurrence of his fainting fits which left him increasingly weak, and few believed that he would live another year. What if he should die while his heir was abroad — and in England of all places? What if the Crown Prince was to have a relapse and be too ill to return home? According to Gerhardt there were reasons to believe that either event was a probability. At the beginning of June the only symptoms of illness that Fritz displayed were almost total loss of voice — already he was writing everything he wished to say on a pad of paper he carried everywhere, in the hope that his gruff whisper would get better with rest — and a sore throat, which was attributed to the constant removal of portions from the swelling. Yet Vicky was so uneasy that on 1 June she spoke privately to Gerhardt, who was very pessimistic. He told her that not

---

*Landgraf was at this time a young and inexperienced surgeon. He was frequently permitted to examine Fritz's throat, but his clumsiness and the time he took exhausted even Fritz's patience until he complained to Mackenzie and Wegner. The authorities in Berlin regarded him as an amateur, for the gloomy medical reports he sent from Britain were never taken seriously.

only every time a part of the growth was removed did it grow again, but also the tumour was suppurating, and the right vocal cord was beginning to deteriorate. If this was the case, and if Mackenzie could not cure it, the only hope of saving Fritz's life lay in an operation, which would not have the same chance of success that it would have had a fortnight before. All he could hope was that Mackenzie was right and that his treatment would be successful, for they had 'nothing else to suggest'.[15] Torn between so many conflicting opinions, Vicky found it doubly hard to suppress her anxiety and keep a calm head in front of her husband, but she told herself that they were doing the right thing in going to the Jubilee; 'one cannot be kept a prisoner here, or be prevented from following a useful course by the fear of what might happen.'[16]

It was in high spirits that they left for England, accompanied by the doctors. Little did Fritz realise that he had said goodbye to his father for the last time. With them they secretly took a large collection of their private papers for storage in the inviolable safety of the archives at Windsor, a cautious move which was later to prove significant. On their arrival at London they made for the Queen's Hotel, Norwood, a healthier area in which to stay than the centre of the city where they would be in the thick of the dust and the heat. After spending a few quiet days there and attending Mackenzie's consulting-rooms for daily treatment, they moved to Buckingham Palace on 18 June in order that Fritz could have a couple of days' complete rest before the procession to Westminster Abbey.

Although he was spared the ordeals of state banquets and receptions, it gave him pleasure to meet as many of his fellow-guests as possible. One was Constantine, Crown Prince of the Hellenes, who was to marry Sophie two years later. Another was Crown Prince Rudolf, a young man whom Fritz had come to admire greatly. Both had much in common; they were imperial heirs to two of the most reactionary powers in Europe, and they shared liberal convictions that had brought them contempt and political isolation from their fathers' goverments. Rudolf had visited Berlin in March for the Emperor's birthday festivities, where he had been entertained at the Neue Palais and spoken forthrightly to his hosts on his distrust of Russian policies, particularly with regard to the Tsar's behaviour over Bulgaria. His forebodings of the country's expansionist ambitions and a desire to see the rest of Europe in a strong mutual alliance impressed Fritz greatly, partic-ularly as the Austrian ministers kept him so much in the dark and he too had to learn from secret meetings with his liberal allies. Rudolf's distrust of Bismarck and Willy, five months his junior, bound the Crown Princes closer together. In his less pessimistic moments, Fritz was tempted to speculate on the harmony that Germany and Austria could bring to Europe when they both succeeded their fathers.*

---

*Fritz's premature death and Willy's subsequent accession contributed in no small way to Rudolf's despair which led him to commit suicide with his mistress at Mayerling in 1889.

The sun poured brightly through Fritz's bedroom windows as he awoke from a deep untroubled sleep on the morning of Tuesday 21 June, feeling a little better and the swelling less tender when he gently touched it with his little finger. Vicky's smile on seeing how happy he appeared was less forced that it had been for weeks, but still she prayed that the day's ceremony would not prove too tiring for him.

Soon after eleven in the morning the procession began through London streets richly decorated with triumphal arches, evergreens, flags and brightly-coloured drapery: six cream-coloured horses pulling an open landau containing the Queen, a plump little figure in a black dress and a bonnet trimmed with white lace and diamonds, accompanied by Vicky and the Princess of Wales. As they came into view the bands stationed along the route from Buckingham Palace to Westminster Abbey struck up a rousing march. Following the coach and its escort of Indian cavalry came the Queen's three surviving sons, five sons-in-law and nine grandsons. Mounted on a white charger Fritz in his striking uniform of the Pomeranian Cuirassiers, his eagle-crested helmet, silver breastplate and Garter star glinting in the sunshine, towered above them all.* His brother-in-law Lord Lorne later likened his appearance to 'that of one of the legendary heroes embodied in the creations of Wagner'.[17] Public knowledge of his illness had swelled his popularity with the Londoners, whose cheering broke into a deafening roar as he saluted. Yet it did not escape the notice of the more keen-eyed among them that he looked thinner than usual.

He was just as observant himself while riding in the procession. After his death, the small pocket book he had been carrying in his uniform that day was found. Under the same date, he had made a note of many of the things he had seen in the streets on his way: the ambulance arrangements, drinking troughs for horses and dogs, and cabmen's shelters.[18] No explanation has ever been given, but taking into account his improved spirits during the stay in London it seems likely that he believed he would get better. Already looking forward to his accession and coronation, he was determined to ensure that the festivities would be more carefully planned than they had been for the coronation of Tsar Alexander II, where he had been surprised by the lack of attention to detail. The Jubilee arrangements, therefore, had given him several ideas which he would see were carried out when his time came.

Following the service at the abbey, all the princes and princesses moved forward to the Queen to pay her homage. When she stepped down from the coronation chair at the end, Fritz happened to be standing near her;

---

*His magnificent bearing on the occasion led to rather unflattering but all-too-true comparisons between him and the portly Prince of Wales, to the latter's detriment, in the *Pall Mall Gazette*. Some London clubs found the remarks so insulting that they banned the paper, thereby giving its sales to their members a healthy boost.

impulsively she embraced him, lingering on his arm in a moment of deep emotion which words could not translate.

He went to bed in the evening feeling tired but well and, above all, happy at having taken part in the procession. Both he and Vicky had been haunted by the prospect of his suffering a relapse or, worse still, being exhausted after leaving the abbey. That he had taken the exertion well was a good sign. How easy to think of what might have been — if the Emperor, Bismarck and the doctors had proved obstinate and forbidden him to attend, and if he had had to content himself sadly with being left behind at Potsdam to read accounts of the festivities in the newspapers. Despite the physical strain involved, his presence in London on the glorious occasion was the best medicine that anyone could have given him.

They stayed in London for a few more days, and were rewarded by continued fine weather. On the day after the procession they visited a children's fete in Hyde Park, taking a keen interest in the stalls and amusements prepared for the Queen's youngest subjects. But nothing brought a smile to Fritz's face more readily that afternoon that the little girl who, when presented to Her Majesty by the Prince of Wales, claimed proudly that in seven years she had never missed a day's attendance at school.[19]

Nevertheless Fritz's throat was still congested, and he had to continue daily treatment at Mackenzie's surgery. On 28 June the doctor removed all that was left of the growth, whereupon Wegner placed it in spirit in a sealed flask and sent it to Virchow at Berlin. On examination it proved nothing further about the disease; the professor's report could advance no new information. But away from the intolerable mantle of Berlin intrigue and argument, and surrounded by the reserved optimism of Vicky and the care of Mackenzie, Fritz believed that he was on the way to recovery. Count Seckendorff, who had in May described the doctor's arrival at Potsdam as 'such a blessing',[20] reported that his master was 'doing well, and we all hope that Dr Mackenzie's treatment will cure him entirely.'[21] It was in high spirits that they went to see the Golden Square Throat Hospital* and talk to the patients. One of those he spoke to was a little girl sitting up in bed nursing a doll, and he asked her whether she or the doll was the patient. Completely undeterred by the kindly but imposing figure of the imperial German heir standing by her bed, she replied simply, 'Sure I don't know which it is, my dear.'[22] The memory of this incident frequently made Fritz smile during the next few weeks.

---

*It was in aid of the this hospital's funds that Vicky commissioned Rennell Rodd (later Lord Rennell of Rodd), then a Councillor at the British Embassy in Berlin, to write a short biography of Fritz the following year. See foreword, p.7

From the hotel in Norwood they went to Osborne. The summer weather was so fine that they could spend most of the daylight hours outside, strolling around the gardens and lawns which reminded them of distant carefree days. Or Fritz would sit in his wicker chair beneath the shade of a cedar tree beside the tennis court, a cup of tea in his hand and his Italian greyhound lying beside him, while Vicky and Moretta played tennis with Seckendorff and Rowland Prothero, son of the local rector. On the hottest days they would go down to the beach, where Fritz sat on the sand while Vicky bathed in the sea. Yet every now and then, their uncertainty about the future made it impossible for them to relax completely. Over forty years later, when their niece Marie of Edinburgh — by then Queen Dowager of Roumania — wrote her memoirs, she recalled her uncle and aunt as she saw them at Osborne when a girl of eleven. Pretending to bombard her and her sisters with sand and dry seaweed, Fritz 'was jolly and yet one somehow felt he was condescending', while Vicky's forced gaiety was apparent; 'her smile had something in it of sunshine when the weather is not really warm.'[23] Marie should have realised that they had more on their minds than simple pleasures of the seaside.

Later that summer they moved to Scotland. Staying in the Fife Arms at Braemar, they drove daily the few miles east to Balmoral. The pure air of the Scottish Highlands had the intended effect and Fritz temporarily became stronger, his voice steadily improving. He saw the Queen regularly and she was relieved to see how much better he looked. She did not know that Dr Mark Hovell, a senior surgeon at the throat hospital who was in attendance at Braemar, had examined him and was convinced that the growth was malignant. Although not so highly qualified or internationally famous as Mackenzie, there is evidence that Hovell was possible the most skilled of all the doctors who attended the royal patient, but was brought in so late that Mackenzie was completely in command — in Britain at least — by the time he arrived. Having neither the self-assertive qualities or the unguarded conviction that he was right, he said nothing for the time being. But Mackenzie was still as confident as ever, and his hope was infectious. In August, Fritz wrote of him that 'he left me at the end of two days so well satisfied that he remarked he considered my sufferings at an end even though I undoubtedly required special care with rest and silence for a long time in order to avoid a relapse.'[24] The emphasis on the note of caution was missed by nobody, but all the same Fritz was deeply grateful and anxious that his mother-in-law should acknowledge this in some way. On 7 September, therefore, the Queen invited the doctor to lunch at Balmoral, and afterwards knighted him at an improvised ceremony in the drawing-room. She still had her misgivings and doubted his suitability, but to refuse Fritz's request for recognition of his services would have been tantamount to telling him that he was doomed. After laying down the sword she asked

Mackenzie searching questions about the illness. It disturbed her that he could tell her so little.

It was not only the Queen who was uneasy. At Berlin the court, which had with unconcealed reluctance allowed its heir to go to England for the Jubilee — but not indefinitely — was wondering when he would return home. The doddering Emperor was sometimes so weak that it was obvious he would not last much longer. Besides, what was his son doing in the hands of a British doctor whose diagnosis was openly believed to be wrong? Even liberal circles feared that Willy was gaining too much influence in state affairs during his father's absence — not that Fritz's presence at Berlin had made much difference before — and were impatient for their champion to come back and divert some of the attention from his son. Backed by Mackenzie, Vicky put her foot down: 'it would be madness to spoil Fritz's cure while he is in a fair way to recovery, but not well yet!'[25]

German opinion was the least of their troubles; quarrels were closer than they had thought. On one of the last days in Scotland a row broke out between Seckendorff and the Chamberlain Count Radolinski, a dishonest self-seeking Bismarckian who had been chosen to replace the faithful von Norman in Fritz's suite. Like the other servants whom the Chancellor had placed in the heir's employment over the passing years — with the notable exception of Seckendorff — Radolinski was a seemingly devoted man whose attention came not from a desire to serve Fritz and Vicky, so much as from the necessity of secretly sending Bismarck a weekly report of the household, and Vicky's conversation in particular. In her anxiety she was completely deceived by his faithful manner, as was Fritz to some extent, until Seckendorff warned her to be more circumspect. At the same time, he told her that Radolinski was doing his best to get rid of him. To support his campaign he had resorted to typically Bismarckian vilification; Vicky, he insisted, was Seckendorff's mistress in more ways than one. During their sojourn in the Highlands he told Sir Henry Ponsonby, Queen Victoria's secretary, that Vicky and her servant were lovers, and that she had prevented the operation on her husband so she could keep him alive just long enough to sample the privileges of being Empress — then she would be left with an imperial dowry, and Seckendorff. Ponsonby was wise enough not to fall for such ridiculous stories and cold-shouldered the man after that but other tales, though equally false, were far more easily believed. The Queen was sometimes taken in, and later found reason to ask her secretary why her daughter found it necessary to take Seckendorff everywhere with her, even up the slopes of Lochnagar.[26] Well might Vicky and Fritz have been entitled to ask why her mother had trailed her late attendant John Brown around so much.

As summer turned into autumn the Scottish weather became damp and cold, and Mackenzie stressed the need for avoiding Berlin over winter. Early in September, the entourage said goodbye to the Highlands and left for Toblach in the Austrian Tyrol. For Fritz, it was goodbye to Britain for ever.

CHAPTER 15

San Remo, 1887-88.

On arrival at Toblach Fritz was enchanted with the scenery, of mountains and pinewoods, but the air was too cold for him. Before long he began to cough badly, look pale and suffer from insomnia. After one particularly bad night when he coughed so severely that Vicky dreaded he might die within hours, a telegram to London brought Mackenzie and Hovell out at once. The former reminded everyone that he had told them the Tyrol would be too damp in autumn, so they moved south to Venice and later Baveno, on the shores of Lake Maggiore. The sun shone brilliantly and Fritz was in better shape by the time his fifty-sixth birthday came around. All the children except Willy and Charlotte came to join them, acting a short play and performing on the piano, just as they had done in happier days at Potsdam. He was so obviously gladdened at this demonstration of affection towards him that Vicky had to force herself to remain cheerful while keeping secret a most unwelcome piece of news. She had received a letter from a friend that morning asking her to bring Fritz back to Germany at once; there was talk of a plot to exclude him from the succession, contrary to the law, and put Willy in his place. Sadly she tore it up to prevent anyone, most of all Fritz, from seeing it.[1]

Undoubtedly part of the concern, sometimes bordering on anger, of the Berliners for their beloved heir — who was popular with everybody except the reactionaries — stemmed from the lack of public relations. Catherine Radziwill believed that the greatest mistake Vicky ever made was to keep from the public genuine knowledge of his condition; the people would have pitied her and admired her courage if only they could have shared her trials with her instead of being left to guess and listen to idle rumour.[2]

Unfortunately she had to choose between either being completely open, or else keeping her agonies to herself in order that her husband should not suffer unnecessarily from seeing alarmist reports in the press. Already there were too many of these, and she tried her hardest to examine the papers before he received them, in order to help him avoid the prophecies of gloom which would depress him and therefore undo weeks of effort on her part to keep his spirits up. Sooner or later the public would be bound to know what danger he was in, but she was not to be blamed for drawing a veil of secrecy over his progress for as long as she did. With her judgment blunted by worry, she was bound to make the wrong choice — if indeed an alternative 'right choice' existed.

Already the papers were arguing. On Fritz's birthday the *Reichs-Anzeiger*, the official gazette, issued a statement that he was better, though it was necessary for him to spare his voice as much as possible and spend the winter in a warm climate so that, as far as possible, he could avoid catching cold.[3] Some of the other papers, inspired partly by the Bismarcks and partly by the grumbling doctors, promptly contradicted the news of his improvement and announced that he was suffering from cancer — which amounted to little more than vague confirmation of the widespread rumour — and the less respectable right-wing press promptly revived the fictitious law which forbade an incurably sick man to wear the Prussian crown. The Liberal papers fought back, and so the vicious circle continued. Despite Vicky's vigilant attempts at censorship Fritz's eyes naturally strayed, and he was 'dreadfully annoyed at all the foolish articles about himself.'[4] It might have been better for him if he had been merely annoyed; to be more accurate, in his fragile state he was more depressed than anything else. Such gloom and doom could only continue to sap what vitality was left in him, and thus reduce his chances of ultimate recovery.

Before long their attention was diverted by most unexpected news. A Frenchman died at about this time, leaving Fritz the whole of his fortune, totalling several million francs. He had been so embittered with the French government that he was determined to demonstrate his contempt for his country by bequeathing his wealth to the heir of the nation's enemy. Without hesitation Fritz declined to have anything to do with it.

Within weeks there was a further setback. He did not improve at Baveno, and Vicky put it down to the humidity. At the beginning of November they moved further south to the Villa Zirio at San Remo, on the Italian coast and close to the French border. The area was famous as a health resort; one of Queen Victoria's former art instructors, the painter and humorist Edward Lear, unsuccessfully sought a cure there, and by coincidence died at San Remo the following February. The villa consisted of two storeys and a basement, Fritz's apartments being a suite of rooms facing east and west, in order to catch the sun. The house stood on a mountain slope above the Riviera road, in an idyllic setting of palms and fruit trees, to say nothing of roses and other flowers which bloomed all winter. Above all it belonged to an Italian; the Berlin press had made much of the fact that the house at Baveno was leased to them by an Englishman.

But Fritz did not improve here either. He lost both colour and appetite, and the heat iritated him. Vicky had to have his bed placed in a warm but sheltered area of the terrace and sit by his side fanning him. It horrified her to see how little interest he suddenly had in anything or anyone — even her.

Then one morning, within a week of their arrival, she discovered that new swellings had appeared on his throat, and he found it a strain to sit up. She was panic-stricken, and Mackenzie was summoned once more. He examined him the morning after his arrival at the villa, discovering a new growth on the larynx which was larger than the previous swellings, and which had a distinctly malignant appearance.

No longer could the doctor talk lightheartedly of a cure. He told Fritz that the disease was more serious than he had thought; half-expecting it, Fritz wrote on his pad - his voice having gone for good — to ask if it was cancer. Mackenzie gravely replied: 'it looks very much like it, but it is impossible to be certain.'[5] With composure Fritz thanked him for being so honest. But when he and Vicky were alone, his self-control went and he burst into tears. 'To think that I should have a horrid, disgusting illness! that I shall be an object of disgust to everyone, and a burden of you all!'[6] It was tantamount to a death sentence, and with the dwindling of hope began to crumble what remained of the dreams of 1858. That he survived Mackenzie's statement for as long as he did is a tribute not only to Vicky's fiercely protective instincts in sustaining the will to live in him, but also to his refusal to admit defeat though so little hope remained.

While the staff at the local telegraph office doubled and reporters flocked from all corners of the world to the Riviera — there were 'some fifty reporters of different newspapers' there in February[7] — the calumnies at Berlin increased a hundredfold. For over twenty years the aristocratic Junker circles at court and the arch-conservatives had waited for the chance to get even with Vicky, for what they considered to be unwarranted interference in their politics and their country. Their Crown Princess, they asserted, had so set her heart on becoming Empress that she had kept the gravity of her husband's illness a secret, afraid of their both being passed over in favour of their eldest son. She had refused to listen to German doctors, preferring to summon an Englishman. Both of them had given him falsely optimistic hopes about his condition and she, to satisfy her own whim, had dragged him to London where he had exhausted himself in her mother's Jubilee procession. Furthermore, they had conspired to distrust their colleagues, thus preventing an operation on the sick man while such a step might have saved his life.

How little truth there was in any of these allegations. It was correct that Fritz and Vicky had eagerly awaited their accession to the throne in order to help inaugurate their principles for a more democratic and cultural regime, but she knew that they could not be set aside in the succession, no matter what his physical condition. They had been assured of this most emphatically by one of their most unforgiving enemies. From that point of view, therefore, there was nothing to be gained by shielding the truth. On the other hand, it was a deliberate falsehood to put out the story that Vicky had called Mackenzie of her own accord; she had not even heard of him before the German doctors mentioned his name, but Bergmann and Gerhardt did not intend to lose face by confessing that they were responsible for his appearance in the first place. Unfortunately Mackenzie's own attitude did nothing to help her. Bearing in mind his ambitious personality, it is more than likely that he preferred to believe that he had been summoned to Germany by the Crown Princess, not by mere fellow-doctors, and far from trying to dispel this impression, he apparently told this to others, including his official biographer H.R. Haweis. As for giving Fritz false hopes, her answer was mere commonsense: 'you know how sensitive and apprehensive (she wrote to Queen Victoria), how suspicious and despondent Fritz is by nature! All the more wrong and positively dangerous (let alone the cruelty of it) to wish him to think the worst! We should not keep him going at all, if this were the case.'[8] Finally, the allegation that she had conspired with Mackenzie to the detriment of German medical knowledge was given the lie by a letter which the doctor published in the Munich *Allgemeine Zeitung* on 31 October, in which he stressed that he had never been opposed to entering into consultation with his German colleagues; 'should any unfavourable symptoms unfortunately develop, I should be the first to ask for the cooperation of one of your countrymen.'[9]

But the most articulate of Vicky's enemies slandered her with little restraint and a good deal of imagination. While Bismarck kept reasonably silent, Waldersee, Willy's most ardent flatterer (with an eye to the future) proclaimed that she 'scarcely seems a responsible being, so fanatically does she uphold the idea that her husband is not seriously ill'.[10] On the same theme Lucius von Balhausen, Minister of Agriculture, later remarked in his memoirs that she resembled her mother, who had refused almost to the end to believe that the Prince Consort was sinking in 1861, went for a drive, and came back to find him dead.[11] Such irresponsible lies go not only to prove to what a pitch the reactionaries had worked themselves up, but also to show how little their writings can be regarded as historical evidence.

Fritz had always been popular in Prussia. All but the most spiteful of his political opponents were prepared to forgive him his liberal leanings to some degree in view of his distinguished military career; the worst that they said of him was that he was feeble and lacked a will of his own, though in their eyes this more often turned to pity for him, for having Vicky as his wife. His Bismarckian secretary Colonel Sommerfield wrote in 1885 that, thanks to her, he was now 'a mere cipher'.[12] The only circle who hated him as much as they loathed her were the representatives of the Christian Socialist Movement, led by the vindictive court chaplain Adolf von Stöcker. Their anti-Semitic ideas had always been deplored by liberal thinkers, the Empress Augusta for one, as 'absolutely unchristian'.[13] Fritz naturally shared his mother's view, and when at a court ball a few years earlier he had met a young Jewess who was dreading the prospect of being ignored, he detailed his friend Count Bernstorff — later German Ambassador to the United States — to dance with her. Vicky had shown her lack of prejudice by accepting the honorary chairmanship of a newly-founded orphanage for Jewish girls in Berlin. With his obstinacy and a tendency to be swayed by toadies looking forward to the reign of the next Emperor but one, it was only to be expected that Willy would range himself opposite his parents and identify himself with the anti-Semitic movement. In December 1887, he attended a meeting of Stöcker's mission at the Waldersees' house at which it was planned to extend the movement to cities throughout Germany. Entering into the spirit of it with his characteristic flamboyance and lack of forethought, Willy made a speech declaring that Christian Socialism was necessary to bring back people to Christianity who had lost their faith, and at the same time to get them to recognise the absolute authority of the monarchy. Bismarck found the speech almost as ludicrous as did Fritz and Vicky, and said so. It brought him a stinging rebuke that in Germany the Emperor, not the Chancellor, was master.

When Willy was not playing the Emperor at Berlin, he was acting out the part elsewhere — San Remo included. In the view of one of his more recent biographers, Michael Balfour, he accepted too unquestioningly the verdict of his flatterers that his father was being mishandled by Mackenzie and, excited by the prospect of premature power, tried to exert some influence out of a sense of duty.[14] Yet is may be said with equal justification that he had inherited Bismarck's creed of an eye for an eye, and he was still smarting from his experiences at the Jubilee. Having arrived in London with Dona in a bad temper, he had been further irritated by the lack of attention he received; the court had been far more interested in his father's health than in him. Then at the Windsor Castle state banquet, he had been so offended at being placed next to an African princess that he left early and retired to bed in a huff. Several months had passed, yet he was still seemingly awaiting the chance to pay his parents back.

It soon came. As the result of public criticism of Mackenzie two more doctors, Professor von Schrotter from Vienna and Dr Krause from Berlin, were sent to the villa to replace Gerhardt and Bergmann, to whom it was made clear that their services were not required any longer in view of their handling of the case. They examined Fritz, and after all doctors present — Mackenzie included — had held a consultation agreeing that the disease was cancer, they declared that two alternatives were possible: either tracheotomy (an incision in the windpipe, which would avoid danger of suffocation), or total removal of the larynx, a dangerous operation which would result in permanent loss of voice at the very least. Whatever course was taken, it would only prolong the patient's life for months rather than years. Then came the moment for them to break the news to Fritz. As they were ushered into the sitting-room he stood with composed dignity, giving a nod and a gentle smile that betrayed no emotion. Vicky was beside him, white as a sheet but determined for his sake not to give way. Schrotter, acting as the doctors' spokesman, told him of their conclusion, without mentioning the word cancer but leaving them in no doubt as to what was inferred, and then offered him the choice of tracheotomy or removal. Calmly he wrote on his pad that he and Vicky wished to be alone for a while, in order that they could decide. Together they selected tracheotomy, should it become necessary; Fritz felt that an Emperor mutilated by the removal of his larynx would be incapable of carrying out his duties. His resigned attitude made it clear that he knew himself to be doomed, but only if he was threatened with suffocation would he submit to a splitting of the larynx. Now that he knew the truth, he seemed if anything a little less depressed than before, when he had been bowed down by the uncertainty. Later in front of the servants and doctors, he apologised for feeling so well under the circumstances.[15]

It was just at this time, when he was confined to his room upstairs reading or writing in the long hours when was sleep was denied him, that Willy chose to put in an appearance. With him he brought yet another doctor, Schmidt, who was to examine Fritz and take a report back to Berlin with him. Whoever sent them is purely speculative; whether one, encouraged by public opinion and egged on privately by the other, decided to take matters into his own hands, or whether the Bismarcks sent them, is not known. It certainly had little to do with the Emperor, who was sliding further into senility. Whatever the circumstances, Willy was too full of his own importance when he arrived to make allowance for his mother's frantic state of mind. Without qualms he told her to get his father up and dressed so that he could take him back to Berlin for an operation. She would not hear of it, and struggling to restrain her temper she suggested that they should go for a walk together. To this retorted that he had no time, as he would be too busy speaking to the doctors. She answered that they had instructions to report to her and not to him, whereupon he insisted that he was acting on the orders of his grandfather, and to see that the doctors were not interfered with in any way.

Now she could simmer no longer. The sight of her son impudently standing with his back half turned to her, as good as telling her what to do in the presence of the household, was more than any woman in her desperate situation could stand. In her own words she 'pitched into him with ... considerable violence.' She declared that she would report his behaviour to Fritz and see that he was forbidden the villa in future;[16] with that she swept regally out of the room. Rather taken aback, he sent Radolinski after her to tell her that he had not meant to be so rude, but he had come as the

Emperor's representative — so he said — and was only doing his duty. The air cleared, she answered that she bore him no grudge, but would not put up with any interference; the head on her shoulders was every bit as good as his. However it was obviously only a truce, and on his return to Berlin he snarled that his mother had treated him like a dog. Forty years later, chastened by abdication and a decade of exile, he regarded the scene more objectively: 'she saw everything in shadows, everything hostile, saw want of sympathy and coolness where there was only a helpless silence.'[17] How much unpleasantness might have been saved if only he could have exercised similar maturity of judgement at the time.

Now that the press could announce with authority that Fritz's disease was 'carcinomatous', the journalists gradually shed their inhibitions.* When Vicky was not sitting with him talking soothingly or renewing ice bandages around his throat she forced herself to read the papers, having made him promise that he would not look at them first. They did not make pleasant reading for her; in particular, the attacks on Mackenzie made her seethe with anger. Whatever his faults — notably pride, which prevented him from admitting that he might have been wrong — he certainly knew how to handle them in the darkest hours of their life together. His tactful behaviour should have been an example to the other doctors, though unfortunately this was not the case. To them it was second nature to argue like prima donnas in the sickroom, never stopping for a moment to consider the feelings of a patient who detested anything approaching a quarrel. The anti-Semitic circle came out with the most imaginative and vicious slander of all; the Scottish doctor was really a Jew, they whispered, his real name being Moritz Marcovitz. Later when Vicky had let fly at him in a heated moment, Bergmann coupled his name with that of Seckendorff as Vicky's lover, another monstrous assertion as Mackenzie was a happily married man and devoted to his family.

   That was not all. She suspected, not without good reason, that the worst of the reactionary clique at Berlin were doing their best to see that Willy would succeed his ailing grandfather on the throne. Bismarck's attitude, according to Sir Frederick Ponsonby, was one of 'sympathetic interest'[18] in the invalid at San Remo; even if he did nothing to encourage actively or discourage the cruel slanders against Fritz and Vicky, he was wise enough to understand that it was in his interests to control the young man's arrogance

---

*Confirmation of Fritz's cancer was leaked to the papers. After he was told by the doctors at San Remo, correspondents were asked by Dr Schrader and Count Radolinski not to divulge the news. The intention was to prepare the German public gradually by a series of cautiously-worded bulletins which would make the patient's state generally known without shocking his own feelings. This plan, however, was frustrated by the immediate publication of a private bulletin to the Emperor in the *Reichs-Anzeiger*. The doctors' worst fears were realised, for Fritz saw it and was extremely upset.

the best he could. It was the sycophantic throng of Waldersee and the Foreign Minister, Baron Friedrich von Holstein, who wanted to see their Crown Prince excluded from the succession, and thereby ingratiated themselves with Willy in order to reap the finest rewards he might bestow when he should eventually ascend the throne. It could be argued that Vicky's fears were groundless — she had no concrete evidence to prove that any movement to pass over Fritz was afoot, but such rumour, counter-rumour and intrigue as that which filtered through to San Remo was unnerving to say the least.

It was no mere rumour, however, when their son was almost as good as promoted to Regent. About a week after the cancer diagnosis, the Emperor gave his grandson the authority, if and when he himself became incapable, to sign state papers on his behalf. Basically it was a reasonable idea; the old man was so senile that he could barely wield a pen to sign his name, let alone grasp the gist of a lengthy legislative document. But it would have been only common courtesy to consult Fritz first, not to let him hear of it as a *fait accompli.* He was furious at the time when an assistant of Bergmann was sent to them on orders from Berlin, in spite of an earlier telegram from Vicky that he should not come. That same morning a notification of Willy's impending duties, signed by Bismarck, had been delivered, but Vicky hoped that by playing for time she could wait for a more opportune moment to break it to him. But Henry arrived a couple of days later, pulling a letter from his pocket written by Willy, smugly describing his position as *Stellvertreter des Kaisers.** For Fritz this was the last straw, and he met it with his first flash of genuine anger for a long time. He became excited and talked a good deal — he could still 'speak' in a hollow whisper — which he had been warned not to do, and insisted that he would go straight back to Berlin and confront his father, son and the Chancellor regardless of the consequences. He was not having them look upon him as already dead. It took Vicky, who was just as angry, an almost superhuman effort to calm him down. If this callous treatment was calculated to wear down the spirit of the heir and destroy in a few minutes the delicate work of several weeks' careful nursing by his wife and chosen doctors, it could hardly have been more cruelly successful. Henry was too weak to understand that he was being used as a pawn in the game. He blindly took the popular view that his father was being killed by his mother and the English doctor, and although 'as obstinate as a mule',[19] it took Vicky only a day or so to talk him out of his uncharacteristic bout of pomposity.

Now that all hope of peace and quiet had gone for good, they found more comfort in the company of their welcome visitors than anything else. Baron von Roggenbach was a frequent caller, and few did as much to keep Fritz's

*Literally 'the deputy Emperor'.

flagging spirits up as this tactful Liberal who talked with reserved optimism on the future of Germany as a constitutional power as he played chess or backgammon with the heir to the throne. Much as he believed in the superiority of German medical skill and privately distrusted Mackenzie, he had to admit that the Scot had 'behaved honourably and straightforwardly here'.[20] The Grand Duke and Duchess of Baden and the Prince of Wales came too, as did the Duke of Edinburgh and Vicky's eccentric sister Louise, Marchioness of Lorne, but nobody has left a more graphic description of her ill-fated hosts than Lady Ponsonby, who as a maid of honour had judged Fritz a little harshly in the idyllic days of his engagement.* She arrived at the villa early in December to find him not only up and about, but with a deceptively fresh colour and good appetite. With reluctance she asked not to be seated next to him at evening dinner, as she could not prevent him talking; 'if one tries to avoid this by talking oneself, then he will answer. If one is silent, then he will begin the conversation.'[21] In front of others he tried hard, and often succeeded, in giving the impression of being reasonably well, but Lady Ponsonby stayed long enough to see that they had been taken in. A few days later, he broke the rules by picking up a paper to read a gloomy report on his health. Listlessly he pointed it out to Vicky, asking why they had to take every ray of hope away. Trying to sound cheerful she told him not to take any notice, then she went into the adjoining room (where Lady Ponsonby was already) and broke down completely.[22]

Vicky's courage paid off, and sometimes Fritz was quite hopeful; he knew that he would not fully recover, but the doctors had told him that the disease could perhaps be held at bay for a couple of years if not more. 'In no way do I despair, and hope, even if only after long and careful treatment, I shall be able to dedicate all my energies to my country as before.'[23] But the improvement was not maintained; one day he would be well, the next much worse. In mid-December Mackenzie was recalled from London by a telegram informing him of a sudden increase in the growth. On hurrying out to San Remo and examining the throat he announced that he could discover no dangerous symptoms present, and although there was a small new growth on the left vocal cord, the general appearance of the larynx was much better than it had been the previous month.

Fritz never failed to be deeply touched by the sympathy shown him from the outside world. The *Reichstag* sent him a telegram wishing him recovery soon after the vital diagnosis, and Sunday 27 November was chosen as a day of prayer for him in all the English chaplaincies throughout Germany. A visiting British clergyman, Bishop Wilkinson, preached a sermon at Berlin on the divine cure of the nobleman's son at Capernaum. A deaf-mute freely offered to have his own sound larynx removed and inserted in his Crown Prince's throat, but the surgeons had to admit that such an operation was

*See p. 34 above.

Empress Victoria, 1888

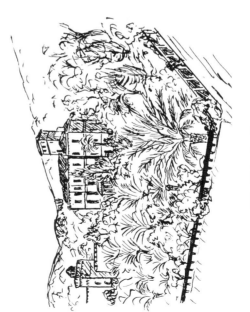

Villa Zirio, San Remo

beyond their skill. 'Infallible remedies' travelled hundreds of miles from well-wishers to the villa: whisky and oatmeal from the Scottish Highlands, ground oyster shells from England, a bag of live worms from the United States, and carbolic acid from France, to say nothing of medicines, ointments, and bottles of mineral water. Never having been superstitious he was not tempted to touch half of them, but it moved him beyond words to think how many people wanted to help him.

Over Christmas and the new year he appeared to rally. They had two trees, one obtained locally and the other sent by some German farmers from the Black Forest 'to give the Crown Prince a breath of German air'.[24] At eight-o'clock on Christmas Eve the household gathered in the large room opening onto the balcony, to be joined by Lady Ponsonby and her daughters, and the Italian Ambassador at Berlin Count Launay. Fritz and Vicky then appeared arm-in-arm, the folding doors opened, and the room was flooded with light as the guests gazed wide-eyed at both gaily-decorated fir trees, ingeniously places in a setting of roses, camellias, violets, geraniums and lilies, all freshly gathered from the gardens. Every guest and humble servant had been remembered and Fritz happily took his share in leading them up to the tables, heaped with presents, in the centre of the room. No amount of trouble was too much for those who had so loyally stood by him in his agony. In the morning they attended divine service, and in the afternoon a party of schoolchildren assembled in front of the villa to sing carols; deeply moved at the sound, he walked out onto the terrace to thank them.

But in the first week of January his condition deteriorated again; a growth had formed on the right of the larynx, he became feverish, had painful spasms of coughing, and slept badly. At one point he coughed up part of the growth, which was immediately sent to Virchow for diagnosis. It contaned no evidence of malignancy, a vaguely encouraging sign, but he continued to feel wretched and depressed.

On the night of 8 February his condition swiftly worsened. When daylight streamed through the windows he was gasping so violently that he begged for an immediate tracheotomy; without it, he would undoubtedly suffocate. The operation was performed that afternoon by Bergmann's assistant Bramann. Trembling violently Vicky waited outside the room, with Moretta and the widowed Grand Duke of Hesse comforting her. When it was over she was relieved to find him looking tolerably well and smiling bravely, although he could not speak, and the sound of breathing through the canula — through which he had to breathe in future — distressed her. Later he dozed fitfully, while she sat by his bedside writing to her mother. It had been a fearful ordeal for her, and even Charlotte and Henry, who had just arrived at the villa, seemed moved to pity by their mother's distress; they were 'very nice'.[25]

The same could not be said of Willy. Swaggering around Berlin boldly in the uniform of the General commanding the Second Infantry Brigade of Guards, his twenty-ninth birthday present, he seemed convinced that William II would succeed William I. Bismarck had written perceptively in January that the value of Fritz's reign would lie in the fact that his son 'would have time to settle down and learn'.[26] After the tracheotomy the press ran riot once again, and in the ensuing alarm it was widely rumoured that Fritz was dead. Willy's immediate reaction was allegedly to go to Bismarck and ask him to be as loyal a servant to him one day as he had been to his grandfather.

Bergmann returned the day after the operation. With him came Radolinski, who set the tone for the next few days by telling everyone how surprised he was to find Fritz still alive. Then Bergmann quarrelled with Mackenzie on the type of canula to be used, and voices were raised on all sides as the other German doctors came to the defence of their ally. Mackenzie remarked coldly that he was only staying at the request of the Crown Prince and Princess, and he could not agree with Bergmann's treatment; the latter, who had given up trying to be civil, growled that he was doing his best 'to keep this abominable colleague within the bounds of decency'.[27]

Fritz, most upset by the row, was heartily glad when they had gone and the temperature had cooled. If he did not improve, then he got no worse. Ten days later with understandable if pathetic optimism, Vicky wrote that he was 'turning the corner and beginning to mend'.[28] Another few weeks, she said, would set him up completely. It seems likely that her optimism at this stage was an act put on to bolster up their spirits, but unfortunately her desire for peace and rest during which time the patient could recuperate was not to be granted. The German doctors had been unable to resist the temptation to drag yet another colleague into the case, and on 26 February Professor Kussmaul arrived; he was not a laryngeal specialist and his only virtue — from the German point of view — seems to have been his nationality. His attempt to examine Fritz's throat was all too obviously amateur. All he could deduce was that the lungs were quite sound, therefore he needed no other proof that cancer was present. Vicky was stung to righteous indignation at Kussmaul being forced upon Fritz, as if too many doctors had not been brought along already. When she told Bergmann sharply that all they needed was for Mackenzie to adjust the tubes and treat the throat, he told her brutally that Fritz would never recover and could only rapidly worsen. To her request that he should wait a fortnight before returning, he agreed with 'a pitying incredulous smile'.[29]

Meanwhile, back at Berlin the old Emperor's strength was declining fast. Only a month away from his ninety-first birthday he was permanently tired, fainted regularly, and was more often preoccupied with the Franco-Prussian war or the Napoleonic struggles of his adolescent years than the present. Vicky had sent him for Christmas a portrait of Fritz, painted in oils by herself, and he would stare at it insensibly, murmuring, 'my son, my poor Fritz', with tears running down his withered cheeks. Sometimes he was convinced that his son was dead, and at other moments he talked of going to visit him at San Remo, where bulletins on his own health were arriving half-hourly, but his physicians would not hear of it. Fritz's thoughts were often with his father too. During those unhappy days so long ago, when both men had argued heatedly, he had never lost his filial affection; this love was often at the root of his subsequent unhappiness. As Vicky tenderly broke the news to him that the old man was sinking, he had at least the consolation of knowing that he had always been a loyal son.

Dutifully, but without a trace of emotion, the Empress Augusta sat beside her husband. Confined to a wheelchair, she had become a raddled, emaciated creature crippled with palsy, little more than skin and bone beneath her make-up and jewellery. It was common knowledge that she had been far from well for several years, and in 1881 she underwent a serious operation for breast cancer which had saved her life but left her a complete invalid. In the drama over her husband and son who were seemingly racing each other to the grave, it was whispered by some that she too lay at death's door. If any feeling stirred in her heart, her witch-like face betrayed nothing as she held the hand of a husband whose love she had never known. With them was their daughter, wearing mourning for her son Louis who had died suddenly in February. The Emperor lay on his back in a narrow camp-bed, wearing his beloved white jacket and old red scarf that had seen almost as many winter campaigns on the battlefield as he had himself. His bedside table was laden with bottles and glasses, but no medicine could prolong the already eventful life of this nonagenarian, one of the few survivors of the eighteenth century. By 8 March the people of Berlin knew that their tenacious old Emperor was not much longer for this world. During his last hours that night, as he lay muttering incoherently in his sleep and waking moments, his mind wandered back over the long past. A little before the end on the following morning, at a signal from her mother, Louise went to his desk and fetched the miniature that had stood there for so long — a portrait of Elise Radziwill. Placing it in his feeble hands, she watched his fingers close gently round it as a barely discernible look of peace came to his face. Shortly after eight o'clock, he was dead.

CHAPTER 16:

Accession, 1888.

Fritz was taking a walk in the grounds of the villa on the morning of 9 March when he was handed a telegram addressed to His Majesty Emperor Frederick William. Replacing it unopened on the salver for a moment, his eyes filled with tears before he could bring himself to read the message so obviously implied.

Minutes later, all members of the household were gathered in the drawing-room. Wearing his General's uniform and accompanied by a tense Vicky, the new Emperor entered the dignified but sad company. Seating himself at the table, he wrote out the announcement of his accession as Frederick III, following in the Prussian tradition.* Next, putting his pen down, he removed from his jacket the ribbon and star from his Order of the Black Eagle, and pinned it onto Vicky's dress. Unable to control her feelings any longer, she fell into his arms and wept unashamedly. When she had regained her composure, he took his pad and wrote a message for Mackenzie to read: 'I thank you for having made me live long enough to recompense the valiant courage of my wife.'[1] Her bravely smiling face throughout the months of anguish had not fooled either of them. Before the morning was over he sent his mother-in-law a telegram to express his desire for 'a close and lasting relationship between our two nations'.[2]

One of Vicky's first thoughts as Empress was the pathos of Fritz succeeding to the long-awaited throne 'as a sick and stricken man'.[3] It was mortifying beyond words to think of him coming into his inheritance in such tragic circumstances. But stricken or not, the date of departure for Berlin could not be postponed indefinitely. Mackenzie warned that the journey could be dangerous for his health, but Fritz replied that there were occasions when it was the duty of a man to take risks; as Seckendorff was to write a fortnight later, 'hope for the best and prepare for the worst'.[4] Early next day the suite left by train amidst glorious sunshine; everybody was in

---

*He had wanted to reign as Frederick IV, thereby implying the connection with the medieval Hohenstaufen Emperors of Germany, but Bismarck respectfully pointed out that he was Frederick III of Prussia and the same should hold for his imperial title to avoid confusion. With this both the new Empress and Crown Prince agreed. Frederick III of Hohenstaufen had reigned as Emperor of Germany, 1440-93; Frederick II (the Great) was King of Prussia, 1740-86.

mourning, and in addition Fritz had a brown woollen scarf around his neck.

The journey was broken at Leipzig, to let Bismarck join the imperial company. It was a strange moment for both men; one had done much to make the other's life a misery, but for once they were meeting on very different terms. On the evening of 11 March they reached Berlin in a swirling snowstorm. Fritz had stood the journey well, but the contrast between the freezing winter conditions at the capital, and the eternal sunshine to which they had waved goodbye a day before, was enough to give anyone a cold at least.

Whatever the state of his health, his mind was still as alert as ever. After taking up residence in Charlotte's and Bernard's apartments at Charlottenburg, which had more of a country setting than the Schloss at Berlin and was therefore considered better for him, one of his first duties was to confirm Bismarck in his position as Chancellor. At the same time he issued a proclamation to the statesman published in the *Reichs-Anzeiger*, summarising his aims on every subject from the maintenance of peace and religious toleration to education and the economy. Composed by Fritz himself, it was carefully worded so as to give offence to neither Bismarck nor his liberal foes. There were no doubt a few naive members of the *Reichstag* who had hoped for the Chancellor's dismissal at the beginning of the new reign, but they were outnumbered by those who appreciated that such an action would provoke a severe constitutional crisis, and leave the Emperor with an intolerable situation which even a fit sovereign would find a burden to handle. In any case, Fritz and Bismarck shared a mutual admiration of sorts for each others' qualities, hidden though it was, and in her more rational moments Vicky would have been the last to deny the inescapable truth: neither they as individuals, nor the Empire, could do without the present Chancellor. Even if they wanted to, they foresaw the potential futility of sending him on his way; as Waldersee wrote callously on their arrival in Berlin, 'everyone who is overthrown now will rise again soon'.[5]

But Fritz's energy as he received official deputations on his accession and guests who had come for his father's funeral astonished those who had believed the worst they had heard or read. From a distance, Prince Hohenlohe thought him looking not so much ill as thin and rather sallow, and his eyes rather prominent; only on closer observation could one notice his suffering expression.[6] Although he was so obviously unwell, and had to write on his pad instead of speaking, the sight of him as he stood before them so bravely and upright in his uniform inspired hope (or occasionally fear) that he might recover his health after all.

The late Emperor was buried on 16 March, a day of intense cold. The Prince of Wales, Crown Prince Rudolf of Austria and the Tsarevich

Nicholas were among the foreign royalties who followed the hearse, drawn by six black-plumed horses to the sound of muffled drums, through the crisp snow and frost on the road to the family mausoleum. Fritz had badly wanted to attend, and it took Vicky and Mackenzie no little effort to dissuade him. Deeply depressed and restless, he watched the long procession from the window of the palace. Seeing Willy as chief mourner, he wrote on his pad, 'that is where I ought to be,'; as the hearse passed beneath the window he broke down completely, and soon after retired to bed. After a good night's sleep, he had to content himself with a short funeral service in the Charlottenburg chapel the following day.

For the first few weeks, his routine was carefully arranged so as to enable him to perform the duties of a monarch as far as possible, without over-exerting himself. Every morning he breakfasted in bed, then dressed and went downstairs about half-past nine to either his study or the palace orangery. After the bright sunshine and semi-tropical gardens of San Remo, the latter was an unattractive building. It had not originally been constructed as an orangery, and the glasswork occupied only one side. The orange trees were old, thick-stemmed and covered with leaves, making the interior very dark and gloomy. Here he worked on state business, reading the papers, or writing letters till lunch. After eating he rested for an hour or so, then received visitors — usually Bismarck, and occasionally Willy. When they had departed, he concluded his business and wrote up his diary, dined at eight in the evening, and retired to bed between half-past nine and ten. Either Mackenzie or Hovell was in constant attendance all day and within call at night in case they were needed. Sometimes the battle against his condition proved too much for Fritz, and overcome by exhaustion he would drop what he was doing, lie down on his couch and close his eyes for a few moments. But in view of the appalling headaches he suffered, fits of coughing, and the morphia he needed to sleep, his devotion to duty was outstanding. One can feel nothing but admiration for a man who, broken by years of misfortune and tragedy, and wasted by disease to a mere shell, tried so valiantly to work as he considered befitted an Emperor; and nothing but compassion that this should have been his fate. Mackenzie noticed that when he felt worse than usual he worked harder than ever; having 'an almost overwhelming sense of the duties of his position', he seemed resolved literally to die at his post. The doctor never discouraged him from working, not only as he knew what disappointment such an order would cause, but also because he realised that the mental effort sustained him and diverted his thoughts from his condition.[7]

'The trial laid upon us is a very heavy one,' wrote Vicky to Lord Napier, 'and it is not easy to meet it with all the courage and energy necessary — One tries to keep a stout heart, and hopes on, that things may improve! The

Emperor is able to attend to his business, and do a great deal, but not being able to speak is, of course, most trying.'[8]

Among the new Emperor's first official actions was the decoration of those whom he considered had served him and Prussia loyally. Nobody objected to his making his former Chief of Staff Count von Blumenthal a Field-Marshal, but when he awarded the Black Eagle to the President of the Supreme Court of Justice Dr Simson, and to the Minister of Justice von Friedberg, there was an outcry in Berlin, especially among the anti-Semites. The latter were both of Jewish descent, and soon it was said that Germany was being ruled by 'Cohen I, King of the Jews'.[9] It was in his working with Friedberg, too, that Fritz encountered the first opposition of his reign. He wanted to leave the mark of a new era and of his own reign of toleration in some way, and grant an amnesty for political refugees and offenders, but Bismarck and the ministers brushed this aside as being a potential disservice to Germany. In the end a curtailed amnesty of sorts was granted, but Fritz was in no state to force his wishes through against a mass of threatened resignations, all from reactionaries who would bide their time and wait for the next reign.

However, such threats of clashes were nothing to the trials of the new Empress. There were many Liberals and close friends who understood and sympathised with her, but they were in almost as precarious a position as she was. A despicable few were guided less by loyalty than by the instinct of self-preservation, such as General von Winterfeld, formerly a trusted friend who during her widowhood was to play a leading part in her persecution; their closest friends were being watched carefully and had to be extremely circumspect in their contacts with the Emperor and Empress. Dr Ludwig Bamberger, Deputy Leader of the *Freisinnige*, was one of the most reliable of their advisers, but such was the state of intrigue in which they were surrounded that he and his Sovereigns could only communicate by means of letters discreetly delivered to each other by the widowed Baroness von Stockmar. It is pathetic to think that Fritz ascended the throne in such circumstances which rendered him a virtual prisoner to his Chancellor; if Bamberger had called at Charlottenburg to talk, Bismarck would have easily found some way to make him regret it. Well-meaning relatives who continually offered advice had little idea of the cruel situation. Queen Victoria, revolted by what she heard of the conduct of Willy, Dona, Charlotte and (sometimes) Henry, told Vicky to send for them and 'threaten them with strong measures'; the Crown Prince 'and his odious ungrateful wife' should be sent on a journey to find their level.[10] Nothing would have pleased her or Fritz more, but they knew it was impossible; any attempt to remove them from the scene, be it a hastily-arranged mission to one of the other European courts or anything else, would have met with instant outcry.

Her devotion to Fritz was mercilessly attacked. Because he could not speak she had to be with him almost constantly, especially when receiving visitors, and as she always pointed out to them how well he was looking, it was asserted that she wished to give the impression that his life — and therefore his reign, under her power-hungry English influence — would be a long one. When the news of his apparently reasonable condition leaked out, Herbert Bismarck concocted a new falsehood; he spread the rumour that Fritz was a mere living vegetable, his mind completely gone. This was later elaborated on to the extent that he was dead and the Empress was concealing the fact in a bid for power. Even more widespread was the allegation that she was demanding to be appointed Regent, to which Willy declared that neither the family, Prussia, nor the German Empire, would allow themselves to be ruled by a woman. The future Chancellor Prince Hohenlohe remarked that if every rumour he heard was true, then it would take a royal commission to protect the Emperor against the Empress.[11]

If the official government circles scorned Fritz and hated Vicky, their attempts to poison the peoples' minds bore little fruit. This was clear at the end of March, when at last the weather was fine enough for him to venture outside. The rousing reception which greeted them as they drove from Charlottenburg to Berlin in an open carriage one sunny day was reminiscent of that which had been accorded them on their arrival in the city after their wedding thirty long years earlier.

A couple of days later the Battenberg crisis reared its head once more; Vicky was anxious to settle Moretta's and Sandro's future together. That she behaved unwisely in so doing cannot be denied, but it is hardly reasonable to blame her for attempting to conclude the matter favourably while she had some chance of success. Exhausted by the strain of the past few months, and desperately worried by thoughts of what the future might hold in store, she was in no state to face her problems with the logic of a clear mind, especially as her emotions tended to overtake her when a member of her own family was involved. Ever since Sandro's abdication she had cherished the idea of the marriage being fulfilled, a wish that had not been dimmed by the eventful eighteen months which had elapsed. Yet Fritz was still not in favour of his daughter being married to the ex-sovereign prince, a scheme so firmly opposed by nearly everyone except his wife and her family. There had been moments when they had all but talked him round to their view, but now he knew that he was dying he was not inclined to let Moretta marry in the teeth of such controversy. Willy and Bismarck, he knew, would take revenge on them both when he died. Moreover, Sandro's position was miserable; he had no money, no country, and no future to offset his promising but abruptly-terminated reign. He would not be able to keep a wife brought up in an imperial family, and Fritz could not afford to provide for them financially. But Waldersee's often-repeated allusion to 'a frightful scene between the

Emperor and Empress'[12] at the beginning of April is pure fiction. Certainly Sandro had never been forgotten; Fritz had personally written him a friendly letter from San Remo in October, though mainly to assure him of his hopes for recovery, and not of his daughter's devotion. Moretta's feelings are shrouded in mystery; Vicky's vehement stand makes it quite possible that the young girl's role was that of dutiful daughter, but her strictly factual memoirs give no indication of her emotions at that time.

Such were Fritz's and Vicky's feelings. Sandro had equally strong views; he was now as determined to be as free of the business as he was to stay away from Bulgaria. Since that fateful night in August 1886 he had been living quietly as a private citizen in Darmstadt, with his attentions discreetly focused on a rather different quarry — a local opera singer, Johanna Loisinger. Gradually he decided that he would be happier with her than with the princess whose affections had provoked so much ill-feeling throughout Europe, but letters from Count Radolinski made it plain to him that Vicky had not given up hope. Not wishing to keep up false pretences, he wrote to Vicky in December 1887 and told her that, in view of the unfavourable circumstances, he was forced to ask her 'to help to bring this situation to an end'.[13] Yet Vicky saw this as being written in fear of the old Emperor and Bismarck, and did not yet concede defeat.

So stood the situation in April 1888. After consulting Vicky, Fritz invited Sandro to Berlin with the intention of discussing the marriage and bestowing on him some military command, probably that of the Brigade of Guards. According to Moretta, her father gave her his consent personally, 'and how lovingly we embraced one another. I believe he planned to bring about the marriage there and then.'[14] It was at this stage that Bismarck entered the fray, telling Fritz angrily that such a move would embitter Russo-German relations, and if the invitation went ahead then he would resign at once. Fritz therefore had no option but to cancel Sandro's visit.

The Chancellor had several motives for objecting to the revival of the uncomfortable business. The first was the still widespread if absurd belief — with seemingly no confirmation — that his son Herbert fancied Moretta, and that his father approved. The family pedigree alone ruled out Herbert's chances; his parents had been created Prince and Princess as recently as 1871, while Sandro's father had been born a prince. Yet if this was the case, then no wonder Vicky was so impatient to send Moretta to the altar with Sandro. The second reason was the most obvious; Bismarck could not resist any chance of thwarting Vicky's dearest wish out of spite, and if Fritz was on his wife's side, then a vendetta against a dying man was too good an opportunity to miss. The third reason is a more complex one, being concerned with the tangled web of Russo-German relations. As a private citizen Sandro had no direct political standing, save as a possible future threat to the Tsar's peace of mind; he was still popular in Bulgaria, where an active group of anti-Russian politicians wanted him back. His successor Prince Ferdinand of Coburg, a distant paternal relative of Vicky, allegedly powdered his face and had such a delicate constitution that he could only consult lady doctors.[15] If Sandro did win his Hohenzollern princess, his position would be firmer and subsequent demands for his reinstatement would grow louder. Although tongues were wagging in Darmstadt, few others knew about Johanna Loisinger, and those who had heard him voice his intention of staying away from Bulgaria shrugged it off as being simply the histrionic outpourings of a man who would soon forget. Only the family knew how much his ordeals had permanently undermined his health. Whatever Sandro's future, Bismarck ranted and raved that the Tsar would lose all confidence in his relations with Germany if the marriage went through, and even a visit by Sandro to Berlin would be interpreted as a hostile demonstration. Here the Chancellor was wide of the mark. When Lothar von Schweinitz, German Ambassador in St Petersburg, tried to sound out the Tsar's feelings on the issue, a message came back that the latter had expressed himself as never being so satisfied with relations between the empires as he had been at Fritz's accession and proclamation. Nikolai Giers, the Russian Minister, added that if Sandro did come to Berlin, 'although we would regret it, we would be convinced that neither the Emperor nor the Chancellor would change their policy of friendship towards Russia.'[16] This was a considerable shock to Bismarck, unaccustomed as he was to hearing what he did not want to hear, but he consoled himself by muttering to the press about the threat of a war with Russia which could only be to British advantage. His final objection was so extraordinary that it would not be worth serious consideration if it had not been alluded to by the historian Erich von Eyck: belief that the Battenberg marriage was part of a plot by Vicky to make Sandro German Chancellor, no less. The Prince would have been well suited to a position in the army, but nobody would have thought of promoting him to the Chancellorship, least of all of a power like Germany. Vicky had no more intention of doing so than Queen Victoria ever had of summoning Bismarck to be her Prime Minister. Somehow he fancied his personal power to be in danger, and saw ghosts.[17]

So what bound the arch-reactionary Tsar to the liberally-minded German Emperor? Alexander III's distrust of the young Empire had arisen largely because of his wife's attitude to the aggressive Prussia which had decimated Denmark in 1864, but her sister Alexandra had come to realise that Fritz could not be tarred with same brush as his fellow-countrymen, an attitude which the Tsar, for all his contempt of democracy, soon shared. Added to this was his respect for family relationships. Because of his warm regard for the Prince of Wales, he was appalled when Willy had proffered his unsolicited remarks against his 'untrustworthy' Uncle Bertie. Thereafter his contempt for the young man resulted in his high esteem for Vicky and Fritz, notwithstanding the former's passionate outpourings against him after his cruel treatment of Sandro.

To return to the present situation, Bismarck had won his point by insisting on the cancellation of Sandro's visit, but he was still not satisfied. Later that week he had an interview with Vicky in which, exercising his deceptive charm to the utmost, he told her in vague terms that the marriage might be possible sometime in the future. Clutching at straws and relieved beyond measure, Vicky was utterly taken in. Yet it was on the same day that a virulent campaign in the right-wing press against her, Fritz and Queen Victoria had been unleashed by the Chancellor. A dumbfounded public was made to believe that he was on the verge of handing in his resignation, because of them.

That the Queen was about to step into the breach was well known. Ever since the autumn she had cherished her intention of visiting her stricken son-in-law again. If the Emperor William had not died in March then they would have met at San Remo, for she had arrived at Florence within a fortnight of Fritz's accession. When she publicly announced her intention of coming to Berlin, the Bismarcks were furious — to them this could only mean one thing. Temperatures rose everywhere as letters and telegrams travelled in hot pursuit between London, Berlin and Florence. Lord Salisbury, having received an apprehensive note from Sir Edward Malet, British Ambassador in Berlin at this most unenviable time, tried to persuade the Queen to shelve her plans for visiting the city, but no horde of choleric statesmen could make her change her mind. As she was at pains to point out, her journey was to have no political significance, and she was therefore privately a little irritated when the Emperor Francis Joseph insisted on receiving her officially en route at Vienna. She had come north with the sole intention of seeing Fritz again, as she recorded in her journal on 20 March ('I am determined . . . to visit dear Vicky and Fritz, if only for a day'[18]), over a week before the revival of the Battenberg affair.

In fact, unknown to all but a few confidantes, she too was against the match. Her main objection was her grandson's attitude; Sir Henry Ponsonby reported to his wife that she would only welcome the marriage if the new Crown Prince would welcome Sandro as a brother-in-law. His recent letter to the unhappy suitor, telling him that if he married Moretta then he (Willy) would consider him the enemy of his family and country,[19] made his attitude clear. She had guessed Sandro's feelings about this, for on 12 March he had written sadly to Vicky to say that only if he succeeded in winning the new Crown Prince's favour could he foresee a happy solution.[20] His brother Henry was equally decided in his opinion; he recognised that Sandro could not possibly afford to keep a wife comfortably in his present state, let alone an imperial princess; if he tried, he would almost certainly be expelled from Germany and ruined.

Not until she was at Florence, after she had written to Vicky to dissuade her from encouraging the marriage, did the Queen hear about Sandro's second love — probably from Henry. On the morning of 24 April, with Beatrice and Henry, the royal train drew into the station at Berlin; the Queen went straight to Charlottenburg and the sickbed. As Vicky ruefully noted, it was the first time she and Fritz had had her under their own roof as a guest.

It was a sad meeting for he was losing ground, and rather the worse for recent sleepless nights. But the sight of his beloved mother-in-law cheered him as he sat up in bed, propped up on his pillows, his weary eyes lighting up with joy as trembling hands held out a bouquet of forget-me-nots and French fern from their garden. She sat beside the bed, holding his hand and talking about the family, while he wrote at intervals on his pad and passed it to her. Not until she was able to speak to Vicky alone did she tell her of the romance between Sandro and Johanna; Fritz never learnt of it. With his will he left a letter to Willy dated 12 April, stating that in the event of his death, he gave his consent to Moretta's marriage and charged him as Emperor to see that it took place; in order to 'obviate any political difficulties', he renounced his wish to give Sandro an army commission or decoration. Vicky was desperately afraid of upsetting him by telling him what had happened, and he went to his grave believing that Sandro would indeed become his son-in-law, if Willy was to change his mind and prove agreeable.*

Despite Lord Salisbury's fears that his sovereign would be exposed to fierce anti-English demonstrations in the street, she was enthusiastically received every time she was seen in public. The crowds cheered her small but unmistakably regal figure and showered the carriage with bouquets as she rode through the street. Whenever Vicky took the seat beside her mother, shouts of 'Long live the Empress!' were evident too. The Queen's greatest success in Berlin, however, was her meeting with Bismarck, which took place at his request the day after her arrival. Malet had told Ponsonby that he would be 'greatly pleased at such attention from the Queen.'[21] When it was over he acquitted himself by commenting to Busch that she had 'behaved quite sensibly',[23] but he was not nearly so patronising while waiting for her; the mere thought of coming face to face with her made him quite ill at ease, as he fussed over little details of etiquette. Where exactly would she be in the audience chamber, and would she be sitting or standing? He was quite relieved when Ponsonby finally led him to Vicky, who escorted him to her mother.

---

*Sandro married Johanna in 1889 and they had two children. He died of peritonitis in 1893.

Generations of writers have regarded the meeting of both personalities with no little excitement and imagination. It has even been said that she was bewitched by the Chancellor and persuaded to join in the chorus against Sandro;[24] nothing is further from the truth. Far from producing the legendary parson from her bag or the bridegroom from her trunk, they did not even mention the Battenbergs. The hour they spent talking was kept to relatively uncontroversial matters. She mentioned Willy's inexperience; Vicky's 'hard fate'; their only other meeting, at Versailles in 1855, which she was flattered he remembered. Most important of all he assured her that he was not contemplating any form of Regency, as it would upset Fritz; 'it would be cruelty'.[25] At the end the 'Iron Chancellor' walked out of the room, smiling with admiration and mopping his brow: 'What a woman! One could do business with her!'[26] It was no idle praise from a man to whom women in positions of power were as much an anathema as Britain and her parliamentary traditions, let alone one whom he had denounced as a representative of that hated petticoat government.

On the last day of her visit the Queen saw Fritz again as they exchanged kisses, photographs and presents, and she told him in a perfectly natural manner that he must repay the visit as soon as he felt better. It was a difficult way to say goodbye, for she knew that only a miracle could make this possible, but then in such poignant circumstances it was hard to know just what to say. With a ready smile and a wave of her hand, she took her leave for the last time of the son-in-law on whom so much had depended. As he sank back on the pillows and watched Vicky go to see her off at the station, his smile faded and the habitually doomed look reappeared on his face.

CHAPTER 17

The Last Few Weeks, 1888.

By now Fritz knew that he was sinking steadily, and for this he had only Bergmann to thank. On 12 April, nearly a fortnight before Queen Victoria's visit, he had a severe attack of coughing, which was relieved by a slight adjustment to the canula. Mackenzie was called, and after consulting Krause and Wegner he decided to try a shorter tube. When this failed to bring more than momentary relief, he chose a different canula altogether and out of professional courtesy invited Bergmann to come to Charlottenburg as soon as possible, to see him insert it. The latter arrived late in the afternoon, wildly excited and thinking from the note that an emergency had arisen. According to Hovell, who was by no means uncritical of Mackenzie, the German doctor's breath smelt heavily of alcohol; his excitement, and the way he swayed from side to side, bore this out.[1] On being led into Fritz's room, where he was writing at his desk, his breathing audible but laboured, Bergmann removed the shorter canula from his throat and replaced it with a new one. It went into the patient's neck, but no breathing came out; instead he had a sudden violent fit of coughing. The doctor tried again, but in the same rough and ready manner, and with the same result. The canula, instead of going into the windpipe as it should have done, was forced in front of it, into the neck tissues, causing heavy coughing and haemorrhage. At this second failure, just as a grim-faced Mackenzie was about to insist on taking over, Bergmann (who had merely been invited to watch) conceded defeat and sent for his more capable assistant Bramann, who had been outside in the carriage waiting to be called if necessary. He replaced the canula properly, but the damage had been done; Fritz continued to cough and bleed for several hours, and Bergmann's clumsiness left him weaker than before. During the evening he asked Mackenzie specifically to prevent Bergmann from carrying out any further operations on him. Bergmann proceeded to write to Vicky asking her rather unnecessarily to relieve him of the duty of working as Mackenzie's adviser, to which the latter's answer was equally to the point; after what he had witnessed, he respectfully warned that he would withdraw from the case altogether if Bergmann was allowed as much as to touch Fritz's throat again.[2]

After Queen Victoria's visit, a ray of sunshine in the sickroom, there was very little that gave him the will to fight against his illness, other than the reassuring presence of Mackenzie and Hovell, and the devotion of his wife and younger daughters. His weakening condition did not blind his perception of Vicky's iron courage. By April she could only sleep fitfully when exhaustion overtook her, and every morning at half-past six she was by his side, before he awoke. On stirring he mouthed the words 'tell me', and she told him 'every tiny little thing I had done, seen and heard the day before, what I had thought, hoped and imagined'.[3] At times he would feel slightly better and his temperature would subside. On such occasions, when the weather was warm enough, they would have a tent erected in the garden and a seat on the lawn screened by shrubs and trees; here he could lie outside and enjoy the fresh air.

Occasionally the Dowager Empress, 'really rather a ghastly sight' (in Queen Victoria's words), would be brought along in her wheelchair to sit by her son and talk to him in her shaking voice. Neither of them had much in common by now, Augusta's interests extending little beyond court functions and the gossip which she had always loved, but Fritz had always been devoted to her and was grateful for her company when she could spare it. One sad characteristic bound them together; physically both were shadows of what they had been in their younger days, and only will-power kept them alive.

He enjoyed nothing more than the days when he felt strong enough to drive into Berlin with Vicky and the girls. For he had only to show himself at the railings of the palace for the crowds, anxiously awaiting each bulletin on his health, to cheer; when he ventured through the streets, his subjects would wave their handkerchiefs and raise their hats in the air in their enthusiasm for the Emperor whose life was said to be hanging by a thread. Women would throw flowers into the carriage, and mothers would lift babies or small children to catch a glimpse of his face. In recognition he would raise his cap as often as his energy would permit, until a sudden coughing fit necessitated them turning off briefly into one of the city palaces for the bandage to be renewed. The widespread sympathy and admiration were testified to by the bouquets delivered daily to Charlottenburg, whether expensive blooms from Berlin's most exclusive florists, or humble bunches of primroses and violets from less wealthy but equally devoted well-wishers. One morning a lady bought up the entire contents of a basket of fresh violets from a street vendor and sent them to her Emperor, a footman coming out and giving her his thanks.[4] The Junkers' contempt for their master was nothing to the love of the middle class and poorer citizens, who if they were content to accept the Chancellor's despotic regime were just as glad to welcome the war hero who might not be spared to occupy the imperial throne for long. Some of the better-informed were not completely ignorant of Willy's unfeeling behaviour to his parents, and loved Fritz all the more because of it.

His mind remained clear, enabling him to study the newspapers and state documents passed to him with the keen interest of a ruler determined to do his duty. He was saddened by the news of flooding in East Prussia, and although he had to send Vicky to represent him on a visit to the distressed areas, he made a personal gift of fifty thousand marks to help the victims. Social conditions caused him concern, and he wanted to alleviate slum areas in the cities by greater state expenditure on housing the poor; 'in this way part of the so-called social question would be solved'.[5] Bismarck had not neglected the lower classes either, but his own tentative steps towards socialism were motivated by absolutist principles; he rejected the idea of factory inspection and statutory limitation of working hours, but he favoured the method of insuring employees against accidents, sickness, redundancy and old age. His philosophy was too revolutionary for some of his contemporaries, although much of it anticipated the twentieth century's welfare state, and it was too transparent for the more discerning Liberals. They saw that the Chancellor's real aim was to make workers feel more dependent on the state, and therefore on him.[6] Fritz's honest intentions of improving social conditions had no such strings attached. As far back as 1863 he was discussing the socialist movement with his mother, and agreed with her that 'self-help would prove the best means of combating distress';[7] one would have much less to fear from the fanaticism of early socialists if one made good some of the grievances of these would-be revolutionaries. With a more liberal ministry they would have been put into practice.

It grieved him that he was unable to carry them out, alongside many other plans he and Vicky had made. When asked about rebuilding the Berlin cathedral, a scheme with which husband and wife had been concerned during a previous visit to Italy, he wrote sadly on his pad that it was 'all over and done with'. At a ministerial meeting, he asked the Finance Minister Adolf Scholz how long it would take the mint to produce the new coins bearing his likeness. On being told that they would not be ready for two or three months, he raised his hands and the look of despair on his face told that he knew he would not live to see them. But some of his ideas still bore fruit. He appointed an army commission to devise new rules for drill and training regulations which drafted some of the military reforms he had intended, in time for him to give his assent. He also wanted to introduce a new uniform for the imperial navy, and gave Henry responsibility for choosing the designs submitted.

Bismarck's attitude towards Fritz was almost beyond reproach; believing that he now had Willy more firmly in his grasp, and with Bergmann's assurance that his master would not survive the summer, he could be patient. He gave the impression of a man who would do what his sovereign wanted if only the ministers would let him, and although Fritz was not deceived he was too weak to argue. It was Willy who irritated him the more. The new Crown Prince, it is said, was resentful of his father being allowed to assume the throne in such a state, until a friend placated him by saying that an interregnum would benefit him. His parents' reign, he was told, would see them both blundering so badly that he would be all the more welcome as Emperor when his time came; whereupon he settled down contentedly to distributing busts and signed photographs of himself. This may or may not be true, but he certainly proved himself an undesirable son and heir during his father's reign. It might be too harsh to say that he was being thoroughly spiteful, and impatient for Fritz to die; yet the best that can be said for him is that he was weak and allowed himself to be led far too easily by his toadies.

This 'weakness' was responsible for some incidents which were unfortunate if not downright cruel. At Bismarck's birthday dinner on 1 April he made a speech comparing the state of Germany to a regiment whose general had been killed and whose second-in-command lay badly wounded, therefore the soldiers should flock to the standard of their junior lieutenant. Fritz read a report in the papers the following day, and wrote to Willy reprimanding him for his disloyalty and asking him to avoid making any similar statements in future. Willy got his own back on his father a few days later, by ostentatiously inviting Bergmann to dinner after his withdrawal from the case following the quarrel with Mackenzie. Without a thought for the future consequences for herself, Vicky prevented their unfilial son for a time from visiting Fritz when he was weakest, as she knew he would only upset him. Yet she was pathetically fair to him when writing to her mother, putting all blame on the coterie 'whose main endeavour is as it were to paralyse Fritz in every way'. Only if she avoided 'all subjects of importance' did mother and son get on well together.[8]

Although far from the devoted son he made himself out to be in later years, Willy could occasionally feel sorry for his parents, and one incident during his father's reign does him credit. When Waldersee, scoffing at the 'petticoat government being exercised indirectly through the sick Emperor', told him he should pay no heed to orders he had coming from Charlottenburg, Willy reminded him that he had like all other German officers sworn an oath to their Emperor. He would continue to obey His Majesty's commands, even if they included placing Waldersee himself in front of a sandheap and shooting him.[9] Such loyalty was sadly all too rare.

News of Vicky's devotion and courage leaked out, and the *Freisinnige* party member Eugen Richter gallantly came to her defence whenever the *Reichstag* was in session. On 26 May he delivered an impassioned speech accusing the government of doing everything possible to insult their Empress, and asked Bismarck what he would do if taunted with just one-hundredth part of the calumnies she had to bear.[10] Members from the right-wing parties tried in vain to shout him down, but after he had finished several of them stood up to announce that they never had the slightest desire to offend her. Fritz's heart warmed as he read an account of Richter's speech the next day, but Vicky was worried that the government might eventually take it out on her.

On 24 May, Queen Victoria's birthday, Fritz was present at one more family occasion, namely the wedding of Henry and Irene at the Charlottenburg chapel. In spite of the day chosen, it rivalled in gloom the sad ceremony of the bride's mother at Osborne which he had attended so many years earlier. He had been fairly well for the previous few days, and had enjoyed making all the arrangements, seeing to the invitations, and welcoming the bride with her father and family the morning before, but on the day itself he was not quite so strong. Moreover, it brought back several unhappy memories; seeing the three younger girls in white bridesmaids' dresses reminded him and Vicky of Moretta's tragedy, a wound which the press had not helped to heal by continuing to speculate as to whether her brother's wedding would be made the occasion for announcing that her betrothal to Sandro would still take place. That neither Sandro nor his father had been invited to the ceremony should have made the answer clear. The sight of Irene, too, reawakened memories of that terrible winter when Alice's death had been followed by that of Waldie. He sensed that this would probably be the last 'festive gathering' he would ever attend, and it was hard for him to share the gaiety provided by electricity which lit up one porch of the castle, or the brightness of the charming flower arrangements. The guests — including the Prince of Wales in his Prussian regimental uniform, the Grand Duke and Duchess Serge of Russia,* and Prince and Princess Louis of Battenberg — all sensed this and found it hard to smile convincingly.

The ceremony unintentionally started without the groom's father. Everyone had assembled and was waiting for him to arrive, while he was waiting to be fetched when they were ready. Eventually the court chaplain Dr Kögel was about to begin the address when the door opened and Fritz entered, wearing his general's uniform with the Hessian Order and the Star of the Garter, his collar open to facilitate breathing through the canula, and a stick in his hand for support. He took his seat quietly on the right of the altar, between his mother and Vicky. At the gentle dignity of his appearance, looking so thin and pale, the latter almost choked in keeping back her tears. When the bridal couple exchanged rings he stood up, and as the organist played the closing voluntary he walked out unaided.

His presence at the wedding excited plenty, and very varied, comment from guests. Field-Marshal von Moltke, now a sprightly eighty-seven,

*Irene's sister Elizabeth and her husband.

spoke for many when he said that he had seen many brave men, 'but none as brave as the Emperor has shown himself today'.[11] On the other hand, Herbert Bismarck told the Prince of Wales afterwards that a sovereign who could not take part in debates should not be allowed to reign. For the sake of Anglo-German relations the Prince controlled himself, but on returning to England he told the Queen angrily that he had felt like throwing the insolent young man out of the room.[12] Official reports in the government-controlled newspapers mentioned eagerly how the Empress had forced her husband to attend, having built up his strength with wine and stimulants, and that those sitting near him in the chapel could hear his piteous gasps for breath; quarter of an hour later they saw him in his invalid chair in plain dress, utterly exhausted.[13] Such accounts were grossly exaggerated, but the day had obviously taken its toll of his remaining strength. He had stood the occasion without so much as coughing, and afterwards he drove around the park in his pony carriage for an hour and a half, but that evening his temperature rose and he had to spend the following day in bed.

On 29 May Willy made amends by leading his Guards Infantry Brigade in a march past his father in the palace grounds.* Fritz sat watching from his open carriage in full uniform, but huddled up in his cloak. It was a trial for him to be seen in such a pitiful state by his troops, to say nothing of thus being reminded that he was prevented from taking part in this or any similar occasions as a reigning Emperor. He did not cough during the march past, but when the troops were ordered to dismiss he felt very weary. From that day he went steadily downhill without any of the temporary improvements which had followed Bergmann's angry exit.

Two days later he visited the family mausoleum where his father had been laid to rest. It was a heartrending occasion, as he knelt painfully before the massive coffin. It had been a cruel fate, too, which had left him such a miserably brief reign after the old man's death. To this emotional experience the doctors attributed their patient's low spirits and worsened physical condition in the evening.

On the following day, 1 June, the court moved from Charlottenburg to Potsdam. Here Fritz had been born, and here he had spent nearly every summer of his married life. More than anywhere else in Germany, except perhaps for the little cottage and farm at Bornstädt, the Neue Palais was his home. As they travelled there on the royal steamer *Alexandria*, he lying on a couch on deck with Vicky sitting beside him, the sun shone brightly and the banks were lined by cheering crowds. It was as if the well-wishers, waving

---

*It is uncertain whose idea the parade was. Willy later maintained[14] that his father had requested it, while Vicky was to write that their son 'meant well, but it was most unfortunate, for Fritz only agreed with the utmost reluctance'.[15]

and throwing flowers, had a premonition that this was the last time they would see their Emperor. At the Spandau bridge, where the rivers Spree and Havel met, a group of school-children tossed so many flowers onto the deck that it took two members of the suite half an hour to collect them all. As Moretta, Sophie and Mossy welcomed them on landing and helped their father into the carriage which was to drive them to the palace, he was evidently very happy to be home at last. Just before he and Vicky walked inside, he wrote on his pad that he wanted it to be known as Friedrichskron.*

Their old home had never looked more lovely to them than it did in the days following, all the more so as they knew that they had so little time left together on earth; 'the sun is always said to shine more beautifully just before setting.'[16] Fritz was certainly deteriorating fast; his sleep and appetite were poor, and meals were 'a torment'. It had been arranged that he would go to Homburg later in the summer in an effort to improve his health, but with each passing day it became increasingly evident that he would not last this long.

Yet this slow death did not put an immediate end to everything he enjoyed. On the warmer days he would sit or lie on the balcony and admire the view, and sometimes they would go driving around the estate to see once again the trees and flowers which they had carefully tended for nearly thirty precious years in which only their love and devotion to each other had remained the same. Indoors, he continued with his work as far as possible. He signed documents, wrote letters, and read the papers from beginning to end, pointing out to Vicky with his finger or pencil anything that impressed him particularly. 'What will become of me?' he asked her on 11 June, four days before the end. 'Do I seem to improve? When shall I be well again? What do you think? Shall I be ill long? I must get well, I have so much to do.'[17] This pathetic but heroic struggle against the ravages of disease certainly prolonged his life and gave him a slender chance of survival that was in complete contrast to the brief illness of his father-in-law; with the Prince Consort's example before her, it is hardly to be wondered that Vicky entertained for so long the possibility that her husband might recover.

It was during the week after their arrival at Friedrichskron that he carried out the only important political act of his reign. The Minister of the Interior, the anti-Semite Robert von Puttkamer, was one of the most reactionary members of the government, and had been responsible for the official proclamation of the Emperor William's death in March without any allusion to his successor. To this Fritz could turn a blind eye, but when the Minister's guilt of bribery in a series of by-elections was proved, Bamberger

*One of William II's first acts as Emperor was to restore to the building its original name, undoubtedly as an insult to his mother and the memory of his father.

quietly sugested to Fritz that he should be asked to resign. To dismiss a colleague of Bismarck's was easier said than done, but when the Chancellor called upon Fritz to sign an bill prolonging the life of the *Reichstag* from three to five years in order to maintain a recently-gained Conservative majority, the latter made his assent conditional on Puttkamer's departure. Fritz had won, but Bismarck spitefully held an ostentatious banquet two days later at which the ex-Minister was guest of honour. Privately the two men were too alike to be really friendly, and Puttkamer was an uncomfortable colleague whom the Chancellor suspected was waiting to step into his place, but the dinner party was a typical Bismarckian gesture — a deliberate act of defiance to get even with his dying master.

On the Sunday after Puttkamer's dismissal, the choir of the Twelve Apostles Church in Berlin asked if they could sing their Emperor some choral music. It was arranged that they would stand outside his sitting-room, where he could sit and listen. When they started their performance Vicky was standing with them, but as they began an anthem Mackenzie beckoned her back, as Fritz was in tears; hearing it for the first time as Emperor had affected him deeply. When the choir had finished he wiped his eyes and, unaided except for his stick, got up and walked towards them to offer his thanks. It was a moving scene and there was hardly a dry eye in the place.

Even at this final stage, he was still capable of making a physical effort when duty demanded. On 12 June his old friend King Oscar of Sweden arrived unexpectedly at Potsdam. Vicky begged him not to tire himself, but he wanted to receive his fellow sovereign properly. Putting on his uniform, which literally hung on him, carrying his helmet in one hand and leaning on his stick, he walked slowly into the sitting-room and listened for a few minutes to his guest's conversation about his recent Spanish travels. But the King did not stay long; he was appalled at his host's wasted appearance, haunted expression, and greying thinning hair. It was the last time Fritz was ever on his feet, and from then on he was confined to bed.

By now Vicky was all but overwhelmed by the change in her husband, hardly sleeping and rarely leaving his room except to hide the tears she could not hold back. On the day of King Oscar's visit, she had a flash of slight optimism; there was 'not much hope left'.[18] By the next day, the 'not much' had changed to 'no'; she could no longer maintain her valiant facade. 'I feel so like a wreck, a sinking ship,' she wrote to Queen Victoria, 'so wounded and struck down, so sore of heart, as if I were bleeding from a thousand wounds.'[19] For that morning, some food had gone down the wrong way in Fritz's throat and eventually through the canula. Mackenzie was alarmed, and obtained a tube through which he could be fed milk, but it was too late to do anything about the food. It had gone into the lung and caused an inflammation, which sent his temperature soaring and weakened him still further.

From now on he was perpetually exhausted, though one important action was not beyond him. In the afternoon he removed a key from the chain he always wore around his neck and pushed it down the front of Vicky's dress. He made his meaning clear by pointing to a small black cashbox which contained family papers. She promised to look after it, and he smiled; now all his private papers were safe. The remainder had been taken to London with them before the Jubilee, except for a few in a parcel which was handed by Mackenzie the next day to an American corres-pondent who was invited to Potsdam so he could collect and deliver it to the British Embassy in Berlin. There it was passed by the Ambassador to the British Attaché, who was to be responsible for seeing that it reached Windsor. It arrived there within a week, by which time the elaborate precautions were proved to have been justified.

On the same day (13 June), Fritz received for the final time the man who had relentlessly blighted his life for so long. The Chancellor was calling, so he said, to discuss the matter of Puttkamer's successor, for which Vicky asked him to write everything down on paper so Fritz could read it first. After he had talked to his Emperor and was about to leave, Vicky returned to the latter's room and he beckoned them both to his bedside. Taking his wife's hand and placing it in that of their inveterate foe, he gave them an appealing look which no words could express. 'Your Majesty may rest assured,' said Bismarck, looking into Fritz's eyes, 'that I shall never forget that Her Majesty is my Queen'.[20] But Vicky had seen too much of the man's capricious nature to believe that she could trust him; to him, words were only words and not promises. For once the actor in him was lacking as she led him stiffly out of the room. She saw no sorrow or sympathy in his face, instead a look of ill-concealed triumph. 'Fritz after all was finished, so why waste time in sentimental lamentations!'[21]

At three o'clock on the following morning, she was woken from a troubled sleep by a gentle sound in her room. It was Mackenzie to say that Fritz's pulse had become weaker and faster, his breathing was rapid and though suffering no apparent pain or discomfort, he was in a feverish state. Going downstairs quietly so as not to wake anyone, she stood outside his door; to go in at such an unusual hour would alarm him. He was restless, tossing about from side to side, coughing every quarter of an hour, and the air went loudly through the canula. By dawn he had improved a little, but she hardly left his bedside all day.

At nine o'clock the three younger girls came to say good morning. It was Sophie's eighteenth birthday, and with a supreme effort her father placed into her hands the bouquet he had ordered as her present. He looked so deceptively cheerful for a moment that she thought he must be getting better. It was his wish that Vicky should try and do something on his behalf to amuse her, and he wanted them to go and play in the Pfaueninsel, but birthday or no birthday it was not a time for mother and daughters to try and enjoy themselves. Later in the day, telegrams were sent to the honey-mooning Henry and Irene in Silesia, and also to Charlotte and Bernard. Willy and Dona came too, followed by a vast suite; they proceeded to bully Fritz's servants and choose their rooms as if they owned the place already. Vicky was too distraught to pay them much attention.

During the night, she fetched a chaise-longue and placed it by his open door in the passage. Here she lay during the hours of darkness, getting up from time to time to see how he was. Still he tossed about, coughing and struggling for breath.

The morning of 15 June dawned fine and clear, just like the days when they would eagerly have driven around the estate. Instead, it was with a sense of grim foreboding that the family gathered in the sickroom with the servants, some of whom never left their master's side. The appearance of Werner, who had been asked to sketch the Emperor William's features immediately after death, was to the newspaper correspondents 'a sign more eloquent than bulletins'.[22] The German doctors showed little emotion as they waited for the inevitable end. Only Mackenzie, weary from working long hours and wheezing with his recurrent asthma, looked unhappy. Ironically Hovell had been called back to England a week earlier to another deathbed — his father's. Fritz was not blind to the suffering borne by this most faithful of servants. As Mackenzie stooped over him to change the canula Fritz laid his hand gently on the doctor's chest, and though too weak to mouth the words he longed to say, looked up into his face with a mute glance of tender sympathy, as if to apologise for causing him physical suffering as well.

Vicky would have given anything to spend these last moments alone with her beloved husband, but it was a privilege not granted to a reigning Emperor and Empress. He dozed for short periods, and when he regained consciousness it was usually to write with faltering hand a question on his pad, or with difficulty to mouth a few words; there was still so much he wanted to know. How was his pulse? Were the doctors satisfied with his condition? Could he see the King of Saxony? Vicky asked if he was thirsty, and when he nodded his head she gave him some white wine on a sponge. Then she asked if he was tired, and he nodded again. Towards mid-morning his strength was plainly ebbing. His eyes took on a different look, and when she held a light to his eyes he did not blink. She took his hand, but he let it drop limply. In a surge of emotion, Moretta knelt down by him weeping and put her arms around him; very soon he was conscious again. He coughed hard, took three deep breaths, gave a jerk and closed his eyes tightly as if something was hurting him, then lay still. His last struggle was over.

Almost numb with shock, Vicky took down from the wall a withered laurel wreath she had given him in 1871 and laid it on his chest, then his cavalry sabre which she placed on his arm, kissed his hands and folded them. 'In this way I took my last farewell of the best husband in the world. Oh, why, why did I have to bear this?'[23]

Two months later, in a letter to Lord Napier, she wrote a simple but moving epitaph: 'As a Man, as a Soldier, a Prince, a Patriot, he did his duty and was worthy of praise; as a Husband, Father, and Son, as a Master and a friend, he was loved and respected, and he is cruelly missed! His Country has lost its pride and its hope, and every good work its protector and supporter!'[24]

Epilogue.

It would be beyond the scope of this biography to mention all the trials which beset the Emperor Frederick's family, especially his widow, after he died; a few must suffice. During his last hours, Prince William was placing a secret guard around the palace, so that on becoming Emperor he could prevent anyone from leaving without a permit. His intention was to prevent the removal of any private correspondence belonging to his parents, knowing that it would not show him in a particularly favourable light, but though his soldiers ransacked all the desks they could lay their hands on, they found nothing. As Fritz had ensured, all papers were in safe custody. The funeral on 18 June at the Friedenskirche was a travesty, the clergy talking and laughing with Herbert Bismarck as if they were attending a party. The Chancellor had gone back to Varzin to look after his estate, his crops mattering more to him than the thought of paying his last respects to the man over whom he had triumphed so often. Vicky and her daughters could not face the official funeral, and by this time they had fled to Bornstädt for a private service of their own.

The bitter argument which broke out on Fritz's death between Mackenzie and his German colleagues culminated in a pamphlet by Bergmann and the others (but significantly excluding Virchow) defending themselves. Mackenzie was persuaded, rather against his better judgment — and Vicky's too — to answer it with his angry though hardly exaggerated *The Fatal Illness of Frederick the Noble*. By its publication he alienated much of his British support and he died in 1892, his health and practice ruined.

The medical controversy was nothing to the affair of Fritz's war diary. After the Franco-Prussian campaign, he showed some of his writings to Heinrich Geffcken, a friend from university days who was now Professor of Political Science at Strasbourg. Geffcken had with Fritz's approval copied extracts for his personal use, and in the autumn of 1888 he was so angry at the continued posthumous attacks on his old friend that he published them in the *Deutsche Rundschau*. For the first time, the public could read about their late Emperor's nationalist beliefs, his desires for German unification, and Bismarck's hesitation during the tense days at Versailles, not to mention his bribery of King Ludwig. The Chancellor was beside himself with rage; Geffcken was arrested on a charge of treason, and although no case could be brought against him and he was released from prison, it marked the beginning of a savage witch-hunt against Fritz's partisans. Roggenbach, Morier and others shared part of the professor's fate; their houses were broken into, and their private papers seized.

Bismarck's reign as Chancellor came to an abrupt end in March 1890, two months after the death of the Dowager Empress Augusta, following a row with the young Emperor on his prerogative rights. He died in 1898 after writing a series of deceitful and embittered memoirs, one volume of which was considered so inflamatory that it was withheld from publication until the collapse of the Empire. Vicky briefly contemplated returning to England for good, but though frequently going back to stay with her mother, she accepted that her rightful place was in her husband's country. At length she built herself a large country-house-cum-palace at Kronberg, which was named Friedrichshof in his memory. During her widowhood she continued to look after her charities with unflagging energy. The differences which had separated her from her headstrong son healed to a degree, although there was never any formal reconciliation as such. She died on 5 August 1901 from cancer of the spine, joining Fritz and their two younger sons in the Friedenskirche mausoleum. Thirteen years later, almost to the day, Britain declared war on Germany. William was forced to abdicate after the defeat of his armies in November 1918 and the Empire crumbled into a republic; he lived in peaceful Dutch exile until June 1941, dying at the age of eighty-two.

It has been said, time and time again, that the Emperor Frederick's token three months' reign was a tragic turning-point in European history — so often, in fact, that sooner or later it is bound to lose its effect and be seen as the dated judgment of an earlier generation. Yet it is an inescapable truth that if he had ascended the throne in March 1888 in good health, then the subsequent tale would have been very different. Bismarck would have remained in power at first, but his new Emperor would have surrounded himself with capable and respected Liberals such as Roggenbach, Bamberger and Richter; he did in fact make a list of the *Reichstag* members he would have chosen for his cabinet, and the courage with which they faced the wrath of Bismarck and William II shows that they would have been equally faithful servants as ruling ministers. The liberal reforms they would gradually have introduced would have within months precipitated a clash with the Chancellor, who would soon have had no option but to resign. The treaty with Russia would almost certainly have been renewed in 1890, for even if Fritz's accession had not been received so warmly in St Petersburg, and even if he had maintained his distaste for Russian reaction and the Tsar's treatment of Sandro, he would have given peace a higher priority than his personal feelings. At the same time he was one of the few Germans capable

of commanding French respect, as the Parisian press unanimously demonstrated on his death, and with the support of a party which did not hanker
after imperial conquests, some if not all of the French-speaking territory
ceded at the treaty of Frankfurt would have been restored to France.

Nobody was blind to the shadow which William's accession cast across
Europe at the time, particularly towards the humiliated but recovering
France. 'It is just possible that had (Frederick) lived he would have postponed the war of revenge so long that the revenge itself would have ceased to
be a great desire with Frenchmen,' ran the leader of the *Western Morning
News* on 16 June 1888. 'It is different now that (William) is chief of the State
. . . the hope of revenge revives in its full force today . . . Kaiser Frederick
might have postponed war by sapping the strength of the sentiment which
leads to it . . .(William) will postpone war only by increasing a fear which
Frenchmen have for the German army.'[1] Prophetic words indeed.

Above all it is beyond doubt that the fear Britain had of Germany in the
1870s and 1880s would have vanished almost overnight with Fritz's accession, the resultant goodwill between both nations being sealed with an
Anglo-German alliance. Bismarck made some efforts to reach an understanding with Lord Salisbury's government in 1889, but his merciless
persecution of the Empress Frederick over the previous few months made
his timing ludicrously inappropriate, for with it German standing in
England dropped even lower. With Frederick instead of William on the
throne, Lord Salisbury and his cabinet would not have thought twice.
Proclaiming as late as 1911 that he adored England, and being on the best of
terms with his cousin George V, William responded halfheartedly to offers
of alliance with England at several stages of his reign. Had he meant what he
said, he would not have given in so easily to his anti-English ministers when
they protested.

Those who have seen the Great War in perspective have come to the
unavoidable conclusion that, more than anything else, it was the result of
two related factors. One was the labyrinth of continental alliances ensuring
that if one country was attacked then another would come to her aid,
bringing with her another one to draw the sword on behalf of either the
victim or the aggressor, and by the process of chain reaction continuing until
most of Europe was in one camp or another; in simple terms, this is what
happened in 1914. The other factor was the headstrong and provocative
behaviour of William II, who prided himself as the Supreme War Lord and
had seen Prussia assert her military supremacy in Europe with three
victorious wars during his formative years. If we try to accept the German
point of view and demolish the theory of Edward VII as the 'peacemaker
King', instead assigning to him much of the guilt for the war, we must
still remember that Edward was only driven into creating a political
climate necessary for bringing about the protective alliances against his

nephew's empire (as modern historians readily point out, he can hardly be credited with having made the alliances himself) through dread of British isolation and fear of Germany's sabre-rattling image. For the latter William must be held partly responsible, and not even his most ardent apologists can hold him blameless for the naval arms race which was a contributory factor to the outbreak of war.

What would have been the picture if Frederick had reigned for, let us say, a decade or more? He would have helped to give the German Empire a far less military image, and this would surely have heralded peace throughout the greater part of Europe for many a year. The Balkan unrest in the early twentieth century and the Austrian Archduke Francis Ferdinand's assass-ination at Sarajevo need not have had nearly such far-reaching consequences, for Britain, France and Russia would have had no need to ally themselves against Germany. This had not in so many words been their aim at the time, but this was how the situation appeared in the summer of 1914. If William had ascended the throne in middle age, having outgrown his impetuous younger days, and inherited a more democratic Reich, he need not have spent his declining years in exile. Whether the Hohenzollerns, like the ruling dynasties in Britain and the other remaining European kingdoms, would have survived the currents of socialism and republicanism that toppled so many monarchs is impossible to predict, but had it not been for Frederick's untimely death Germany might still be reigned over by his descendants. And if only his son had not been persuaded by the reactionary anti-British elements in his government from accepting frequent offers of British friend-ship, but come to an alliance, then he would have spared himself the horrifying dilemma in August 1914 when he realised that Germany and Austria were in one power bloc, Britain, France and Russia in the other.

Many a doubt has been expressed as to whether Fritz would have been able to steer Germany into more constitutional and democratic channels. Bismarck's comment that the 'extreme Liberals' would have been greatly disillusioned by the attitude he would have taken with those who wished to see a limit to his personal prerogative and the conduct of his government under liberalism,[2] a distorted view, has been echoed by writers ever since. Theo Aronson believes that the Chancellor was so thoroughly entrenched in his position by 1878, the year that Dr Nobiling nearly brought Fritz to the throne, that the latter would have had a hard task in altering the conviction held by most of his subjects that might was right and 'force had become the most important thing'.[3] In exile his eldest son wrote that his father 'was an authoritarian in his bones, and not too tolerant of opposition'.[4] Hardly a fair statement from a man who threatened to put a bullet through the head of his sister's Battenberg suitor if he set foot in Berlin against his wishes, or who sent a German expeditionary force to suppress the Chinese Boxer rising in

1900 with orders that anyone who fell into his men's hands fell to their swords. His inference that he did not believe his father to be more than half-heartedly committed to liberalism cannot be taken at face value, for a good deal of William's memoirs must be regarded with as much circumspection as those of Bismarck; his assertion that he was 'inwardly outraged'[5] at the hostility against his mother during her husband's reign is unfortunate to say the very least. For like his eldest brother-in-law (Edward VII) and the even more tragically-fated Crown Prince Rudolf of Austria, Frederick realised that the monarchy could not afford to stand still in a changing world and survive. His respect for the constitution, his interest in improving conditions for the workers and the poor, his abhorrence of anti-Semitism, his intelligent study of the radical press, and above all his political opposition to the father he so loved and feared, all make nonsense of certain judgments on him.

Michael Balfour suggests that forces at work throughout Germany were strong enough to have frustrated even a healthy Frederick, and doubts that he had either the inclination or stamina to dominate.[6] Were these forces strong enough? It is true to say that the majority had come to accept Bismarck's philosophy of blood and iron, but Gerhard Masur, who was born and bred in the Germany of William II, has inferred that the middle classes would accept anything within reason: 'To remain calm was the first duty of a citizen.'[7] They would have acquiesced no less in a more democratic empire at the turn of the nineteenth century. If Frederick was not one of nature's 'dominators', he would still have provided the necessary guidance for a change of political climate. The hypothetical 'Gladstone ministry' would have been to the 1890s what Bismarck, Holstein and their circle were to the 1880s.

Golo Mann expresses similar ideas when he says that it was impossible for one man to correct the faults in the social structure of the Prusso-German state. Indeed — but it was surely not beyond the radical and progressive ministers that the one man would have appointed to support him. Another point Mann makes is that Frederick was 'the slave of class traditions'.[8] What nineteenth-century monarch, autocratic or otherwise, was not? Edward VII was as well, but after his mother's death he cleared away much of the rigidity and inaccessibility that had characterised the throne during her reign. Unlike him Frederick was no society leader, but he had endeared himself to his soldiers and the common people, such as the humble Bornstädt villagers, without remaining too aloof from them. He was extremely popular in his homeland as Crown Prince, even before his illness brought him widespread sympathy. According to Crown Prince Rudolf, commenting with remarkable insight at the age of fifteen, 'monarchy has lost its old power and clings to the trust and love of the people'.[9] Although he was speaking of the rule of his father, Emperor Francis Joseph, his words could equally have applied to

Germany. William I was loved by his people, it is true, but like Queen Victoria at the end of her reign he had become something of a legendary, remote figure. His son, whose kindly presence and sincere interest in the nation, would have retained their trust and love while at the same time dispersing something of the mustiness which surrounded the throne. It is difficult to say the same for *his* son, who as Edward VII said had to be reminded that he living at the end of the nineteenth century and not in the middle ages.[10] It cannot be easy for a country to love a sovereign who visits a colonial exhibition and, catching sight of the house of a negro King with his enemies' skulls impaled on poles outside it, exclaims 'If only I could see the *Reichstag* strung up like that!'[11] Undoubtedly he did not mean what he said in such bombastic utterances, which were legion, and he was not as black as he was painted by the British and allied press in 1918. This is not the place to argue how good or how bad a sovereign William II was, but it must be said that, in sharp contrast to his father, he was not the man to occupy a throne in an age when the growth of republicanism was a reality for monarchs and monarchists throughout Europe.

We must not overstate the case; it would be exaggeration to believe that Frederick would have been a 'citizen King'. When Prince Charles of Denmark was elected King of Norway in 1905 and took the title of Haakon VII, he shocked the British court by proposing to travel around the streets of Oslo in a tram, because he reckoned that moving among his subjects with the utmost simplicity was an effective way of winning popularity and combating republicanism. Sir Frederick Ponsonby, who was to provoke the wrath of the ex-Emperor William in 1928 with his publication of *Letters of the Empress Frederick,** told Haakon to 'get up on a pedestal and remain there'.[12] Frederick would have agreed.

In both Britain and Norway monarchy survives. It would very likely have done so in Germany too, had he been given the chance to reign while still fit and healthy. At least he would have been able indirectly to prevent Germany from suffering the evils that befell her after 1918; he would certainly have helped to inaugurate an era of European peace which would have made the years 1914-18 as settled as the pre-Bismarckian era. And it would have been left for historians to speculate on what might have been the outcome for Europe if his impetuous son William had after all ascended the throne at the age of twenty-nine.†

---

*See Foreword, p. 8.

†See 'If the Emperor Frederick had not had cancer' by Emil Ludwig. It takes the form of a 'fantasy' in which the author writes what course he believes history would have taken if Frederick had recovered from what proved to be a minor throat ailment in 1887, and reigned until August 1914, having maintained peace with Russia, held a formal reconciliation with France, and introduced parliamentary government into Germany.

Did Frederick Die of Cancer or . . .?

The rumour that Frederick's disease was partly or wholly venereal in origin has been mentioned too often, and by too many modern reliable authors, to be ignored completely. To be dismissed as mere scandal-mongering would savour of whitewashing him, and it would be impossible to prove the matter one way or the other. One's chances of finding any letters mentioning syphilis are slight to say the least; we frequently read of Queen Victoria's family having destroyed individual correspondence of a potentially embarrassing or painful nature, and any mentioning him as having syphilis would have been the first to be consigned to the flames.

So what evidence is there to suggest this? After the crucial consultation in November 1887 Dr Moritz Schmidt, who had been present, mentioned cryptically in an university lecture that the Crown Prince had a disease 'of contagious origin', and when reports appeared in the Parisian press that it was venereal, Frederick asked Mackenzie to deny them. After his death a biography, *Drame Impérial*, appeared by a Paris journalist, Jean de Bonnefon. It alleges that the Emperor had surrendered to the charms of a Spanish woman in 1869 while at Suez for the canal opening; symptoms appeared about a month later, and he was given rather primitive treatment by the Khedive's physician. The same book, however, tells that the Crown Princess slapped Mackenzie's face when he diagnosed cancer, and the style throughout is of the 'popular press' level — hardly a guarantee of authenticity. It is just as possible that Frederick was suffering partly from some very obscure non-venereal disease, with symptoms similar to those of syphilis, but which confounded the best brains of the 1880s and could only have been diagnosed with certainty in the light of twentieth century advances in medical science. Venereal disease had such a high incidence at the time that it was often used as a credible slander against one's enemies; Prince Alexander von Battenberg was accused of having it when the Russian court was trying to discredit him before his enforced abdication.

Mackenzie appears to have believed the disease to be syphilitic; he concealed his knowledge out of loyalty to his patient, but shortly before his death in 1892 he confided the secret to his assistant Dr Pierce, who told the author Robert Scott Stevenson that he was certain syphilis of the larynx was present before cancer. It is, however, impossible to discount the theory that

Mackenzie was deliberately misleading the others. Although it cannot be proved, Fritz's larynx may have betrayed no signs of disease before the onset of cancer. The doctor was a highly skilled man, but at the same time a very proud one, and the mention of syphilis may have been an attempt to cover up errors of judgement. What is certain is that the whole case, and the protracted rows after the Emperor's death, left him a broken man. This would have been a natural way of fortifying his injured pride. Against this argument may be set Dr Schmidt's conviction that the illness was 'the result of an infection which had remained in the system for many years', but Schmidt was the only doctor to put forward this view, and for that reason alone the idea seems remote.

Finally, let us consider the Empress's attitude. As a wife who placed an extremely high value on her husband's fidelity, it is easy to imagine what disgust she would have felt if he had strayed from the straight and narrow with such devastating results. She would have presumably been sympathetic with him; but hardly so devoted to the final tragic end, had his troubles been caused by a furtive liaison in Egypt or elsewhere. That their last child Margaret, born in 1872, was the healthiest and most long-lived of all their daughters (she died in 1954 aged eighty-one), is further evidence in her father's favour.

So many doctors attended him — and so few agreed on anything — that it is impossible to establish anything beyond the fact that he had cancer of the larynx. Yet heredity may have played a part in the disease, for most of the Hohenzollerns were possessed of extraordinary longevity, his father and son for example. There was however a history of cancer in the family, as Mackenzie observed; a maternal aunt and his cousin Prince Frederick Charles both died from it at a similar age, though in the latter's case a fondness for the bottle must have played a not inconsiderable role. It is interesting to note that Tsar Alexander III looked with disfavour on a projected match between the Tsarevich Nicholas and Princess Margaret as her father's death from cancer meant a risk of tainted blood appearing in the Romanov family; he never lived to appreciate the irony of this as Nicholas married Princess Alix of Hesse, who as a carrier of haemophilia brought such tragic results for the dynasty. Moreover, the Emperor William II underwent an operation for a growth on the larynx in 1903; although the events of fifteen years earlier made him feel very uneasy at first he soon recovered, but his voice was left flat and lifeless. One can therefore fairly safely discount the theory of syphilis, but hereditary factors may well have been partly responsible for Frederick's illness and untimely death.

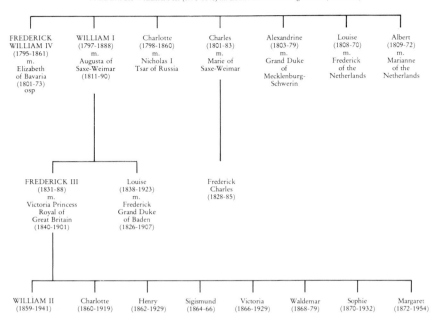

FREDERICK WILLIAM III (1770-1840) m. Louise of Mecklenburg-Strelitz (1776-1810)

FREDERICK WILLIAM IV (1795-1861) m. Elizabeth of Bavaria (1801-73) osp

WILLIAM I (1797-1888) m. Augusta of Saxe-Weimar (1811-90)

Charlotte (1798-1860) m. Nicholas I Tsar of Russia

Charles (1801-83) m. Marie of Saxe-Weimar

Alexandrine (1803-79) m. Grand Duke of Mecklenburg-Schwerin

Louise (1808-70) m. Frederick of the Netherlands

Albert (1809-72) m. Marianne of the Netherlands

FREDERICK III (1831-88) m. Victoria Princess Royal of Great Britain (1840-1901)

Louise (1838-1923) m. Frederick Grand Duke of Baden (1826-1907)

Frederick Charles (1828-85)

WILLIAM II (1859-1941)

Charlotte (1860-1919)

Henry (1862-1929)

Sigismund (1864-66)

Victoria (1866-1929)

Waldemar (1868-79)

Sophie (1870-1932)

Margaret (1872-1954)

THE HOUSE OF HOHENZOLLERN: partial table.

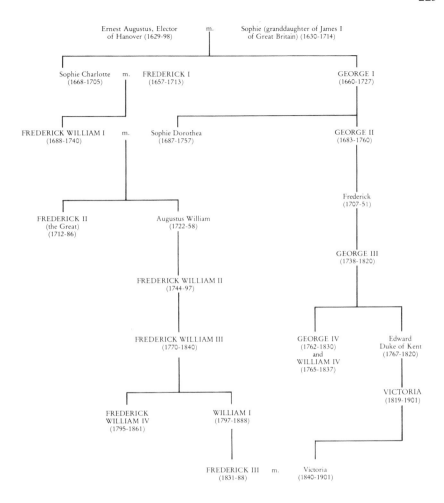

THE HOUSES OF HOHENZOLLERN AND HANOVER: partial table.

The Children of the Emperor Frederick.

1. William, born 27 January 1859; 1881, married Princess Augusta of Schleswig-Holstein-Sonderburg-Augustenburg (1858-1921), 6 sons, 1 daughter. Ascended throne 1888 as German Emperor and King of Prussia; abdicated 1918. 1922, married Princess Hermine of Reuss (1887-1947). Died 4 June 1941.

2. Charlotte, born 24 July 1860; 1878, married Prince Bernard of Saxe-Meiningen (1851-1928), 1 daughter. Died 1 October 1919.

3. Henry, born 14 August 1862; 1888, married Princess Irene of Hesse (1866-1953), 3 sons. Died 20 April 1929.

4. Sigismund, born 11 September 1864. Died 18 June 1866.

5. Victoria, born 12 April 1866; 1890, married Prince Adolf of Schaumburg-Lippe (1859-1916); 1927, married Alexander Zubkov (1900-36), no issue by either marriage. Died 13 November 1929, having begun divorce proceedings against second husband.

6. Waldemar, born 10 February 1868. Died 27 March 1879.

7. Sophie, born 14 June 1870; 1889, married Constantine, Crown Prince of the Hellenes (1858-1923), who reigned as King 1913-17; abdicated and temporarily restored 1920-22, 3 sons (all of whom ascended the throne), 3 daughters. Died 13 January 1932.

8. Margaret, born 22 April 1872; 1893, married Prince Frederick Charles, later Landgrave, of Hesse (1868-1940); 6 sons, including 2 pairs of twins. Died 21 January 1954.

Reference Notes.

Abbreviations

DC	*Dearest Child*, edited by Roger Fulford
Diaries	*Diaries of the Emperor Frederick*
DM	*Dearest Mama*, edited by Roger Fulford
EF	*Letters of the Empress Frederick*, edited by Sir Frederick Ponsonby
EFS	*The Empress Frederick writes to Sophie*, edited by Arthur Gould Lee
EL	*My Early Life*, William II
FL	*Further Letters of Queen Victoria*, edited by Hector Bolitho
IOL	India Office Library (Napier Letters)
Memoir	*The Empress Frederick: a Memoir*, Anon.
PC	*Letters of the Prince Consort*, edited by Kurt Jagow
QV	*Letters of Queen Victoria* (with series and volume number)
RA	Royal Archives, Windsor
Recollections	*Recollections of Three Kaisers*, Anon.
Sal MSS	Salisbury Manuscripts
WD	*War Diary of the Emperor Frederick*
YDL	*Your Dear Letter*, edited by Roger Fulford

Authors (and titles, where necessary to avoid confusion) of books are given in every other case. All sources are fully cited in the bibliography.

Chapter 1

1 *Recollections* 27
2 Bülow 17
3 Tschudi 62
4 Bennett 97
5 Poschinger 16
6 Ibid. 18
7 QV I ii 106
8 Poschinger 17
9 Ibid. 21
10 *PC* 136
11 Poschinger 28
12 Ibid. 37

Chapter 2

1 QV I ii 3
2 Barkeley *Empress* 12
3 Radziwill 47
4 Masur 47

5   *FL* 25
6   Rodd 37-38
7   William II *Ancestors* 265
8   *PC* 233
9   *QV* I iii 147
10 Longford 260
11 Prince Frederick William
    to Prince Albert
    22.10.1855, RA
12 *The Times* 3.10.1855
13 Corti *Empress* 24
    (hereafter Corti
    unless otherwise
    specified)
14 Rodd 46-47
15 As 11 above

Chapter 3

1   As Chapter 2, 11 above
2   Poschinger 67
3   Longford 262
4   Ibid. 264
5   Rodd 49
6   Ponsonby M. 241
7   Poschinger 79
8   *Illustrated Times*
    4.7.1857
9   *QV* I iii 253
10 Corti 36
11 *Memoir* 52
12 Corti 36
13 Ibid. 37
14 *Memoir* 68
15 Ibid. 68
16 *PC* 288

Chapter 4

1   Radziwill 55-56
2   *DC* 21
3   *PC* 290
4   Albert 162
5   *PC* 294
6   *DC* 73
7   *PC* 296
8   Tschudi 170-71
9   Bennett 76

10 *PC* 307
11 Corti 47
12 Poschinger 113
13 Ibid. 115

Chapter 5

1   Fulford 269
2   Poschinger 116
3   Corti 83
4   *DC* 191
5   Eyck F. 244
6   Bennett 92
7   Ibid. 93
8   Ibid. 96
9   McClintock 35
10 *DC* 238
11 Ibid. 244-45
12 Corti 62
13 *PC* 353
14 Queen Victoria's
    Journal 26.9.1860,
    RA
15 *DC* 277
16 Ibid. 261-62;
    Wiegler 194
17 *QV* I iii 424-26;
    EF 28-30

Chapter 6

1   Radziwill 42
2   Bennett 104
3   *DC* 309
4   Tschudi 180
5   Battiscombe 23
6   Bennett 104
7   *QV* I iii 457
8   Wiegler 203
9   *DC* 367-68
10 Ibid. 372
11 *Memoir* 152
12 Ibid. 153
13 Ponsonby M. 242
14 Corti 76-77
15 *DM* 88
16 Corti 85-86
17 Ibid. 87

18 *DM* 62
19 Poschinger 131
20 *DM* 102
21 Wiegler 209
22 *DM* 92
23 Corti 89-90
24 Bennett 119
25 Taylor A. 51

Chapter 7

1 Bennett 124
2 Lee I 147
3 *DM* 113
4 Ibid. 135
5 Corti 99
6 *DM* 128
7 Ibid. 164
8 Ibid. 186
9 Corti 102
10 Wiegler 216
11 Poschinger 140
12 Ibid. 142
13 *DM* 225
14 *EF* 41
15 Corti 104
16 Ibid. 106
17 *EF* 44
18 Wiegler 218
19 *EF* 47
20 Corti 110
21 Ibid. 112
22 Busch III 238
23 Corti 113
24 *DM* 272
25 Corti 114
26 Ibid. 115

Chapter 8

1 *DM* 249
2 Corti 123
3 Ibid. 121
4 Ibid. 124
5 Ibid. 133
6 Ibid. 119
7 *Memoir* 211
8 Ibid. 200

9 Lee I 256
10 Rodd 63
11 Taylor L. 509
12 *EF* 57
13 Battiscombe 76
14 Longford 350
15 *YDL* 58
16 Corti 145
17 *YDL* 68
18 *EF* 61
19 *Diaries* 48
20 Poschinger 279
21 Taylor L. 171
22 Corti 153

Chapter 9

1 Corti 158
2 Taylor L. 241
3 Poschinger 289
4 Corti 161
5 *YDL* 177
6 Poschinger 309
7 Corti 139
8 Barkeley *Empress* 123
9 Kurtz 37
10 *YDL* 149
11 *Diaries* 88
12 Taylor L. 250
13 Rodd 95
14 *Diaries* 143-44
15 Ibid. 142
16 Ibid. 181
17 Rodd 95

Chapter 10

1 *YDL* 273
2 Corti 170
3 *YDL* 285
4 *EF* 80
5 Ibid. 80
6 Rodd 104
7 Ibid. 108
8 Poschinger 321
9 Rodd 115
10 *Diaries* 211
11 *WD* 115

12 Ibid. 202-03
13 *Diaries* 234
14 *WD* 223
15 Ibid. 168
16 *Diaries* 195
17 *YDL* 249
18 Eyck E. 178
19 *WD* 238
20 Horne 75
21 Corti 180
22 Bennett 185
23 *WD* 265
24 Ibid. 210
25 *EF* 126
26 *YDL* 316

Chapter 11

1 *YDL* 322
2 *EF* 89
3 *QV* II ii 155
4 Poschinger 352, quoting
   The Times
5 Taylor A. 137
6 *EL* 59
7 Poschinger 361-62
8 Haslip 252
9 Poschinger 363
10 Fulford *Darling Child*
   94-97
11 Corti 187
12 Ludwig 12
13 *Recollections* 96
14 Ponsonby A. 251
15 Hough 56
16 Bennett 87
17 *EF* 123
18 Ibid. 144
19 Ibid. 138
20 Poschinger 375-76
21 *EL* 5
22 *PC* 347
23 *EF* 174
24 Bennett 210
25 Balfour 80
26 Longford 386

27 Radziwill 144
28 Crown Princess to
   Lord Napier 30.12.1876,
   IOL
29 Lee I 432

Chapter 12

1 Lee I 485
2 Steward's diary,
   Hatfield House,
   June 1878
3 Wiegler 367
4 McClintock 192
5 Radziwill 149
6 Wiegler 372
7 Radziwill 150
8 Bennett 204
9 Radziwill 153
10 *Recollections* 76
11 Radziwill 96-97
12 Crown Princess to
   Lord Napier 14.4.1879,
   IOL
13 Poschinger 417
14 *Memoir* 279
15 Buchanan 94
16 *EF* 179
17 Battiscombe 159-60
18 *QV* II iii 169-70

Chapter 13

1 *EF* 191
2 Eyck E. 275
3 Massie 82
4 Bennett 215
5 Daisy of Pless 195
6 Lee I 478
7 Corti 219-20
8 *EF* 214
9 Balfour 94
10 Poschinger 399-400
11 *Diaries* 283
12 Ibid. 305
13 Ibid. 323
14 Radziwill 178
15 Bennett 228

16 Corti 225-26
17 Epton 166
18 Aronson 126
19 Corti 219
20 Hough 52
21 Magnus 186
22 Longford 394
23 Victoria *My Memoirs* 67
24 *EF* 202-03
25 Hough 79
26 Crown Princess to
     Lord Napier 26.12.1886,
     IOL
27 Corti 231
28 Ludwig 21
29 Crown Princess to
     Queen Victoria
     11.10.1886, Sal MSS
30 Crown Prince to
     Queen Victoria
     22.1.1887, Sal MSS

Chapter 14

1 Blunt 208
2 Radziwill 180
3 *EF* 266
4 Stevenson 67
5 *EF* 226
6 Corti 242
7 Ibid. 241
8 Ibid. 242
9 Stevenson 82
10 Mackenzie 27
11 Corti 308
12 *EFS* 218
13 Corti 243
14 Longford 499
15 *EF* 237
16 Ibid. 239
17 Lorne 346
18 Rodd 168-69
19 Taylor L. 458
20 Count Seckendorff to Lord
     Napier 27.5.1887, IOL
21 Count Seckendorff to Lord
     Napier 27.6.1887, IOL
22 Mackenzie 51-52

23 Marie of Roumania 36-38
24 Corti 246
25 *EF* 242
26 Longford 503

Chapter 15

1 Bennett 235
2 Radziwill 189
3 Stevenson 90
4 *EF* 249
5 Mackenzie 63
6 *EF* 260
7 Magnus 200
8 *EF* 260-61
9 Mackenzie 63
10 Ludwig 46
11 Barkeley *Empress* 213
12 Magnus 202
13 Wiegler 77
14 Balfour 111
15 Mackenzie 66
16 *EF* 256
17 *The Times* 23.2.1929;
     Ponsonby F. 114-15
18 *EF* 266
19 Ibid. 264
20 Ponsonby M. 261
21 *EF* 267; Ponsonby M. 260
22 Ponsonby M. 265
23 Corti 257
24 Poschinger 440
25 *EF* 275
26 Corti 259-60
27 Ibid. 262
28 *EF* 277
29 Ibid. 277

Chapter 16

1 Stevenson 110
2 *QV* III i 390
3 *EF* 287
4 Count Seckendorff to
     Lord Napier 22.3.1888,
     IOL
5 Corti 268

6   Wiegler 447
7   Mackenzie 173-74
8   Empress Victoria to
       Lord Napier 31.3.1888,
       IOL
9   Corti 270
10 Longford 505
11 Ludwig 50
12 Ibid. 49
13 Corti *Alexander* 267
14 Victoria *My Memoirs* 74
15 Buchanan 141
16 Eyck E. 302
17 Ibid. 303
18 *QV* III i 394
19 Ponsonby A. 293-94
20 Corti *Alexander* 278
21 *EF* 302
22 Ponsonby A. 297
23 Busch III 187
24 Taylor A. 233
25 Corti 289
26 *FL* 268

Chapter 17

1   Stevenson 123
2   Mackenzie 148-49
3   Corti 290
4   *Recollections* 107
5   Corti 293
6   Taylor A. 204
7   Tschudi 192
8   *EF* 311

9   Nowak 21-23
10 Barkeley *Empress* 250
11 Radziwill 218
12 Corti 278
13 Ludwig 50
14 *EL* 294-95
15 Corti 279
16 Ibid. 296
17 Ibid. 279
18 *EF* 314
19 Ibid. 315
20 Corti 297
21 Ibid. 298
22 *The Times* 16.6.1888
23 Corti 302
24 Empress Frederick to
       Lord Napier 11.8.1888,
       IOL

Epilogue

1   *Western Morning News*
       16.6.1888
2   Poschinger 450-51
3   Aronson 259
4   *EL* 5
5   William II *Memoirs* 21
6   Balfour 62-63
7   Masur 47
8   Mann (Penguin edn) 406-07
9   Barkeley *Mayerling* 27
10 Magnus 209
11 Balfour 159
12 Ponsonby F. 193-94

Bibliography.

I. Manuscript Sources

Napier Letters. Letters from Crown Princess Frederick William (later the Empress Frederick) and Count Götz Seckendorff to Lord Napier of Magdala. India Office Library and Records, European Manuscripts (F114/16).

Royal Archives. One letter from Prince Frederick William to Prince Albert. Windsor (RA129/86).

Salisbury Manuscripts. Steward's Diary, Hatfield House, and two letters from the papers of the 3rd Marquess of Salisbury (Box F114).

II. Books

The place of publication in each case is London unless otherwise stated.

ALBERT, Harold A. *Queen Victoria's Sister: the Life and Letters of Princess Feodore* (Robert Hale 1967)

ALBERT, Prince Consort *Letters of the Prince Consort, 1831-1861;* selected and edited by Kurt Jagow (John Murray 1938)

ANON. *The Empress Frederick: a Memoir* (James Nisbet 1913)

ANON. *Recollections of Three Kaisers* (Herbert Jenkins 1929)

ARONSON, Theo *The Kaisers* (Cassell 1971)

BALFOUR, Michael *The Kaiser and his Times* (Cresset 1964)

BARKELEY, Richard *The Empress Frederick, Daughter of Queen Victoria* (Macmillan 1956)

BARKELEY, Richard *The Road to Mayerling: Life and Death of Crown Prince Rudolf of Austria* (Macmillan 1958)

BATTISCOMBE, Georgina *Queen Alexandra* (Constable 1969)

BENNETT, Daphne *Vicky, Princess Royal and German Empress* (Collins Harvill 1971)

BIRD, Anthony *The Damnable Duke of Cumberland . . .* (Barrie and Rockliff 1966)

BLUNT, Wilfred *The Dream King: Ludwig II of Bavaria* (Hamish Hamilton 1970)

BUCHANAN, Meriel *Queen Victoria's Relations* (Cassell 1954)

BULOW, Bernard von *Memoirs 1897-1903* (Putnam 1931)

BUSCH, Moritz *Bismarck: some Secret Pages of his History,* 3 Vols. (Macmillan 1898)

CORTI, Egon Caesar Conte *Alexander von Battenberg* (Cassell 1954)

CORTI, Egon Caesar Conte *The English Empress: a Study in the Relations between Queen Victoria and her Eldest Daughter, Empress Frederick of Germany* (Cassell 1957)

DAISY, Princess of Pless *The Private Diaries of Daisy, Princess of Pless, 1873-1914;* edited by Desmond Chapman-Huston (John Murray 1950)

DUFF, David *Hessian Tapestry* (Frederick Muller 1967)

EPTON, Nina *Victoria and her Daughters* (Weidenfeld and Nicolson 1971)

EYCK, Erich *Bismarck and the German Empire,* 2nd edn. (Allen and Unwin 1958)

EYCK, Frank   *The Prince Consort: a Political Biography* (Chatto and Windus 1959)

FREDERICK III, German Emperor   *Diaries of the Emperor Frederick during the Campaigns of 1866 and 1870-71 as well as his Journeys to the East and to Spain*; edited by Margaretha von Poschinger (Chapman and Hall 1902)

FREDERICK III   *War Diary of the Emperor Frederick, 1870-71*; edited by A.R. Allinson (Stanley Paul 1927)

FREYTAG, Gustav   *The Crown Prince and the German Imperial Crown* (George Bell 1890)

FULFORD, Roger   *The Prince Consort* (Macmillan 1949)

GRANT, A.J. and TEMPERLEY, Harold   *Europe in the Nineteenth and Twentieth Centuries*, 6th edn. (Longman 1952)

HASLIP, Joan   *The Lonely Empress: a Biography of Elizabeth of Austria* (Weidenfeld and Nicolson 1965)

HORNE, Alistair   *The Terrible Year: the Paris Commune 1871* (Macmillan 1971)

HOUGH, Richard, edited by   *Advice to a Grand-daughter: Letters from Queen Victoria to Princess Victoria of Hesse* (Heinemann 1975)

KLESSMAN, Rüdiger   *The Berlin Gallery* (Thames and Hudson 1971)

KURTZ, Harold   *The Second Reich: Kaiser Wilhelm II and his Germany* (Macdonald 1970)

LEE, Sir Sidney   *King Edward VII*, 2 Vols. (Macmillan 1925-27)

LONGFORD, Elizabeth   *Victoria RI* (Weidenfeld and Nicolson 1964)

LORNE, John Marquis of   *VRI: her Life and Empire* (Harmsworth 1901)

LUDWIG, Emil 'If the Emperor Frederick had not had Cancer' (In *If it had Happened Otherwise*, edited by J.C. Squire, 2nd edn. Sidgwick and Jackson 1972)

LUDWIG, Emil   *Kaiser Wilhelm II* (Putnam 1926)

McCLINTOCK, Mary Howard   *The Queen Thanks Sir Howard: the Life of Major-General Sir Howard Elphinstone* (John Murray 1945)

MACKENZIE, Sir Morell   *The Fatal Illness of Frederick the Noble* (Sampson Low 1888)

MAGNUS. Philip   *King Edward the Seventh* (John Murray 1964)

MANDER, John   *Our German Cousins: Anglo-German Relations in the Nineteenth and Twentieth Centuries* (John Murray 1974)

MANN, Golo   *The History of Germany since 1789* (Chatto and Windus 1968/ Harmondsworth, Penguin 1974)

MARIE, Queen of Roumania   *The Story of my Life Vol. 1* (Cassell 1934)

MASSIE, Robert K.   *Nicholas and Alexandra* (Victor Gollancz 1968)

MASUR, Gerhard   *Imperial Berlin* (Routledge Kegan Paul 1971)

NELSON, Walter Henry   *The Soldier Kings: the House of Hohenzollern* (Dent 1971)

NOWAK, Karl Friedrich   *Kaiser and Chancellor: the Opening Years of the Reign of the Emperor William II* (Putnam 1930)

PONSONBY, Arthur   *Henry Ponsonby, Queen Victoria's Private Secretary: his Life from his Letters* (Macmillan 1942)

PONSONBY, Sir Frederick   *Recollections of Three Reigns* (Eyre and Spottiswoode 1951)

PONSONBY, Mary   *Mary Ponsonby: a Memoir, some Letters, and a Journal* (John Murray 1927)

POSCHINGER, Margaretha von *Life of the Emperor Frederick;* edited with an introduction by Sidney Whitman (Harper 1901)

RADZIWILL, Catherine *The Empress Frederick* (Cassell 1934)

RODD, James Rennell *Frederick, Crown Prince and Emperor: a Biographical Sketch Dedicated to his Memory* (David Stott 1888)

STEVENSON, R. Scott *Morell Mackenzie* (Heinemann 1946)

TAYLOR, A.J.P. *Bismarck, the Man and the Statesman* (Hamish Hamilton 1955)

TAYLOR, Lucy *'Fritz' of Prussia: Germany's Second Emperor* (Nelson 1891)

TISDALL, E.E.P. *She Made World Chaos: the Intimate Story of the Empress Frederick of Prussia* [sic] (Stanley Paul 1940)

TSCHUDI, Clara *Augusta, Empress of Germany* (Swan Sonnenschein 1900)

VICTORIA, Princess, later Empress Frederick *The Empress Frederick writes to Sophie, her Daughter, Crown Princess and later Queen of the Hellenes: Letters 1889-1901;* edited by Arthur Gould Lee (Faber 1955)

VICTORIA, later Empress Frederick *Letters of the Empress Frederick;* edited by Sir Frederick Ponsonby (Macmillan 1928)

VICTORIA, Princess of Prussia *My Memoirs* (Eveleigh, Nash and Grayson 1929)

VICTORIA, Queen *The Letters of Queen Victoria.* 1st series edited by A.C. Benson and Viscount Esher, 3 Vols. (John Murray 1907)/2nd series edited by G.E. Buckle, 3 Vols. (John Murray 1926-28) / 3rd series edited by G.E. Buckle, 3 Vols. (John Murray 1930-32)

VICTORIA, Queen *Darling Child: Private Correspondence of Queen Victoria and the Crown Princess of Prussia, 1871-78;* edited by Roger Fulford (Evans 1976)

VICTORIA, Queen *Dearest Child: Letters between Queen Victoria and the Princess Royal, 1858-61;* edited by Roger Fulford (Evans 1964)

VICTORIA, Queen *Dearest Mama: Letters between Queen Victoria and the Crown Princess of Prussia, 1862-64;* edited by Roger Fulford (Evans 1968)

VICTORIA, Queen *Your Dear Letter: Private Correspondence between Queen Victoria and the Crown Princess of Prussia, 1865-71;* edited by Roger Fulford (Evans 1971)

VICTORIA, Queen *Further Letters of Queen Victoria, from the Archives of the House of Brandenburg-Prussia;* edited by Hector Bolitho (Thornton Butterworth 1938)

WIEGLER, Paul *William the First, his Life and Times;* edited by Constance Vesey (Allen and Unwin 1929)

WILLIAM II, Ex-German Emperor *My Ancestors* (Heinemann 1929)

WILLIAM II *My Early Life* (Methuen 1926)

WILLIAM II *My Memoirs, 1878-1918* (Cassell 1922)

WOODHAM-SMITH, Cecil *Queen Victoria, her Life and Times, Vol. 1, 1819-61* (Hamish Hamilton 1972)

III. Periodicals

The Illustrated Times
The Times
The Western Morning News

Index

Acknowledgements

I wish to acknowledge the gracious permission of Her Majesty the Queen for the republication of material from the Royal Archives which is subject to copyright; the kind permission of Lord Napier and the staff of the India Office Library, and the kind permission of Lord Salisbury and Robin Harcourt Williams, for access to and use of correspondence.

I am grateful to the following for permission to quote from their books: Macmillan & Co Ltd, for **Letters of the Empress Frederick**, edited by Sir Frederick Ponsonby, and Cassell & Co Ltd for **The English Empress**, by Egon Caesar Conte Corti.

Among those who have helped in some way or other during the writing of this book, I am indebted particularly to Daphne Bennett (author of the invaluable **Vicky, Princess Royal of England and German Empress**) for her advice on specific personal issues; my parents, for constant encouragement, useful criticism, assistance with proof-reading, and my mother also for the line drawings; and Kelvin Osborn, for translation.